p. 160

p. 247-248 "The Judge"

p XIV

Doing Justice

Doing Justice

A Prosecutor's Thoughts on Crime,
Punishment, and the Rule of Law

Preet Bharara

ALFRED A. KNOPF
NEW YORK
2019

THIS IS A BORZOI BOOK
PUBLISHED BY ALFRED A. KNOPF

Copyright © 2019 by Preet Bharara

All rights reserved. Published in the United States by Alfred A. Knopf,
a division of Penguin Random House LLC, New York, and distributed
in Canada by Random House of Canada, a division of Penguin Random
House Canada Limited, Toronto.

www.aaknopf.com

Knopf, Borzoi Books, and the colophon are registered trademarks
of Penguin Random House LLC.

Library of Congress Cataloging-in-Publication Data
Names: Bharara, Preet, author.
Title: Doing justice / Preet Bharara.
Description: New York : Alfred A. Knopf, 2019.
Identifiers: LCCN 2018053931 (print) | LCCN 2018055346 (ebook) |
    ISBN 9780525521136 (ebook) | ISBN 9780525521129 (hardcover)
Subjects: LCSH: Justice, Administration of—United States. |
    Justice, Administration of—Moral and ethical aspects. | Justice. |
    Rule of law—United States.
Classification: LCC KF8700 (ebook) | LCC KF8700.B43 2019 (print) |
    DDC 347.73—dc23
LC record available at https://protect-us.mimecast.com/s/SRzkCBBnp1sp
    YEOxf6uIoQ?domain=urldefense.proofpoint.com

Jacket design by Carol Devine Carson

Manufactured in the United States of America
Published March 19, 2019
Second Printing, March 2019

*For my family
and for the fearless women and men
of the U.S. Attorney's Office for
the Southern District of New York,
the best place I will ever work*

Contents

Preface

This book was written, over the course of more than a year, in the midst of an involuntary career change. I held the position of U.S. Attorney for the Southern District of New York (SDNY) for seven and a half years, extended beyond the usual term at the personal request of President-elect Donald J. Trump on November 30, 2016, soon after his election. Then, on March 11, 2017, I was abruptly fired by President Trump.

Before I left that office, the crises were many and since then they have been and continue to be frequent, even constant. The rule of law and faith in the rule of law, the state of judicial and prosecutorial independence, the meaning and primacy of truth—all are in question and under fire in numerous ways.

Phrases and concepts like "the rule of law" and "due process" and "presumed innocent" seem to do service these days more as political slogans than as bedrock principles. Other honored precepts appear to be slipping too. It seems preferred these days to demonize one's opponents rather than engage them, to bludgeon critics rather than win them over. There is a creeping contempt for truth and expertise. Rigor is wanting everywhere. We swim in lies, never corrected. And the concept of justice seems turned on its head—holding different meaning depending on whether you are a political adversary or ally.

Certain norms do matter. Our adversaries are not our enemies; the law is not a political weapon; objective truths do exist; fair process is essential in civilized society.

It turns out that the law has something to teach us about truth, dignity, and justice. About how to resolve disagreements and disputes—with reason and evidence rather than taunts and character assassination. Much of what passes for argument in the public square these days would be laughed out of court. Politicians and television talking heads would be disbarred for perversions of truth and outright lies. As someone recently put it, federal court is not Twitter.

Many people find this moment in America alarming. There is rightfully a sense of urgency. But amid all that urgency, it is also vital to take a deep breath, to take a step back, to try to understand how justice is supposed to be accomplished. Then study the contrast between the bombast and anger versus the calm thought process. The education is in that contrast.

Early in my tenure as U.S. Attorney, I had this idea of creating a kind of guide for young prosecutors, new and idealistic. People who, in the words of one of my predecessors, Henry Stimson, have "hope and virtue" but neither experience nor training. A guide that was not really about the law as such but about how to find the right way to do the right thing, drawing not from legal texts and treatises but from the real-life human dilemmas that would perplex them every day. And in developing its themes, I realized that it might in fact be a guide to justice generally, not only for practitioners, but for real people who strive and struggle in their homes and offices to be fair and just. I didn't write the book then, for various reasons, but the concept remained in my head and in my heart.

It's my hope that years in the trenches overseeing the finest group of public servants I have ever met lend me some perspective to help people make sense of what has been happening in America.

In putting down these thoughts and stories, I went back to cases and controversies that predate today's legal battles. More important, I went back to basics. What does it mean to be fair and fair-minded? What does independence require, how is truth discovered, how is justice served? What is discretion and how to exercise it wisely? Not in the abstract, but in the messy and meddlesome real world, where we rely on flawed humans to carry out those ideals on the ground.

So this book is about those things, and because it is, it is also very much about the present. Sometimes the best way to address current events is to recall first principles.

For as long as I can remember, I have wanted to advance justice and its understanding. I have been devoted to the mission, cause, and philosophy of it my whole life—personally, academically, and professionally. What it is, what it means, how to accomplish it. How it thrives, how it dies.

When I was in high school in New Jersey, I entered public speaking contests. One competitive category required giving a speech previously delivered by someone else. (It was, I suppose, the super-nerd version of covering a song.) I was fifteen when I came across the defense summation delivered in the *People v. Henry Sweet* trial. The facts were these: Dr. Ossian Sweet had moved his family into a new house in a neighborhood in Detroit. Dr. Sweet was a black man, and his white neighbors didn't want a black family in their midst. It was 1925.

On their second night in the house, an angry mob descended and terrorized the Sweet family. They yelled and threw rocks. In the ensuing chaos, while defending the home, Dr. Sweet's younger brother, Henry, fired a gun into the crowd. A white man was killed.

Henry Sweet found himself on trial not only for his freedom but also for his life. The state was seeking to execute him. Luckily for Henry, his lawyer was Clarence Darrow. In the case of the *People v. Henry Sweet,* Darrow delivered one of the most beautiful summations ever spoken. He talked of course about the facts of the case and argued the law of self-defense. But he also talked about justice generally and spoke eloquently about the plight of black people, only recently officially liberated from slavery.

He said of the African American, "The law has made him equal, but man has not. And, after all, the last analysis is, what has *man* done? And not what has the law done." Ninety years later, that question remains relevant.

Darrow also said this:

> After all, every human being's life in this world is inevitably mixed with every other life and, no matter what laws we pass, no matter what precautions we take, unless the people we meet are kindly and decent and human and liberty-loving, then there is no liberty. Freedom comes from human beings, rather than from laws and institutions.

To this day, no class, no professor, no law book, has ever conveyed to me more powerfully or persuasively what it means to be a justice-seeking lawyer than those words I committed to memory more than thirty years ago. I'm sure, as a pimpled adolescent, I didn't comprehend their full meaning. But the longer I served as U.S. Attorney, the more I came to believe in their vital truth. False allegations, wrongful convictions, excessive punishments, miscarriages of justice are often wholly the result of human failings, not flaws in the impersonal machinery of justice.

Though we are, admirably, a nation of laws, justice can sometimes spring as much from the heart as from the head. That is because the law can unduly elevate the abstract over the actual. Everyone in the system is a person, and while justice is something of an abstraction, it is sought and felt by real human beings.

Smart laws do not assure justice any more than a good recipe guarantees a delicious meal. The law is merely an instrument, and without the involvement of human hands it is as lifeless and uninspiring as a violin kept in its case. The law cannot compel us to love each other or respect each other. It cannot cancel hate or conquer evil; teach grace or extinguish apathy. Every day, the law's best aims are carried out, for good or ill, by human beings. Justice is served, or thwarted, by human beings. Mercy is bestowed, or refused, by human beings.

I went to law school because I longed to be part of the legal community that seeks to do justice in America. I've had many jobs since law school. I worked in private practice for six years following graduation, doing a mix of white-collar criminal defense, securities litigation, international arbitration, and other corporate work. Later in my career, I had the honor of serving as chief counsel to Senator Chuck Schumer on the U.S. Senate Judiciary Committee, where I drafted crime legislation, vetted judicial nominations, and oversaw an investigation (irony alert) into the political firing of U.S. Attorneys.

But the only thing I ever *really* wanted to be was an assistant U.S. Attorney (AUSA) in the Southern District of New York, the premier public law office in the country, if not the world. Sometimes my parents would visit me in New York when I was a young law firm associate, and I would take them for dim sum in Chinatown. As we walked to lunch from the City Hall subway stop in lower Manhattan, I would point to the squat, brutalist concrete building on stilts next to police headquarters and say, "That's where I want to work someday." This was One St. Andrew's Plaza, to my mind a magical address. I got to do that after Mary Jo White swore me in as a rookie prosecutor in 2000, and my life has never been the same since.

The U.S. Attorney's Office headquartered in Manhattan is a storied institution, established at the dawn of our nation, a century before there was even the Justice Department. The first U.S. Attorney in New York, Richard Harrison, was nominated by George Washington in a handwritten document sent to the Senate, along with his choice for secretary of state—Thomas

Jefferson. Its alumni include many who went on to become governors, mayors, cabinet secretaries, and Supreme Court justices. Over the centuries, the SDNY has been responsible for prosecuting every type of federal criminal case—from treason to terrorism, from public corruption to organized crime. In its modern form, it employs over two hundred highly credentialed, mostly young and idealistic lawyers, and an equal number of dedicated staff. Along with ninety-two other U.S. Attorney's Offices, the SDNY is part of the Justice Department, but it has a well-known and vaunted independent streak, as evidenced by its longtime nickname, the Sovereign District.

When I assumed my position as the head of that office in 2009, I sought to embrace the culture I inherited from my predecessors. There was only one admonition and it was constant: *Do the right thing, in the right way, for the right reasons.* And do only that. I repeated that to a generation of public servants as often as I could. It was a good feeling to be in that office. And even though the nature of criminal work meant seeing some of the worst that humanity has to offer, it was the most inspiring and hopeful place I have ever been.

We did not always get it right. We were not error-free. We pursued cases that some people thought were overreach, and we walked away from others that some were dying to see us bring. But I can't recall a time when we didn't think hard about what we were doing, why we were doing it, and whether it was in the interests of justice.

Justice is a broad and hazy subject. It is one of the most elusive and debatable concepts known to humankind, and disagreements over its meaning have spawned revolutions, religions, and civil wars. I do not advance here some grand and novel theory of justice. But what I do suggest is that people will regard a result as just if they regard the process leading to it as fair and if they believe the people responsible for it are fair-minded. It is often said that justice not only must be done but also must be *seen* to be done. Right now, many people in this country do not see fair process, nor do they understand it. There is a crisis of confidence in modern America, but it is not always in the failure of the law or the breakdown of the constitutional process. What we have is a system too often marred by men and women who come to justice with a closed mind, with inaccurate preconceptions, with bias, with self-interest. With a belief that the system is something to beat, to circumvent, rather than as a way to reach the truth.

The approach I lay out applies not only to how federal laws are interpreted and enforced in courts around the country; it also informs how mature, thinking people make decisions in their communities, in their workplaces, and in their homes. This is not a book just about the law. It is a book about integrity, leadership, decision making, and moral reasoning. These are all crucial to the meaning and nature of justice.

The moral quandary of fair and effective punishment, for example, is not unique to life-tenured jurists presiding over criminal cases. It will be familiar to many people—to the regulator who must penalize a rogue company; to the supervisor who must handle a misbehaving employee; and even to the parent who has to discipline an unruly child. What is proportional? What is effective? What will in the future deter that person specifically and everyone else generally? What action is sufficient but not greater than necessary?

There are gaps in the law and oceans of discretion left to prosecutors. Think of all the judgments made every day. Many such judgments occur in courtrooms everywhere, sure. But at work and at home and in school and on the internet, awful and consequential judgments are made *without* the benefit of the imperfect but moderating check of established precedents, binding rules, open proceedings, rights of appeal. How much injustice occurs in all those areas of life? How much closed-mindedness? How much rush to judgment? How much disproportionate punishment? This book is about the fairness of those judgments too.

These questions have no precise or certain answers, and yet every day orderly society demands that they be answered. And every day mere mortals try to meet that challenge as best they can.

PART I

Inquiry

Introduction

Truth is central to justice, and the discovery of truth requires a searching inquiry. In criminal justice, this is the investigation, which is not only the path to truth but also the way to accountability (or exoneration). The fairness, effectiveness, rigor, integrity, and speed of any investigation naturally determine whether justice will be done in any particular case—criminal or otherwise.

Investigations are hard. When people see the final product wrung from the mind and heart of an artist or writer or entrepreneur, they often underappreciate the effort behind it. The painstaking, backbreaking, stop-and-go labor is not necessarily evident in the elegance of the brushstrokes, the clarity of the prose, or the simplicity of the business model. The ultimate consumer knows little to nothing of the false starts, dead ends, winding detours, and other setbacks en route to the final product. The layperson sees the destination, not the journey.

The same can be true of investigations. There's a ready pop-culture phrase to describe how investigations should be done, suggesting it is an easy exercise. "Just connect the dots," people say. The idea that you can always get to the truth through a technique we teach kindergartners has always been puzzling to me.

In connect the dots, so long as you know how to count, you can draw the picture. Even a child can drag a crayon from the first little dot numbered *one* to the next one numbered *two* and so on and so forth until some jagged picture of a cow or a barn

or a house or a dog emerges. No such luck in a real investigation. There's no foolproof guide or order, no guarantee that any
of the work that you're doing—dragging not a crayon across a
page but your feet all over town interviewing witnesses, issuing
subpoenas, looking into financial documents—will yield a clear,
accurate, and actionable picture.

The same with "follow the money," another gross oversim-
plification. This facile phrase was not ripped from the head-
lines of Watergate as popularly assumed but coined by the late
screenwriter/storyteller William Goldman for the film version
of *All the President's Men*. Bob Woodward and Carl Bernstein
themselves never used the phrase. It was invented by a brilliant
Hollywood screenwriter and has become part of the popular
lexicon, but it is not as easy as it sounds.

Since the dawn of financial crime, investigators have known
that you follow the flow of money to whom and from whom
and for what. The problem with phrases like "connect the dots"
and "follow the money" is that they dramatically underestimate
the difficulty, complexity, and length of a standard criminal investigation, especially one that involves what's in people's minds.

The difficulty in investigation is not just complexity. Let's
take something infinitely more complex than connect the dots.
My younger son, Rahm, is obsessed with solving what my generation knew as the Rubik's Cube. I take him to cubing competitions on many weekends. He can solve a three-by-three
standard multicolored cube in an average of eleven seconds,
which, though not world class, is super impressive. The thing
about cubing, though, is this: No matter how much you scramble it, there is a mathematically predictable solution. Depending on how many algorithms you've memorized, you might
solve it in more or fewer moves, but the point is that it is always
solvable if you have enough resolve, memory, and practice.
And there is a preferred, mathematically determined ordering
of steps to complete the puzzle. This is not true for criminal

investigations. There are guidelines, sure, and best practices of course, but there is no predetermined and universal order of steps to take. More important, not every criminal mystery has a solution.

Back to follow the money. People think you find a check, you see who wrote it, you see who cashed it, and you're done. It's rarely so simple. Sophisticated people trying to hide their tracks use lots of accounts, lots of intermediaries. They favor cash, they falsify documents, they create shell companies and fraudulent paper trails. Often there is no record or trace of incriminating transactions at all. That's the heart and soul of money laundering, which can be an especially difficult crime to prove. Many of us have a hard enough time figuring out what's in our own heads, never mind ferreting out what illicit sparks are flaring in someone else's noggin. But that is exactly the challenge in almost every white-collar or corruption case.

Often some of the individual acts that make up the crime are perfectly legal, and indeed fully within the person's authority and job description—like the president firing an FBI director or a portfolio manager trading stock or a congressman voting on legislation. Depending on what *other* facts are true, these actions might be obstruction of justice (was the intent to shut down an investigation?) or insider trading (was the trade made on material nonpublic information?) or political corruption (was the vote bought by a bribe?).

The investigator's orientation matters. The mind-set and motivation are key. You must *want* to find the truth, must *want* to get it right. All too often, people simply want to win, facts and truth be damned. But to begin an inquiry, when justice is the goal, you must not be wedded to any result, must not have a thesis in advance. To be open-minded means proceeding without a theory. You develop a thesis from the facts, not vice versa.

Why is this so important? Once you commit to a theory or a thesis, it's hard to let it go. Psychologists are familiar with this phenomenon. People tend to tune out facts that conflict with their original thesis. They will downplay contrary evidence or, even worse, may not even recognize new facts as undercutting their first belief. First beliefs are sticky. Unproven first beliefs weaken your brain and dull your thinking just as a fever weakens your body. In any given inquiry, without constant vigilance, obvious first principles are at risk of degrading into facile catchphrases. You know them all: keep an open mind, don't prejudge, don't assume, don't jump to conclusions, guard against bias.

This open-minded approach meets resistance because it slows the speed of an investigation. After a horrible disaster or a violent crime, the world understandably clamors for accountability; they want the bad guys caught. The victims have faces; sympathy and empathy naturally pour forth. It's understandable that people want to see the faces of the evildoers. They want culprits, and they want them fast. In the wake of a crime, everyone turns into a NASCAR fan. They want speed, speed, speed.

Speed is an investigation's best friend and also its worst enemy. Speed is your friend because some evidence evaporates like a puddle in the sun. Memories lapse, witnesses walk, documents go missing too. So you want to get your hands on all the nuggets you can in short order.

But undue speed can cause you to overlook evidence or misinterpret it. It can force mistakes. As the Roman senator Tacitus said, "Truth is confirmed by inspection and delay; falsehood by haste and uncertainty." When you are always racing forward, it becomes hard to take a step back. But stepping back can be the key to a case. An investigator must maintain a near-impossible balance between patience and impatience. A burning drive to find the truth quickly is essential, but so is a calm resolve to take your time to get it right.

For sure, the success and quality of any investigation depend on the experience, smarts, resourcefulness, curiosity, creativity, courage, and doggedness of the people conducting it. But it will depend on something else also: their character. I suppose character matters in some way in all professional endeavors. I'd prefer that the baker or pilot or carpenter be blessed with good character, but I'm not sure the cake, the flight, or the cabinet requires more than mere professional skill. Searches for truth and accountability demand something more of the people conducting them: integrity, honor, and independence, among other things.

What follows is not a comprehensive primer on how to investigate misconduct. Rather, in these pages, I describe some success stories and some tales of caution. You will hear about a few cases where the wrong people were accused and others where the truly guilty parties escaped scrutiny for too long. You will learn about the human qualities of the best investigators, like the legendary mob buster Kenneth McCabe, who I believe set the gold standard. You will delve into the art and morality of interrogation and come to grips with the sometimes tawdry use of cooperating witnesses, a.k.a. snitches. You will read about the limits of science, the tendency to human error, the importance of hard work and professionalism, and the power of a single person to deliver (or thwart) justice.

The Truth Is Elusive: The Boys

During the summer of 1989, between my junior and senior years of college, I worked for an hourly wage at my uncle's small insurance business in Long Branch, New Jersey. It was tedious work that involved literally typing thousands of names, addresses, and phone numbers into a desktop computer from the phone book to create a database for mailers advertising my uncle's business. This was not the most auspicious precursor to a distinguished career in the law, so I welcomed any respite from encroaching carpal tunnel syndrome that hot Jersey summer.

One afternoon in August, I got a call from my best friend from high school, Jessica Goldsmith Barzilay, who was also on summer break before her junior year at SUNY Binghamton. The office receptionist, who also happened to be my aunt, transferred the call to the phone closest to my desk. The most pleasant and upbeat personality I know, Jessica has always been quick to laugh and even quicker to make other people laugh. Her face is forever crinkled in a smile.

There was no smile in Jessica's voice on the afternoon of August 20, 1989. It was the first of several devastating phone calls I received from her in the span of a few months. In this first call, she was trying to tell me something, but I couldn't make out what she was saying, because she was crying—not in the ordinary way people weep because something merely sad has happened, she was quaking the way people do when something tragic has come to pass. While she struggled to deliver her unspeakable news, my first thoughts went to her parents, at whose home my brother and I would have dessert every Thanksgiving in a long-running tradition. Next I thought about her two sisters, who had also gone to high school with us.

After a minute or two, Jessica composed herself. The news was about her parents' lifelong friends. "Jose and Kitty are dead," she said. Not only were they dead, but they had been murdered—viciously murdered—their bodies blown apart by shotgun blasts, in their own living room and at close range. They had been eating strawberries and ice cream on the couch, watching *The Spy Who Loved Me*. We learned later that the blasts were so violent, Jose's head was almost severed from his body.

I had long heard about Jose and Kitty from Jessica. Jessica's parents had lived near them for a time when they were all young and poor and trying to make a go of it in Queens. They rented small apartments near each other and did what young, striving couples do. They worked hard, tried to make ends meet, and dreamed big. An inseparable foursome, they spent holidays and weekends with each other, played tennis and Monopoly together. In the years since these humble beginnings, Jose, an immigrant from Cuba, had moved the family to Beverly Hills, grown very successful in Hollywood, and in every way had lived and achieved the American dream. Jose and Kitty had two sons. I'd heard about them too because, growing up, Jessica had a crush on the older one, who went on to Princeton. Both boys were handsome and athletic. Now they were orphans.

On the night of the murders, police received a hysterical call from one of the brothers, who said he had come upon his parents' bodies. Cops sped to the family residence, a $5 million mansion that had once been Michael Jackson's home and before that Elton John's. There they found the younger son on the front lawn, curled up in the fetal position. Inside they found the bloodbath.

I had never met this family, but I felt I knew them well through Jessica's stories over the years. Now I felt searing vicarious grief listening to my friend sob through the grisly details. When Jessica had calmed down enough, I thought it was okay to find out more. Were there suspects? No suspects yet, she said, but the police believed it might be a Mafia killing on account of the brutality. It could have been a vengeance hit, but she had no idea who would want to do such a thing. And for some time, the cops had no clue either.

Eventually, this murder-mystery would become the second most sensational criminal case of the 1990s, eclipsed only by the trial of O. J. Simpson. Kitty and Jose were the parents of Lyle and Erik Menendez, and they had been slaughtered by their own sons. It was a long while, however, before this awful truth became known. And longer still before Jessica and her family would believe it.

Jessica couldn't attend the memorial in Princeton, because she needed to get back for the start of classes. Her parents attended the services—which had to be closed casket—and reported that Erik seemed especially heartbroken over his parents' deaths. Both children, they said, spoke lovingly and eloquently about Jose and Kitty.

I remember the next time Jessica called me in tears. It was months later, in March 1990. I was sitting on the hard twin mattress in my tiny college dorm room with an architect's lamp on, senior thesis coming due, and procrastinating as usual. Her voice was cracking but calmer than it had been in August. She said, "They mistakenly arrested the boys." That's always how she referred to Lyle and Erik. Even now, three decades later, these two men—now well into middle age and serving life sentences for parricide—are "the boys." Frozen in time, pre-murder.

"How could the cops make such a terrible mistake?" she

asked. It wasn't a purely rhetorical question. I was heading to Columbia Law School in the fall, and I suppose she was plaintively asking me to channel some future legal self, to explain how such a profound police error could occur (and how it could be fixed).

I flinched before asking the obvious question. "Jessica, could they have done it?"

Her reply was adamant: "No. One hundred percent no."

I said, "Can you be sure?"

"I know they didn't do it," Jessica said. "I know it, I *know* it." I was convinced.

Months after the arrest, Jessica called again. She had just spoken with one of the boys' aunts. Lyle and Erik had confessed. The boys had killed their parents, they claimed, in self-defense, after what they said was years of mental, physical, and sexual abuse by Jose. And why Kitty? Lyle would later be heard in a taped session with his psychiatrist saying he killed their mother to put her "out of her misery." The confession and change of plea was about to become public, and the Menendez aunt wanted Jessica's family to hear it from her before it was on the news. I asked Jessica how her dad was taking it. "This is worse than losing Kitty and Jose," he had told her.

What followed was a six-year odyssey involving an epic legal battle over the admissibility of the psychiatrist's recordings, fights over the self-defense doctrine, appeals to the California Supreme Court, multiple mistrials, and finally murder convictions of both sons in 1996. All of this would play out in public and transfix the country. The drama spawned multiple books and a TV series. Jessica even testified at the first and third trials.

By the time of the confession, I was a law student. But on that evening when Jessica first learned the truth, we did not discuss the criminal law, didn't speculate about the viability of legal defenses or the possible sentence Lyle and Erik might receive if convicted. What Jessica talked about was her own gullibility, what she had gotten wrong, what she had missed. All those years. What had she not seen or chosen not to see? What pain and suffering had she been blind to? The shooting was not an impulsive heat-of-the-moment act. The crime had been meticulously arranged and planned and then carefully covered up. Lyle went on a spending spree afterward with his inheritance. He bought a Porsche, a Rolex watch, and a restaurant in Princeton.

What signs of monstrosity had Jessica ignored? The deaths were heartbreaking and the boys' role in them excruciating, but what was also gnawing at Jessica was her own misplaced trust, her blindness to even the possibility of what turned out to be the truth. We talked all night, until the sun came up. The boys had done it. Jessica *knew* they hadn't. But they had. She tried to make sense of it. We tried to make sense of it.

Much later, Jessica and her family would recall things that seemed odd and even terrible that might have signaled some roiling family tension below the perfect American dream surface. Jose was a tough dad, uncompromising and harsh with the boys. One time, he drove twelve-year-old Erik to a cemetery at night and left him crying among the tombstones in an effort to toughen him up. There were other stories like that, which Jessica has shared over the decades since. But the boys had turned out so well, everyone believed, that such incidents were forgotten or dismissed—until the murders. Or more accurately, until the boys' *confession* to the murders.

Our all-nighter on the phone produced no epiphanies, save one: *you can't know anything about anybody*. You can't ever really know someone else's mind or someone else's heart, what someone else is capable of. I mean, *really* know. That seems an apparent if depressing fact of life, but it was far less obvious to a couple of twenty-two-year-olds who had yet to live and work in the world.

It was the first moment I realized that anyone could be guilty of anything. There was something shattering about that. Shattering, but also instructive. To this day, when people tell me they *know* someone didn't do it, I think of Lyle and Erik Menendez. It's a sad but necessary reflex in a certain line of work. Because sometimes, all belief and faith and instinct to the contrary, the privileged sons of millionaires massacre their own parents.

Beyond being a version of a coming-of-age story and loss of innocence, my conversations with Jessica deeply informed my time as an investigator and prosecutor. I have not only healthy skepticism of the potential guilt of any suspect but also the necessary converse, skepticism of the innocence of any person. It is common and correct for people to talk about the important presumption of innocence—a legal term relating to trial—in court. The application of that sacred principle is the reason a criminal trial can be conducted fairly. It is why juries can weigh all the evidence and reserve judgment before making a determination.

The investigative phase is different. The presumption of innocence would be a dangerous standard for an investigator. The investigator has to keep an open mind about the potential *guilt* of everyone—whether it's someone who's a good friend of the victim or a blood relative or even the privileged, well-to-do sons.

When people talk about bias, it is generally negative bias. It's a concern—a righteous concern—that people might have bias *against* someone of a certain race, ethnicity, or gender that might cause them to unduly suspect a particular person of committing a crime. But the Menendez brothers case, like so many other cases, reminds us of the need for wariness of positive bias too: the belief that an outwardly upstanding citizen or externally successful and wealthy person could not engage in deceit, fraud, assault—or parricide. Positive bias not only causes law enforcement to overlook suspects but, perhaps even more important, causes otherwise thoughtful people to become victims.

A racist white man may cross the street if he sees a young African American man in a hoodie walking toward him at night, but that same man might have willingly parted with his entire fortune by investing with a celebrated, well-dressed, but crooked white socialite investment adviser in whom all of his friends have also put unbounded trust.

So, what does this mean? How are people supposed to live their lives? Perhaps it is untenable for ordinary citizens, when deciding which babysitter to hire, which lawyer to retain, which investment adviser to bring on board, to assume the worst about them, or spend much time investigating all of them. That would be paralyzing in your daily and professional life. But maybe bank clerks and teachers and students and people going about their everyday lives should be skeptical enough to sound the alarm when they see flags so red they're downright crimson. This does not always happen.

Things Are Not What They Seem: "Urbane Cowboys"

How many people in your orbit are crooks or con men? How many people do you judge to be threatening or beneath you because of how they look, dress, or act? How many people do you look up to, emulate, or envy because of a patina of success, power, and wealth? Common sense and prosecutorial experience tell me that neither extreme makes any sense. It is tough to live your life so cynically that with every interaction you think that every person is an impostor and a fraud intent on victimizing you. But blind trust based on outward appearances is foolishly naive. Somewhere between these extremes—for law enforcement agents as well as for businesses, and for individuals too—is a role for healthy skepticism, arm's-length dealing, due diligence, and sensible caution. This is not just well-meaning fortune-cookie advice. It has practical consequences for identifying and curbing terribly malicious conduct that too often goes unchecked, as the world discovered in the case of Bernard Madoff. But mini-Madoffs, less well-known, are everywhere.

My tenth day as U.S. Attorney was a Sunday. I was sitting in my office in jeans and a T-shirt, catching up on the voluminous weekly summary of criminal cases my unit chiefs put together regularly, when my deputy, Boyd Johnson, unexpectedly walked in with one of our fraud unit supervisors, John Hillebrecht. "John needs to talk to you," he said. "We have a situation."

Let me pause to mention that I was blessed to have outstanding deputies throughout my tenure as U.S. Attorney. Boyd, my first, was one of my oldest and dearest friends, whom I promoted from corruption chief to deputy U.S. Attorney on my first day in the new job. Tall, athletic, and likable, Boyd is a keenly intuitive lawyer and an energetic and inspiring leader. We had worked together twice before, in private practice and at SDNY. I trust him like a brother. He was now my guide these first few days and weeks in office. Quick practice point: try if you can to work with your best and smartest friends in life.

After Boyd left, for four years my deputy was Richard Zabel. Rich was basically the smartest guy in the building. He was simultaneously down-to-earth and possessed of a kind of professorial élan. He spoke French and wrote fiction, sported a goatee, and quoted literature. He was an exacting supervisor, a surgical editor, and a priceless confidant. He's the kind of person, for me at least, that after a week you feel you've known your whole life. Moreover, Rich remains the only person I have ever sung to in public, at his farewell dinner. That's all I will say about that.

For my last couple of years in office, Joon Kim was the deputy. Joon is an overachieving product of Exeter, Stanford, and Harvard. He is understated and brilliant, and I lured him back to public service from a seven-figure salary at Cleary Gottlieb. Joon's humor masks a deep idealism. Few people make me laugh as hard as Joon. He was by my side when I was fired and was truly outstanding as acting U.S. Attorney.

The point of this aside is to say that no leader does the job alone. Everything is a partnership, and if you don't choose your teammates well, all hell will break loose.

Back to the situation, which was this: The FBI had very recently begun investigating an Iranian American named Hassan Nemazee for potential large-scale bank fraud. Just a few days earlier, Citibank had notified the FBI of its belief that Nemazee had, based on lies about collateral, fraudulently obtained a loan of $74.9 million. This was not a national security matter. There was no impending danger. So why the Sunday emergency?

The urgency was that, as sometimes happens, a suspect makes highly inconvenient travel plans. Hassan Nemazee was booked on a flight, that very evening, out of Newark Liberty International Airport to Rome, Italy. When a criminal target decides to leave the jurisdiction, the same question always presents itself: Is it a legitimate short-term business trip from which he will return, or is he hinked up and fleeing? Or might he be on alert while out of country and choose not to come back, leaving us with not only a fugitive on our hands but also egg on our faces? This is always delicate. To be fair, the reverse sometimes happens too. Defendants are lost who flee abroad, sure, but unsuspecting criminals, charged under seal, sometimes fly *into* the United States and face prompt arrest. This was true, for example, of an Iranian gold trader named Reza Zarrab, whose sealed indictment ruined his family visit to Disney World. As far as the overall balance sheet of justice is concerned, though no such records are kept, the travel lottery is probably a bit of a wash.

The cleanest way to prevent flight would have been to arrest Nemazee right then. Just a few weeks later, surprised with a similarly sudden travel issue, we hastened—well ahead of our ideal schedule—to arrest the hedge fund CEO Raj Rajaratnam for insider trading when we learned he had booked an international flight. In that case, however, we already had months of wiretap evidence and plenty of probable cause to arrest, though the sudden unplanned arrest on a Friday morning presented logistical and planning hurdles. In Nemazee's case, the investigation was in its infancy. Citibank had its suspicions (representatives had recently asked him to verify his assets, suggesting they would contact his other bank directly), but at this point we were essentially taking Citibank's word that this well-known and upstanding citizen was a grifter. We didn't even have the supporting documents yet.

Nemazee, moreover, was no ordinary target. He was an extremely wealthy, respectable, and prominent businessman, politically connected to every recognizable, national Democrat in the country. There was no hint of wrongdoing in his past. This Iranian American, married with three children, was a monument to the American dream. He graduated from Harvard College and lived a life of generosity and largesse. He had donated more than a million dollars to a range of charities and schools, including Harvard University, Brown University, the Spence School, the Whitney Museum of American Art, and the Council on Foreign Relations. He had given generously to Democrats (Barack Obama, Hillary Clinton, Bill Clinton, Joe Biden, Al Gore, John Kerry, Chuck Schumer) and also to prominent Republicans (Senators Jesse Helms, Sam Brownback, and Alfonse D'Amato). He was well-dressed, well-mannered, and well-read, and he lived in a $28 million apartment on Park Avenue.

To us, that he was politically connected to a particular party was trivial. My office had recently investigated, prosecuted, and convicted another notable Democratic fund-raiser named Norman Hsu. Mine was an apolitical job; Democrats and Republicans were equally in the crosshairs. What was important is that Nemazee had an unimpeachable reputation. While prominent and wealthy people are never above the law, investigators should always take care—while facts are still developing—not to cause undue reputational harm to a mere suspect. That is important not only for the reputation of the target but also for the reputation and credibility of the FBI and the U.S. Attorney's Office. The scenario was sensitive: Let Nemazee go and hope he comes back, or intercede in some way?

We decided to take a middle-ground approach and remain flexible. Two outstanding agents went to intercept Nemazee at Newark Airport. The goal was to avoid the worst-case scenario: Nemazee getting on that plane. Everyone's nightmare is letting

a potential bad guy fly. The agents planned to be polite and cour-
teous because experience teaches that the soft-spoken approach
is usually best, especially in a consensual situation. The agents
would have a calm and respectful, but firm, conversation with
our genteel suspect.

The hope was one of three things would happen to sidestep
the doomsday scenario: Nemazee would lie to the FBI, so they
could arrest him; he would incriminate himself by making some
admission, so they could arrest him; or he would decide volun-
tarily to stay in the country while we sorted it all out.

The agents arrived at the airport hours in advance and
waited until Nemazee was through security to make sure he
had been screened for weapons. What happened when two
well-mannered but armed men, who identified themselves as
special agents from the Federal Bureau of Investigation, surprised Nemazee and explained that Citibank was accusing him
of stealing $75 million through deceit and false pretenses? Well,
in that moment, Hassan Nemazee was nothing if not a perfect
gentleman, calm as a maître d' handling a lost reservation. He
explained patiently to the agents that it was all a big misunderstanding. "I absolutely have the money that I represented to
the bank. It's all a big mistake. I absolutely have the money."
The agents didn't know whether to believe him, but he was
not unconvincing. Notwithstanding what must have been a tremendous shock and inconvenience, Nemazee, cheerfully and
without any outward sign of anger or complaint, complied with
their request to stay. The plane flew without him.

John came back into my office, after a briefing from the
agents, and updated me and Boyd. I thought to myself, "Well,
that's kind of a relief. Worst-case scenario, we've mildly embar-
rassed someone Citibank was wrong about and mildly embar-
rassed ourselves." Not that I was overly focused on outward
appearance, but it was so early and the accusation seemed so
incongruous; I was prepared to believe that he could be guilty or

innocent. Given how calm, cool, and collected he was at the airport, I thought we might have had it wrong. And yet I was also thinking about the Menendez brothers. Things are not always as they seem.

Two hours later, Nemazee's longtime lawyer Marc Mukasey called John and went well beyond the norm for a defense lawyer in the situation. He not only reiterated what Nemazee said—that this was all a big misunderstanding—but also went one step further and vouched for him personally. He explained that he saw Nemazee all the time, that they went to Yankee games together sitting in the firm's seats, and that he was an all-around swell guy. Mukasey said, "He's a friend, not just a client."

Then came the kicker. Mukasey said, "He's going to pay all the money back tomorrow. Is that okay?" My thoughts turned again to how wrong this could have gone had we arrested him. If he was in fact a fraud, if he was in fact living a lie and didn't have the assets that he claimed, then it was a pretty tall order to pay back on half a day's notice $74.9 million. Even monumentally wealthy people would find that difficult because of liquidity issues.

I went to bed that night thinking about something that I had previously understood but that had come into sharp relief as the weekend had progressed: how fraught every decision is along the way to an arrest. Obviously, the decision to charge someone has tremendous import, but even at the investigative phase when things are moving quickly, when facts are not yet clear, when motivation and intent are hard to interpret, when the ball has only just begun to roll, there is a certain kind of fog of war that can envelop the decision makers. This is especially so when circumstances force quick game-time decisions earlier than the natural momentum of an investigation would counsel. Thinking a potential embarrassing moment had been averted, I drifted to sleep.

The next morning, Nemazee was on my mind still. It wouldn't

be the first time that someone had promised to put up quick cash for bail or something else and not come through. But before the clock had even struck noon, Hillebrecht was back in my office. "You know, boss, you're not going to fucking believe this, but he just paid it all back." The full $74.9 million. As if it were nothing. I sat back in my chair and said, "Holy cow." Except I didn't say "cow."

Even while we congratulated ourselves for handling this fairly well, I thought, "Boy, did we almost screw up."

But before John left my office, he looked at me, looked at Boyd, and said, "You know what? Let's see what else is going on here. I'm not sure we know the whole story." John, tall with an angular face, was a monster trial lawyer who had taken down countless made men in the mob; if you wanted to know how to get a piece of evidence admitted, you went to John. His instincts were gold; his hunches were informal probable cause. This hunch, however, seemed improbable at best.

Fast-forward a few hours and John was again in my office. He began the same way he had that morning by saying, "Boss, you're not going to fucking believe this." I looked up. "There's something screwy with the repayment." John and the agent had looked at the origin of the repayment, and the FBI drilled down quickly. The repayment funds had come from HSBC.

After we chased down documents from both Citibank and HSBC in trying to confirm the newly posted collateral, a truer picture of the affable and affluent Hassan Nemazee came into focus. In order to save himself from the allegation of fraud by Citibank, on Monday morning Nemazee had simply strolled into the lobby of another large bank and employed precisely the same stratagem of fakery, combined with the aura of wealth, success, and respectability, and, at the drop of a dime, persuaded a *second* sophisticated financial institution to part with $74.9 million. To do that, I thought, you need clout and cojones both.

That was a fateful decision. The upshot for Mr. Nemazee was

this: in the blink of an eye, he had doubled his trouble because punishment in the federal system is linked to the dollar value of fraud. We could no longer wait. Together with FBI agent Dalynn Barker, John pieced together enough facts to get a warrant for Nemazee's arrest that evening.

The ensuing investigation unraveled a life of lies. Nemazee's bank fraud extended not just to Citibank and HSBC but to Bank of America as well. He had invented financial institutions, forged signatures, and faked documents to assert that he had the financial collateral to substantiate these huge loans, including repeatedly representing that he owned millions of dollars in U.S. Treasuries. He fabricated his office address, phone numbers, bank addresses, and bank representatives. One of his offices at 575 Madison Avenue turned out to be a business that provided a telephone answering service, mail receipt service, and conference rooms. Ultimately, Nemazee pled guilty to defrauding banks of more than $290 million in loan proceeds. Though he lived in a $28 million apartment, drove a blue Maserati, flew a 2007 Cessna 680 airplane, boated in a 135-foot yacht, and maintained other multimillion-dollar properties in Tribeca, Italy, and Katonah, he was not a man of great means. It was all a giant, gold-plated charade.

The reaction to his arrest was interesting. Politicians scrambled to return his donations. Acquaintances and colleagues announced their shock and surprise. In the paper, an anonymous financier friend claimed, with some irony, that he knew Nemazee well: "People really liked the guy—even my wife, who can generally smell a rat from a mile away. But for this fraud, he was one of the nicest, most respectable, urbane, well-read persons you could ever hope to meet." There's a lot in that statement, starting with the gentleman's quaint faith in his wife's—or anyone's—ability to smell a rat. The caveat in his remark is one for the ages: *but for this fraud*.

You may not cry for the victims in this case. They were, after all, three huge, multinational financial institutions: HSBC, Citibank, and Bank of America; two of the three in completely separate circumstances were accused of fraud by my own office. How did they fall for the charms and stylings of Hassan Nemazee? These people had not internalized some version of the lesson of the Menendez brothers: *Things are not always as they seem.* That can be true in the murder of well-to-do parents by their privileged children, and it can be true in highly sophisticated fraud against the biggest banks on the planet.

The likable, respectable, and handsome image of American success caused banks, which are by law required to "know your customer," to skip the simplest of checks. Notwithstanding the huge sums they were prepared to lend, they had never called his cell number, never visited his supposed place of business, and never attempted to corroborate any of the information Nemazee provided. While it is never kosher to "blame the victim," one could and should ask, "Why were these banks asleep at the switch? Why did they make assumptions that would cost the institutions hundreds of millions of dollars without doing the most fundamental check?" It bears some mulling. The disappointing truth is that smart, sophisticated, well-heeled professionals—in a kind of reverse discrimination—make easy (and costly) judgments about people based on appearances, on credentials, and on connections, people who would be unmasked and exposed by even the slightest inquiry. Walk and talk and act a certain way, in a particular elitist and entitled manner, with an air of aristocratic belonging about you, and maybe you can get away with a multi-hundred-million-dollar fraud.

There's another observation here. Hassan Nemazee did a lot of good in his life. In fact, the principal argument made by his lawyer at sentencing before Judge Sidney H. Stein was that this was a good man who had done bad things. This was a good man who had donated money to various charities. This was a good man who supported the democratic process. This was a good man who had raised three successful children. This was a good man who had given so much and helped so many. The fully evil man is rare. More often you find complex creatures capable of great kindness and charity, on the one hand, but also serious fraud and malice, on the other.

Hassan Nemazee is not unique. He was essentially a less famous version of Bernard Madoff. Both manipulated people and fooled them, using a mixture of charm, bearing, social connection, exclusivity. Both easily defrauded smart and sophisticated people and institutions. Here, for example, are some of the "rubes" duped by Bernie Madoff: the director Steven Spielberg; the actors Kevin Bacon, Kyra Sedgwick, and John Malkovich; the Nobel laureate and Holocaust survivor Elie Wiesel; the Hall of Fame pitcher Sandy Koufax; the Mets co-owner Fred Wilpon; the cinema star Zsa Zsa Gabor; the former New York governor Eliot Spitzer; the family of the former U.S. secretary of state Henry Kissinger; the DreamWorks CEO, Jeffrey Katzenberg; Senator Frank Lautenberg; and the International Olympic Committee. It wasn't just individuals but banks too. Also, the Securities and Exchange Commission, which didn't catch the fraud for decades. The point is that Madoff was able to pull the wool over the eyes of billionaires and bigwigs, along with regular folks and families. The losses were catastrophic: tens of billions in wealth and savings.

Madoff did it the same way Nemazee did it. He built a name for himself, which required some trappings: a $7 million apartment on Manhattan's Upper East Side, a $21 million home in Palm Beach, houses in the Hamptons and France, and, of course, *Bull*, the fifty-five-foot yacht. It required being seen, so Madoff cultivated relationships with the right people, and soon, relying on word-of-mouth recommendations, he had access to the exclusive, upper echelons of society. But it wasn't all flattery. Sometimes the charade required a level of smugness; Madoff was known to reject investments that were below a certain amount; that pretense of exclusivity made him even more desirable. Eventually, Madoff's status as a supposedly reputable money manager made him a symbol: it *signified* something to invest with him. And so people did. Unquestioningly.

There are mini-Madoffs everywhere. Take, for example, Ken Starr (not that Ken Starr). The Ken Starr whom we prosecuted was a stockbroker. "Broker to the stars," they called him. Starr was a Manhattan investment adviser who gained a reputation for representing Hollywood's elite, with clients such as Sylvester Stallone, Natalie Portman, Al Pacino, Uma Thurman, and Martin Scorsese. He fleeced many of them.

To gain the trust of his clientele, Starr claimed to be close to respectable businessmen such as Pete Peterson, the co-founder of Blackstone. As *The New York Times* later reported, "He would tell Hollywood figures of his connections on Wall Street, while regaling Wall Streeters with stories of Hollywood." It was a symbiotic fraud. Starr grew increasingly wealthy over the years—purchasing a $7.5 million Manhattan apartment with a thirty-two-foot pool. But Starr, like Madoff, was running a Ponzi scheme; he wasn't investing his clients' money, and he used newer investors to pay off older investors' requests for redemption. Ultimately, he was arrested, prosecuted, convicted, and sentenced to seven and a half years in prison.

Overworked agents with guns and badges, operating at a distance, are not sufficient to keep institutions fair and just; they are not enough to prevent the Madoffs and Nemazees and Starrs of the world from wreaking havoc. What deters that kind of fraudster is the fear that everyone he might deal with will ask questions, will require some proof, will not just take his word at face value. That sometimes can generate unpleasantness and offense, but that's really what it takes. It seems obvious, but people con very sophisticated victims every day, sophisticated victims who don't ask the right questions.

For me, the Nemazee affair was a spine-developing moment. You want to make sure that you're holding everyone accountable for crimes they have committed, but you don't want to embarrass yourself and your office—especially on your tenth day in the job. As much as anybody wants to say that you're not supposed to worry about what other people will think, it is a hard feeling to avoid altogether. If you think what you're doing is right and others either don't understand it or have a political or ideological agenda, then it's much easier to tell them—in your mind—to go to hell. Having a spine means that you can't be afraid to hesitate because you want to get it right, but it's also wrong not to take any action because you are afraid of external consequences. The key is to make sure that prudent hesitation does not turn into paralysis and that responsible aggressiveness does not turn into recklessness. Like anything else in the delivery of justice, at the investigative or any other phase, the approach requires balance. There is no science, no mathematical formula, no precise scale on which you can balance these things, but they must be balanced nonetheless.

Gold-Standard Investigators: The Ethic of the Mob Buster Kenny McCabe

As you pass through the revolving lobby doors of SDNY headquarters at One St. Andrew's Plaza, you walk into what looks like a high-security, state-owned airport lounge. Straight ahead, blue-blazered security officers stand behind two bulletproof panes of glass. Visitors to the office—cops, defense lawyers, messengers, relatives of defendants waiting to co-sign bail bonds—mill about or sit in black pleather chairs arranged in rows on the gray-brown industrial carpet. The only color is provided by a couple of odd art installations. One, an enormous mural taking up the entire left wall, is painted in pastels and depicts the unsmiling faces of five generic but racially diverse professionals. The second looms overhead. Called *Kayaks in the Storm,* it's a collection of painted life-sized boats hanging from the lobby's high ceiling like a mobile over a child's crib. Way off to the right, beyond the panel of "Wanted" posters, is an ever-present wood podium, affixed with a Justice seal and adjacent to an American flag, off duty until the next blockbuster news conference.

You could easily miss it, but the moral center of that lobby is a small upright memorial, tucked to the right of the revolving-door entrance. It marks the contributions of the longtime SDNY investigator Kenneth McCabe, who passed away in 2006 from melanoma.

In an office stocked with ace investigators, Kenny McCabe

was the class act of the lot. Tall, gruff, and Irish, he became a legendary expert on the doings and dealings of the five La Cosa Nostra families—Gambino, Genovese, Bonanno, Lucchese, and Colombo. Kenny knew the name of every reputed boss, capo, soldier, and associate. He knew the associates of the associates. A crime writer once noted that Kenny "was said to be able to tell the rank and standing of wiseguys just by looking at their behavior."

Kenny was right out of central casting. He looked a little like John Wayne. But he was a real-life mob-busting cop. Kenny was the intrepid badge who trekked to mob funerals, mob weddings, and mob christenings, firearm in his holster and camera in his hands, shooting picture after picture for his extensive collection. Not only did Kenny know all the mobsters, but the mobsters all knew him. Sometimes they smiled and waved for the surveillance photos. They greeted him on the street with a nod and a not unfriendly "Hey, Kenny." From time to time, as he took snapshots of people going into and out of churches and social clubs, they would send him a sandwich or cup of coffee.

For years, Kenny sat on the ninth floor of One St. Andrew's Plaza. There he maintained cabinets filled to capacity with his photographs of reputed and convicted mobsters interacting or, in the parlance, "associating" with each other. His photography project was no idle exercise. It was part of the proof that the jury would see and hear about in countless mob cases. One of the keys to making a racketeering case is to document the connections and relationships between and among members of the Mafia. Over the years, hundreds of Kenny's surveillance photos were slapped with yellow government exhibit stickers and entered into evidence at trial.

Kenny testified often as an expert on the workings of the Mafia, explaining to countless juries the command structure of a typical organized crime family, how one became a member of the mob, how the oath of *omertà* was administered and blood drawn from the inductee's finger. He would explain how, if there was a serious beef, you couldn't whack a made man without getting permission.

Kenny was a six-foot six-inch tower of no-nonsense bluntness. I put him on the stand only once, during the trial of an upstate cop who we alleged did favors for Vinnie "the Butch" Corrao, a made member of the Gambino crime family. Armed with obstruction and extortion charges, we approached the cop to get him to flip against Vinnie Butch. But we made two errors. First, we hadn't fully locked down our extortion victim, who ended up recanting (out of fear, we firmly believed). The other error was underestimating a police officer's willingness to roll the dice on the eve of his pension vesting. So, rather than flip, the officer defiantly went to trial. With the extortion charges dropped, we proceeded with somewhat weaker allegations. The judge was Michael B. Mukasey, who later became the U.S. attorney general.

We had wiretaps, but they didn't prove all that much about the cop. I called Kenny to testify about the ways of La Cosa Nostra as he had a million times before. A former cop himself, Kenny didn't flinch at the prospect of testifying against a fellow officer. On direct examination, Kenny was no nonsense, as always. On cross-examination, the defense lawyer made a show of attacking our surveillance methods, especially the use of wiretaps. At one point, after a series of questions about the wire, the lawyer looked at the jury and back at Kenny, then practically screamed, "Mr. McCabe, how would you like it if all of *your* phone conversations were secretly taped by the government?"

Without missing a proverbial beat, Kenny calmly shot back, "I got nothing to hide. Do you?" At least a couple of jurors smiled outright. We ended up losing that trial. When the cop was acquitted, I could not help feeling that I had let Kenny down. Kenny had put away untold high-profile mobsters, but he cared just as much about my little dog of a case as he did about the game-changing ones.

I did not work with Kenny as much as others, but he made a deep impression on me. As U.S. Attorney, I established an honor in his name—the McCabe Medal—to be awarded at the annual office dinner, along with two other decades-old awards, to recognize a law enforcement agent who best personified Kenny's ethic and character. What was it that so distinguished Kenny McCabe? Why should he be not only honored but emulated?

One reason is that Kenny believed in the virtue of work. He didn't take shortcuts, toot his own horn, or blame others for failure. He believed that you just do your job and you do it well. Every day. Even when it's hard. Even when it's dull or even when no one is looking. Even when the work seems small and beneath your title or God-given talent. Kenny took his pictures, made his rounds, followed his leads. He turned over rocks day after day after day, building cases he knew would take years to make or might not ever get made. Kenny was a brick-by-brick guy.

Some years ago, I gave the Class Day address at Harvard Law School's commencement, and I mentioned the baseball pitching great Roy Halladay of the Philadelphia Phillies. I described how, almost exactly four years earlier, Halladay had achieved one of the most rare and difficult feats in all of sports. He pitched a perfect game. Nine innings. No hits. No walks. Twenty-seven up, twenty-seven down. He was perfect, and he is in the history books because of it. Then, four months after *that,* on October 6, 2010, in the very same season, Halladay threw a no-hitter (not quite perfect, but damn close), and he did it in a playoff game. In all of baseball history, only two people have ever thrown a no-hitter in the postseason. Just two.

The Phillies pitching coach, Rich Dubee, was asked by a reporter what advice he had offered his ace. The coach said he had given Roy Halladay a simple instruction: "Go out there and try to be good. If you go out there and try to be good, you've got a chance to be great."

That's it.

Ambitious people tend to think of every endeavor as a ball game in which they're going to pitch a perfect game. It doesn't work that way. People should want to be monumentally successful—and Kenny, it should be said, was a very ambitious cop—but you've got to do it one pitch at a time. Pitch after pitch after pitch. That's what develops into a perfect game or, by analogy, an outstanding career. No one who ever pitched a perfect game in baseball went to the mound that day expecting to do so. Not only is that unrealistic; it is the height of arrogance. Yet people all the time make that very mistake. They want to be great, before they've learned how to be good. The Kenny McCabes of the world know different.

What else? Kenny was an expert. His devotion to tracking and tormenting mobsters was complete, bordering on compulsive. He knew everything there was to know about the Italian Mafia in New York and New Jersey. He simply knew more than anyone else. To develop expertise requires total immersion nearing obsession. If you really want to learn about fish, you have to live in the water, and that's what Kenny did. He lived and breathed the mob, memorized their faces, names, connections, genealogies, beefs, and battles. He took in what even the lowliest associate had to say and made a permanent mental note, knowing that one day that one piece could complete a criminal puzzle.

This kind of commitment is more unusual than you may think. The average good agent or cop does a tour of duty, makes some busts, maybe does decent work in narcotics or gangs or robberies or even terrorism. Then he is moved to another squad or another precinct (or in the FBI's case, even another city), never sticking around to acquire the kind of deep knowledge that can make the long-term difference Kenny made.

Many ambitious people do not have patience, and so their ambition yields little in the way of substantive results. Kenny had the patience of Job and had the collars to show for it. As *The New York Times* wrote in his obituary, Kenny's job was "to help topple godfathers." That he did. He helped put away the boss of the Bonanno family and the acting boss of the Lucchese family. He personally arrested the Gambino boss, Paul Castellano, who was later assassinated outside Sparks Steak House in 1985. And then Kenny arrested the man who ordered that assassination, John Gotti Jr. Kenny McCabe was responsible for locking up more murderous, terrorizing, racketeering mobsters than anyone else in modern times. You don't do that without a steel spine and an iron stomach.

Kenny's work was often the linchpin of a case. When, during a 1990s mob trial, a young federal prosecutor named James Comey badly needed to show a link between a Lucchese family member and a Gambino capo, Kenny immediately identified a 1983 wedding connection. It was Kenny McCabe who, based on his unique underground network, revealed for the first time in open court during a 2004 trial that Vincent "Vinny Gorgeous" Basciano had taken over as boss of the notorious Bonanno family, critical testimony in Basciano's case.

But Kenny had other qualities too; he was honest and fair. No one ever saw Kenny yell, rough up, or mistreat even the worst of the worst mobster. To be sure, sometimes deceit is called for to collar a criminal. We use stings and undercovers and wiretaps. But most of what Kenny did was straight and aboveboard. He took pictures where his targets could see him. He spoke to them on the street like real people, not like the thugs that some of them were. He got people to tell him things, important things that they might not tell any other agent, because they trusted and respected him. As one of my predecessors, David Kelley, said of the wiseguys' respect for Kenny, "The mob is all about playing by the rules. He didn't lie. He dealt with them fairly. They got arrested fair and square."

Kenny was not a pushover; he was not naive. He didn't have to whack anyone with a baton or a baseball bat to get the job done. Kenny's strength was in his character more than in his burly arms and frame. He understood that toughness didn't come from acting tough. Toughness came from being tough. This legendary mob buster didn't need to knock heads or rough up his targets when he put them in his squad car. He didn't need to threaten or bully. It's a mistake too many would-be leaders make. Kenny understood that if you need to say you're tough, then you aren't; if you need to say you are feared, then you aren't. I have seen too many people who manage by intimidation and fear, whose default mode is to bludgeon or belittle. Abusive people are weak, not strong. As the late five-star general and commander in chief Dwight Eisenhower, who was as tough as they come, once said, "You don't lead by hitting people over the head—that's assault, not leadership." Kenny knew better. Real toughness is a necessary trait in pursuing justice: you must be tough enough to persist in a task, tough enough to admit error, tough enough to stay quiet when need be.

Once back in the early 2000s, after our office got a conviction in some mob case, three of us went out for drinks at Yello, a seedy Chinatown bar just off Pearl Street near the courthouse. We all had small kids at the time, three young assistant U.S. Attorneys, still making our way. Kenny had testified at the trial and came along. Over beers, Kenny said something about family that I never forgot. Looking rueful, he said, "Be careful not to spend so much time trying to become a big shot that you don't spend enough time with your kids." That was it, one sentence. The kind of sentence you think about later in life from time to time with a twinge.

Kenny's family revered him. As I started writing this book, I got together with his son, Duke, to hear more stories about his dad. He told me many. One was this: When he was maybe nine years old, Duke had basketball games on Sundays by the Queens Center mall, not far from the Bergin Hunt and Fish Club, in Ozone Park, Queens. That was one of the places where John Gotti and the Gambino gang would consort. After the game, Kenny would take a slight detour in his Oldsmobile Delta 88—nothing but American cars for Kenny—to drive slowly up 101st Avenue to the Hunt and Fish Club, just to see who was around. Kenny would perch a pad on the steering wheel and jot down the names of anyone he saw. He would toss another pad to Duke and make him write down every license plate on the block. And little Duke would dutifully write down the combinations of letters and numbers—sometimes in pen, sometimes in crayon—and present them to his big-shot father. It is one of his fondest memories.

Over the years, thousands of people have traversed that gritty airport lounge of a lobby at One St. Andrew's. Most probably never stopped to read the inscription under the modest five-by-seven-inch picture of Kenny McCabe. This is what it says:

IN MEMORY OF KENNETH J. McCABE
1946–2006

Ken McCabe was a remarkable man, an outstanding investigator, and the one indispensable person in this country's battle against La Cosa Nostra during the 25 years before his untimely death. He was honest, gifted, tough as nails, and, to those who were lucky enough to know him well, as soft as a marshmallow inside his huge and intimidating exterior. He shaped generations of AUSAs, shunned credit and attention, and made it his mission in life to protect the weak. His best friend and the love of his life was his wife Kathy, with whom he nurtured and adored four children, five grandchildren, and their Breezy Point, Queens home. No finer person will ever walk through this lobby.

Kenny McCabe borders on myth because he was uncompromising in everything he undertook. We need more like him.

The Problem of Confirmation Bias:
Latent Fingerprint 17

Initial bad calls made by fallible human beings working in imperfect systems are bound to happen. Those bad first calls can set a course for disaster. Most of the time, however, a disastrous path is reversible—if reconsidered early enough.

But reconsideration is difficult, isn't it? An opinion once formed is hard to abandon. A conclusion once broadcast is hard to withdraw. Witnesses, studies show, stick to their first identification, doctors to their first diagnosis, and lawyers to their first assessment of the merits of a case. But the open mind has to persist beyond the first call in decisions of law and order, of life and death. Every conclusion must be subject to challenge and revision. This is hard because human beings have egos. We are stubborn. That stubbornness can cause tremendous injustice, especially when the stakes are highest—when public safety is at risk. One of the most difficult—but most crucial—things to achieve, in the early stages of pursuing justice, is objectivity. Or as close as we can get to objectivity, which is probably simply separating facts from ego or some other bias.

Consider the case of Brandon Mayfield.

March 11, 2004, saw the deadliest morning commute in Europe's history. Just before 8:00 a.m., terrorists blew up four passenger trains in the heart of Madrid, Spain. There were ten bombs in all, stuffed into backpacks and crammed with compressed dynamite and sharp nails, the nails thrown in for good measure to inflict maximum bloodletting and death. The explosions split train cars in half and ripped human bodies apart. One hundred ninety-one people died, and almost two thousand more suffered devastating injury. It was the deadliest act of terrorism on the Continent since World War II. It was Europe's 9/11.

These particular terrorists, presumed to be Islamic, were not suicide bombers; they detonated their bombs remotely so they might live another day to slaughter even more innocents. The attack birthed not only sweeping panic and outrage but also an epic crime scene—made more urgent because the perpetrators were still at large. Nothing, in my experience, mobilizes law enforcement like a terror attack.

Spain's 3/11, as the day became known, was no exception. While first responders and medical personnel raced to aid the maimed and wounded, the Spanish National Police (SNP) also sprang into action, chasing witnesses and hunting leads. Hundreds of agents fanned out over a wide radius. Within hours, the SNP came upon the kind of jackpot forensic evidence that could lead directly to those responsible for so much death. In an abandoned stolen van, police found a blue plastic bag containing seven copper detonators and the remnants of explosives. They could hardly believe their luck. The detonators were unquestionably connected to the train bombings. And any person who had held that bag was certainly part of the plot and would be brought to swift justice.

Spanish experts who examined the plastic bag for fingerprints could identify only two prints sufficiently clear to be used for identification. Neither of the two usable prints yielded an immediate match within the SNP's database.

Given the urgency and while continuing their own fingerprint review, the Spanish conveyed digital images of the lifted prints through INTERPOL to the premier law enforcement agency in the world—the FBI. Seasoned FBI analysts working in the lab at Quantico went to work. After they ran each image against a database of more than 44 million fingerprints, the initial computer search yielded twenty possible matches. After further examination, FBI fingerprint experts narrowed the match to a single individual. An examiner performed a side-by-side comparison and concluded, on March 19, that latent fingerprint 17 (LFP 17) was a match. A second experienced examiner confirmed that match. A chief in the elite Latent Print Unit made it three for three.

At the time this trio of FBI experts confirmed the match to latent fingerprint 17, they did not know the name, race, residence, or background of the person who matched it. When the FBI first learned the person's identity, there was surprise. This apparent plotter of a heinous terrorist attack that took almost two hundred lives and injured nearly two thousand more was . . . a thirty-seven-year-old white American lawyer living quietly in Portland, Oregon, with his wife and three young children, thousands of miles from the carnage in Madrid. Why were his prints even in the database? Because he had served as second lieutenant in the U.S. Army, honorably discharged after eight years of service.

And yet science had spoken. The match had been made and confirmed. Three times. Clearly the FBI had got its man. A series of other facts about Brandon Mayfield would soon seem to ratify the fingerprint work: It turned out that Mayfield had married a Muslim immigrant from Egypt. Not only that, but he *himself* had converted to Islam. Not only that, but he frequented a particular mosque in Beaverton, Oregon, that had received attention from local authorities. And not only that, but as a lawyer Mayfield had once represented a convicted terrorist—a member of the so-called Portland Seven, all convicted in federal court of material support of al-Qaeda and the Taliban. Although his representation was not in the criminal case—but in connection with a child custody issue—it was notable. The match was making a lot more sense.

Let's count up the strikes against Mayfield: his print was on that blue bag of death; three experts confirmed it; he'd married a Muslim; he'd converted to Islam; and he'd shown common cause with a convicted terrorist. That's almost enough strikes to retire the side.

Agents obtained a warrant from the ultrasecret tribunal known as the FISA court, which oversees certain kinds of surveillance. They began twenty-four-hour surveillance of Mayfield and his family, secretly searched his home, and began delving into every aspect of his life, his work, his friendships, and his travel.

It was at this time that I became personally associated with the case as an AUSA in the Terrorism and Organized Crime Unit. Based on the groundbreaking terrorism cases brought by SDNY in the past (the first World Trade Center bombing, the attacks on the U.S. embassies in Kenya and Tanzania), we rightly thought of ourselves as the most experienced and professional prosecutors of terror crimes anywhere in the country. So if there was an American terrorist jihadist responsible for the deaths of 191 people, we wanted to bring the case. There was only one problem with that plan: Brandon Mayfield lived in Oregon, and the Oregon U.S. Attorney had other ideas. I understood that a turf battle over this alleged American terrorist, Brandon Mayfield, was brewing. But if the Southern District were to take the lead, it would be my case, and Brandon Mayfield would be my defendant. I will admit that I was kind of thrilled.

One might ask, once the fingerprints came back as a match and his background as a Muslim convert and lawyer to terrorists was known, why wasn't Brandon Mayfield charged with a crime on the spot? The reason is that the lack of other hard evidence was disturbing. FBI agents could find nothing else to corroborate his involvement in the bombing. Yes, latent fingerprint 17 matched Mayfield's finger, but there was no evidence that he had ever traveled to Spain or even gone out of the country in the last ten years. In fact, Mayfield's passport had expired the year before and hadn't been renewed. While telephone records showed calls between Mayfield's home and the director of a local Islamic charity, who was on the federal terrorism watch list, there was no evidence of any other connectivity between Mayfield and terrorism.

This utter lack of corroborating evidence was baffling. For weeks, investigators scrutinized Mayfield's life, but the pieces were not falling into place. Moreover, throughout April there was a continuing back-and-forth between the FBI and the SNP. The Spanish, still in hot pursuit of the mass murderers, were doubtful of the Mayfield match. In mid-April, the SNP in fact disagreed with the FBI print assessment, which led the bureau to send an agent to Madrid to hash out the different opinions. After that meeting, the SNP agreed to reassess the prints yet again. The FBI remained confident of its own analysis. Notwithstanding these ongoing issues, exactly eight weeks after the bombing—on May 6, 2004—the FBI took Mayfield into custody because press leaks seemed imminent and they wanted eyes and cuffs on him in case he chose to flee. He was not charged with a crime but jailed on what is called a material witness warrant.

I read about all this on the front page of *The New York Times*. Apparently, we had lost the turf battle. I was not so happy that day.

Mayfield was housed in the administrative segregation unit of the Multnomah County Detention Center and kept in his cell for up to twenty-two hours per day. From the beginning, he maintained his innocence, but of course most everyone does. He claimed he had never been to Spain, that he had nothing to do with the attack, and that it was all a big mistake. There was talk that anti-Muslim bias was fueling the investigation. The FBI for its part trusted in its science—the triple confirmation of the fingerprint match—and rejected any accusation of bias.

And yet, as the investigation rolled on, the FBI could not find a shred of additional evidence. Some developments were, in retrospect, comical. During the search of Mayfield's home, agents seized documents they believed to be Spanish and incriminating; they turned out to be Mayfield's daughter's Spanish homework. A search of Mayfield's home computer yielded research on flights to Spain, housing, and railroad schedules; that turned out to be his daughter's homework assignment on planning a vacation. A Spanish phone number was found written down in the house; that turned out to be part of an effort to find an international exchange program for Mayfield's son.

At this point, Mayfield's lawyer made a smart request. He asked the court for an independent examiner. If the FBI were either biased or inexpert, a fourth fingerprint expert chosen by the court and approved by the defense would get it right. The court appointed a highly respected expert, Kenneth Moses, a veteran fingerprint investigator with decades of experience and countless awards to his name.

But when he compared latent fingerprint 17 with Brandon Mayfield's left index finger, he agreed with the FBI and testified to his conclusion. He too determined that Mayfield's print was on the bag of detonators.

On the very same day that Moses testified—May 19—the SNP told the FBI that they not only disbelieved the Mayfield match but now had definitively concluded that latent fingerprint 17 in fact belonged to an Algerian national (and terror suspect) named Ouhnane Daoud. Specifically, they said, latent fingerprint 17 and another print matched the thumb and middle finger of Daoud's right hand. After some argument between the FBI and the SNP, the next day prosecutors in the Oregon U.S. Attorney's Office requested that the court release Brandon Mayfield to home detention while the agencies tried to sort out the truth.

Mayfield was released but not yet cleared. FBI officials again traveled to Madrid and determined, for the first time, that latent fingerprint 17 was "of no value for identification purposes" and finally, on May 24, rescinded their conclusion of the match with Brandon Mayfield. A week later, on June 1, 2004, the SNP charged Daoud with 191 counts of murder.

Mayfield was officially exonerated. A public FBI apology is about as rare as a $3 bill, but the FBI apologized to Mayfield that day and later paid him $2 million in compensation. The FBI in its statement said, somewhat bureaucratically, "The FBI apologizes to Mr. Mayfield and his family for the hardships that this matter has caused." Mayfield and his lawyer harshly condemned the arrest and treatment. "In a climate of fear," Mayfield said, "this war on terrorism has gone to the extreme and innocent people are victims as a result." Years earlier, ironically, in a law school paper titled "Liberty," Mayfield had expressed his fears that the government could quickly morph into a surveillance machine and impinge on the rights of its citizens.

I will admit, on that date, I was pretty relieved that we had lost the turf battle to Oregon.

Harsh criticism of the FBI was immediate, but not all of it was on the mark. *The New York Times* wrote on May 26, 2004, "The case smacks of a rush to judgment based on flimsy evidence." But that wasn't quite right. Fingerprint evidence is not flimsy. It's definitive if it's done right. But as *The New York Times* also went on to say, "The method itself is not foolproof, and the analysts who provide the final judgment sometimes make the wrong call." This is 100 percent right.

How on earth could the FBI have made such a colossal blunder? How on earth—given the combined expertise, repeated findings, high-profile nature, and sky-high stakes—could such a debacle have happened? The U.S. Attorney's Office somewhat understandably denied responsibility and reminded everyone that they have to depend on FBI forensic analysis. The U.S. Attorney Karin Immergut said, "We are prosecutors. We're not forensic analysts. We rely on the FBI to give us their opinion as to whether or not a fingerprint is a match."

For its part, the FBI did its own internal investigation and came to this conclusion: the initial examiner "failed to conduct a complete analysis" of latent fingerprint 17 that led him to "disregard important differences in appearance between LFP 17 and Mayfield's known prints." Simply put, according to the FBI, it was a problem of initial "overconfidence," "the pressure of working on a high-profile case," and subsequently an unwillingness to go back and reexamine initial findings.

Not only did the FBI undertake an internal investigation, but the Office of the Inspector General launched its own review as well. That report, running to 330 pages, was less kind. What happened? Were the fingerprint analysts bigots? Was there a rush to judgment? Did the pressure to find someone responsible for heinous acts that killed so many undercut careful professionalism?

The truth can be complicated. Everyone agrees that at the time the initial fingerprint matches were made to Brandon Mayfield, analysts did not know the name, background, or religion of the match. The computer finds matches based on an image of the control print and the potential match. Other identifying information that could have caused some unfair anti-Muslim bias was not even in the equation at the time not one, not two, but *three* analysts at the FBI made their call. Not only that, but the match was then confirmed a *fourth* time, *after* the identity was known, by the independent expert chosen by the court and approved by Brandon Mayfield's own lawyer.

So again, what happened? Was it an honest mistake? Was it an innocent mistake? Could it have been prevented? What level of incompetence caused it?

The report of the inspector general (IG) determined that the "misidentification could have been prevented through a more rigorous application of several principles of latent fingerprint identification." Among other things, the IG found, FBI examiners had placed too much reliance on tiny, tertiary points of similarity between LFP 17 and Mayfield's print while at the same time rationalizing small differences, which should have ruled out the match. There was, overall, a lack of rigor and stringent methodology.

But what about the question of anti-Muslim bias? The Office of the Inspector General did not conclude that there was overt bias or anti-Muslim prejudice. However, as other aspects of the print match came into question over time, as discussions with the Spanish grew heated, and as corroborating evidence failed to materialize, the IG did surmise that these other data points about Mayfield (Muslim convert, Muslim wife, terrorist client) dissuaded FBI officials from reexamining their first conclusions. It might not have been direct animus, but it clouded their judgment in a way that caused great pain to an innocent person. It cannot be said that bias didn't play some role.

The FBI, according to the IG, had a culture conducive to confirmation bias. In other words, once one person, viewed as credible and professional, came to a conclusion, subsequent examiners were prone to agree with it. In the FBI print lab, and elsewhere, there was a culture of hesitation to challenge both superiors and first conclusions. But perhaps most important, for our purposes, the IG report found that Mayfield's background influenced examiners' "failure to sufficiently reconsider" their initial identification.

That is worth repeating. An innocent man was accused and forever injured because of a *failure to sufficiently reconsider*. It was not the first error that wrought the injustice. First errors seldom do. It wasn't the second or third error either. Rather, it was the continuing and lazy *persistence* in the first blunder—the mismatch of similar fingerprints by mistake but not with malice—followed by discoveries concerning Mayfield's wife, work, and religion quickly accepted as corroboration instead of coincidence that greased a slow-motion miscarriage of justice through a fog of latent bias and stereotype.

As I said at the outset and as the Mayfield case teaches, reconsideration is difficult, while confirmation is easy. It is much more difficult to keep your mind open when someone else in the chain of command has put forth a credible conclusion, or when you have already decided a thing. Changing your mind is hard, especially if it means going against an expert or a higher-up.

In federal trial practice, there is actually a legal motion called a "motion for reconsideration." Courts almost never grant such motions, but it is a real motion that lawyers make. It's a formal way of saying to the judge who screwed you, hey, I know we were just in your courtroom and we've been through all this, but respectfully we think you got it wrong and could you change your mind please? Good luck with that. Most lawyers understand that it's a long-shot gambit, especially absent significant new facts or a change in the law. Some litigants don't bother making the motion even if it has merit, because they fear irritating the judge still presiding over their case. It may be that most motions for reconsideration should be denied on the merits, but one wonders if the failure rate of such court pleas is influenced in part by the psychology of stubbornness.

There is a complicating factor in the case of Brandon Mayfield. In one sense, yes, there was confirmation bias. But it is also true that there was an extraordinary coincidence. One of the very first points emphasized in the IG report is the remarkable similarity between the two sets of prints—between the innocent Brandon Mayfield and the true suspect, Ouhnane Daoud. The "minutiae," or points of comparison, between them—where the ridges of the print split or end—mirrored each other to a stunning degree. Years later in 2012, the defense's own expert, Kenneth Moses, said in a television interview, "No time before in history had there ever been two fingerprints with fifteen minutiae that were not the same person. Under our past standards, I was right. But I was wrong. I had made an error. And so had every other examiner that looked at the print." The Spanish, of course, had not made that error. Nevertheless, the IG report noted that this degree of similarity "is an extremely unusual circumstance," which was a "critical factor that misled four examiners and contributed to their overlooking other important differences between LFP 17 and Mayfield's fingerprint."

Just as perfect laws have limits, even foolproof science has limitations because the people responsible for the interpretation make errors.

There is an important point here: The worst mistakes are often made in the well-meaning margins. Life-altering errors can be made by smart and competent people of general goodwill. To me this is one of the most frightening aspects of law enforcement responsibility.

People will naturally focus on the crooked cop and the bungling constable. But there is arguably greater danger posed by the small imperfections of decent men and women who fail to maintain excellence, who drift from best practices, who forget to be utterly terrified of getting it wrong. Especially where many people are responsible for the work, accountability is spread as thin as morning frost.

In my experience, it is not simply the rogue operator who can cause the debacle. Disaster often springs from the sum of many tiny errors and miscalculations. That is as true of a criminal investigation as it is of a rocket attack. Minor mistakes, in combination, can alter the focus of an investigation (or the trajectory of a missile) to a degree that the effort ends up destroying the innocent and sparing the guilty. In war, it is called collateral damage; in law enforcement, it is wrongful arrest (or even worse, wrongful conviction).

In many ways, this phenomenon poses the greatest danger to justice because it lurks. It is often invisible, in ways that outright corruption and incompetence are not. It is harder to screen for, harder to protect against, and frequently impossible to explain to a horrified public afterward, in a satisfactory way.

An investigator searching for truth and trying to assure just and fair accountability can never stop examining and reexamining conclusions about any aspect of the case. This is not to say that at each step of the way everyone involved in the case should be paralyzed by fear of making a mistake. But it does mean that even after someone seemingly smarter or more experienced than you has come to a conclusion, that conclusion should not necessarily stand forever. That's true not only in the investigative stage but even after a charge has been brought. Even after an accusation has been filed, fair-minded people must continue to think about new evidence coming to light or the *lack* of incriminating evidence coming to light as their understanding of the facts develops and matures. Was the original decision correct? Was the original conclusion correct?

The law is not perfect. The system is not perfect. And as we see in stories like the Brandon Mayfield case, people aren't perfect either. Justice is never assured, but if each person in the process remembers to be vigilant, rigorous, and open-minded to changing a view, justice is at least more likely.

Judge Learned Hand once, while testifying before Congress, laid claim to a phrase, borrowed from Oliver Cromwell speaking in a wholly different context in 1650. Learned Hand said of that phrase, "I should like to have [it] written over the portals of every church, every school, and every courthouse, may I say, of every legislative body in the United States."

What principle did Learned Hand wish every pastor, teacher, judge, and representative to remember just when crossing the threshold of their places of work? It was this: "I beseech ye in the bowels of Christ, think that ye may be mistaken."

He could have added to his list the portals of every prosecutor's office and every law enforcement headquarters: think that we may be mistaken.

The Need for Rigor:
A Death in Soundview

The return address was 354 Hunter Street, Ossining, New York 10562. That's the address of the maximum-security New York State penitentiary known as Sing Sing. The letter was dated April 11, 2012, and came from inmate 97A7088. That was the number assigned to Eric Glisson when he was incarcerated seventeen years earlier for the murder of a Bronx livery cab driver named Baithe Diop. The letter was addressed to a gang prosecutor in my office who had long since left SDNY, but it nevertheless made its way to the in-box of one of the office's veteran investigators, John O'Malley.

The note from Eric Glisson made a dramatic but not uncommon claim: "I have been incarcerated for 17 years for a crime I didn't commit."

John O'Malley had been a twenty-year homicide cop with the NYPD before becoming an investigator with the U.S. Attorney's Office. His pale blue eyes, the whites often tinged red, had seen just about everything. He had locked up countless drug dealers, robbers, and murderers. As Kenny McCabe was expert in the doings and dealings of La Cosa Nostra, O'Malley and his colleagues in the Violent Crimes Unit had encyclopedic knowledge of the gangs of New York, including the Latin Kings, Sex Money Murder, Bloods, Crips, Trinitarios, Power Rules, Ñetas, Willis Avenue Lynch Mob, and many, many others.

O'Malley cared deeply about homicides, and he knew a lot

about them. I don't mean just in the generic sense. He was knowledgeable about the murder scene in New York, but he also knew a lot about particular homicides—who snuffed out whom, how, where, and why. For that reason, a few years earlier O'Malley told Vanessa Melchiori, the woman who screens the mail for civilian complaints at SDNY, "If you ever see a letter talking about a murder, bring it to me." But for O'Malley's directive to Vanessa, Glisson's letter might well have been tossed, gone forever, an unread message in a bottle.

One mid-afternoon, sitting in his office by the sixth-floor staircase, O'Malley pulled Glisson's letter from the envelope with his large hands. With an increasingly furrowed brow, he read the handwritten lines: "I write because I along with several other people, some of whom I don't know, were convicted of a crime relating to the murder of Baithe Diop on January 19, 1995, in the Soundview section [of the Bronx]." He wrote that the murder had taken place in the middle of the night at Lafayette and Croes Avenues. Glisson had heard that a couple of other men had done it as an initiation into the Sex Money Murder gang. He was taking the rap, he said, for other men's crimes.

Coincidentally, O'Malley had himself grown up in Soundview, had seen the neighborhood change before his very eyes, was personally familiar with the crime scene. The more important coincidence was this: John O'Malley was the principal investigator who dismantled Sex Money Murder, a violent gang that had inflicted all manner of killings, shootings, and knifings upon the Soundview section of the Bronx and elsewhere.

The specific details of the murder described in the letter—victim, time, place, manner—made O'Malley's blood run cold. In his words, it was a "holy shit" moment. Why? Because he had heard it all before. A decade earlier, another man had confessed to something eerily similar, and he'd made that confession to none other than O'Malley himself—the robbery and murder of an unidentified livery cab driver, in that very time period, at Lafayette and Croes.

This seems a good place to remark on a singularly important trait that God has conferred on all the best investigators, like John O'Malley: a steel-trap mind. Light has a better chance of escaping a black hole than a fact does of escaping O'Malley's brain. That quality turned out to be good news for Eric Glisson and his co-defendants.

O'Malley's mind went back almost a decade to his investigation of a member of Sex Money Murder named Gilbert Vega. Vega had been arrested and prosecuted, in 2001, on racketeering charges involving narcotics trafficking and related violence. Some time after his arrest, Vega flipped. Like all potential cooperating witnesses in SDNY, Vega had to submit to a lengthy and grueling series of interrogations and debriefings about his criminal past, known as proffer sessions. Before entering into a cooperation deal with a bad guy, we required that he not only own up to what he was charged with but also admit and plead guilty to all other bad conduct—whether we already knew about it or whether we could independently prove it in court. O'Malley was one of the world heavyweight champions of being able to (metaphorically) punch the truth out of a defendant, which he did through a combination of matter-of-fact honesty and persuasive straight talk.

In 2002 and 2003, Vega proffered about all his crimes before being signed up. As he put the Glisson letter down, O'Malley now remembered one of those proffer sessions. It turns out that during one of the interviews where O'Malley and the prosecutors were sizing up Vega for a deal, in March 2003, Vega confessed to a crime we hadn't known about—the 1995 robbery and shooting of an unnamed livery cab driver, done with an associate named Jose Rodriguez, a.k.a. Joey Green Eyes, on Croes Avenue between Seward and Lafayette in Soundview, located in the 43rd Precinct. Though Vega didn't know his victim's name, his proffer was otherwise detailed. Vega said that he and Rodriguez had been in Harlem visiting a girl Rodriguez knew in the winter of 1994–95; in the early morning, the two of them got into a livery cab with an African driver to return to Sound-view. On the ride home, they decided to rob the driver, directing him to the block of Croes Avenue between Seward and Lafay-ette, across the street from P.S. 107. Vega and Rodriguez pulled guns. An argument and struggle followed, and both men shot the driver. Vega and Rodriguez fled the car, which was still mov-ing slowly up the street before crashing.

In 2003—guided by common practice and his own diligence—O'Malley attempted to corroborate the fact of this apparent 1995 murder so that Vega could plead guilty to it and so the victim's family might have closure. Among other things, he went to visit Jose Rodriguez in federal prison and pressed him about this robbery-murder, to which he had never confessed, although he had also flipped and signed up as a cooperator with SDNY. Upon being confronted with these facts, Rodriguez immediately admitted to the crime and cor-roborated every substantive detail of Vega's account, including time frame, precise location, their respective positions in the cab, the robbery, and the shooting.

Back in 2003, O'Malley had also tried to find the police paper-work on the murder. He called the precinct directly, described the details, and asked, "You guys got something on this mur-der?" They said they had nothing. No one at the 4-3 mentioned the murder of Baithe Diop, though the details were so similar; had someone done so, Glisson might have been cleared back then. O'Malley tried to find a police report or documents relat-ing to the murder of a livery cab driver on January 19, 1995, but he came up empty. O'Malley didn't think too much of it. He knew Vega and Rodriguez hadn't made it up. Why would they? It wouldn't be the first time someone confessed to a mur-der that didn't work out: "Not every murderer sticks around to check the pulse of the victim." Maybe the driver survived and drove into another precinct. Without proof of death—with no body—there was no homicide to admit to. Therefore, on top of the crimes they were already charged with, Vega and Rodriguez also ended up pleading guilty to discharging a firearm in relation to a robbery.

Fast-forward nine full years, to 2012, and O'Malley improbably reading Eric Glisson's letter. He immediately ran Glisson's rap sheet and confirmed that he had been convicted of a 1995 murder whose details seemed to match the crime Vega and Rodriguez pled to. He told one of the chiefs of the Violent Crimes Unit, Margaret Garnett, about his belief in Glisson's innocence. Then, together with Margaret, O'Malley went about the business of confirming that Eric Glisson was innocent.

First, to make sure he had the details right, O'Malley spoke by telephone with both Vega and Rodriguez. Each confirmed the details previously given. Vega also offered up one new fact: they had taken the cabdriver's cell phone and called a few friends afterward before disposing of it.

Days later, O'Malley was on his way to Sing Sing. He appeared unannounced one afternoon at the prison and was shown to one of the private rooms where lawyers meet with their incarcerated clients. It was a tiny chamber, with a concrete floor, a thick rectangular window facing the main meeting room. One desk, four chairs, cheap light in the ceiling. There O'Malley waited. Glisson had no idea who was there to see him.

Glisson walked in, all piss and vinegar, face in a frown. He took one look at O'Malley and said, "Who the fuck are you?" In fairness, the man had been locked up seventeen years for something he hadn't done.

O'Malley didn't blink. He held up the letter and said, "Did you write this?" Glisson saw that it was his own handwritten message for help, and his expression instantly changed. "Yeah," he whispered, twice.

O'Malley said, "I'm from the U.S. Attorney's Office. I know you didn't do this murder. I know who did it." Then O'Malley shook Glisson's hand and apologized to him.

I later asked O'Malley why he said sorry at that moment, and he said, "You know the guy got fucked and it bothered me. It bothered me that I couldn't have caught it ten years ago."

At this point, neither man had sat down. If anyone were peering through the window at that moment, they would have seen Eric Glisson drop to his knees, as if in prayer, and weep. O'Malley helped him up and asked him, "Do you have a lawyer?"

Glisson nodded.

O'Malley said, "I promise I'll call your lawyer when I leave." He shook Glisson's hand and left.

Before O'Malley walked out, Glisson said, "What about the other people?" O'Malley would learn that five other people had been convicted—also wrongly—for Baithe Diop's murder. Glisson said only, "Thank you, thank you." He looked for the first time in almost two decades like a man with hope.

O'Malley called Glisson's attorney, Peter Cross. Cross was not a criminal lawyer, had never tried a criminal case, had never taken on a client accused of a crime. For years, Eric Glisson proclaimed his innocence, but an inmate proclaiming his innocence was hardly unusual and it was not proof. There was a Maryknoll nun who volunteered in the prison named Joanna Chan, whom the inmates called Grandma. She ran a theater program for inmates and taught them Chinese. Soon after meeting Eric, Sister Chan learned his story and believed him. She contacted the only lawyer she knew, Peter Cross. Cross agreed to meet with Eric Glisson at Sing Sing. He told Glisson, "I'll take your case because no one else will. I'm not a criminal lawyer, but the only way to get you out is if we find the guy who did it." Cross added, "We're going to go search for the one-armed killer together," a reference to the movie *The Fugitive*.

One of the first things Cross did was something that the prosecutors who put Glisson and his co-defendants in prison had apparently not done—visit the actual crime scene in Soundview. He went to the apartment window where the sole witness in the underlying case, Miriam Tavares, claimed she saw Glisson shoot

Baithe Diop. He came to this conclusion: the witness was too far away to have actually seen the crime or heard the conversations she described in court. From that bathroom window, the murder had occurred a hundred yards away. There was no way to corroborate the testimony of Tavares, who died in 2002 of a drug overdose. She did apparently have a reason to be angry at Glisson, who claimed they'd had a sexual relationship that did not end well. This fairly quick shoe-leather inquiry made Cross believe that Glisson was innocent.

In 2012, John O'Malley went to the same crime scene, looked out from the same apartment window, and from that vantage point came to the same conclusion: Miriam Tavares was not credible, and Eric Glisson hadn't committed the crime, given this view on top of the confessions of the two cooperating witnesses.

Peter Cross would say, "We shouldn't have had to fight so hard with the Bronx to get Eric Glisson out. They never want to admit a mistake." Cross (rightly) questioned the DA's rush to judgment in the case: "I think they got on a horse early on in this case and they rode that horse and they weren't going to change direction." In other words, they were simply not inclined to *reconsider.*

Eric Glisson was one of six people who were falsely convicted of murdering Baithe Diop and Denise Raymond, a woman who was killed in her home the night before Diop's murder. The NYPD detectives investigating Raymond's murder found the Diop crime scene and concluded the incidents were related. They charged six people for the two murders. The five others were Devon Ayers, Michael Cosme, Carlos Perez, Israel Vasquez, and Cathy Watkins—the only woman in the group. By January 2013, the convictions for "the Bronx Six" were overturned, and the defendants later received $3.9 million from the state. The city agreed to pay the wrongfully accused a total of $40 million in 2016.

———

John O'Malley saw Eric Glisson just one time after he got out of prison. Glisson's lawyer brought him in for a private thank-you to O'Malley. It was not a long meeting. John O'Malley is not a very talkative guy. But he did say this to Glisson: "I hate to use the word 'luck' with you because a guy who went to jail for seventeen years, maybe you don't use that word 'luck.' But for your letter to find its way to my desk is like divine intervention. That's how lucky you are. That letter goes to anyone else, they wouldn't have known anything." It would have been just another letter by just another convicted criminal who was proclaiming his innocence. Dime a dozen.

When asked about O'Malley, Glisson later said, "I thank God every day for John O'Malley. When I looked in that man's eyes, I saw a man who has integrity; I saw a man who was honest."

What went wrong? I don't know the prosecutors in the underlying case. I can't say they were bigots or personally disposed against the six wrongly convicted defendants, but it is impossible to conclude that they discharged their responsibilities well. If the original investigative team had undertaken a conscientious effort to go to that apartment window to see what their witness claimed to see, they might not have been blind to the ultimate truth: that Tavares's testimony was not credible.

Moreover, as Glisson said, "It turns out the police and the district attorney had all the evidence at their disposal to solve this crime from the beginning." That remark was not an overstatement. Glisson had actively fought to appeal his charges and persistently requested documents related to his case—requests that were mostly ignored. At long last he received telephone records from Diop's mobile phone, stolen in the robbery in 1995. Glisson saw that calls made almost immediately after the shooting were to the relatives of Sex Money Murder members. It turns out these were the people whom Vega and Rodriguez had called after they robbed and shot Diop. This was critical evidence corroborating the guilt of Vega and Rodriguez, underscoring the innocence of Glisson and the others. It was never produced to the defense or remarked upon by the prosecution in the 1997 trial.

One fact I learned only recently: In 1995, *New York* magazine published a lengthy, laudatory, glossy profile of the two officers who had "cracked" the case of Diop's murder by arresting Glisson and the others. They were hailed as hero cops, their full-page pictures splashed in the pages of the periodical. You wonder whether this hagiography played some role in their failure to reconsider. After all, not only would a case and convictions be undone, but also a legacy of heroism.

One's understanding of the truth—whether that's the correctness of a fact or the guilt of a person—should never be unalterable. Think of a strongly held, defensible point of view as a block of ice, fixed and solid. When such views are well founded, holding fast to them is commendable. But if new facts come to light—or new revelations materialize—then that block of ice should crack, melt, and even evaporate.

There is such a thing in the law as repose; for certain kinds of crimes, there is an end point to when people can be held liable for their conduct, because most cases must be brought within a set statute of limitations. That's true and right for a lot of reasons: as time passes between a criminal act and its prosecution, memories fade, evidence disappears, witnesses vanish. But repose works in one direction only. Prosecutors need to be morally vigilant and never be resistant to accepting credible, exculpatory evidence no matter how much time has passed.

There's something of a paradox here because we ask—even demand—people to accept the judgments of juries. We expect people to respect the rulings of the court. We trust our prosecutors and our law enforcement officials to get it right. After all, whatever one may think about the prosecution in the Diop case and the error in bringing charges against six innocent people based on flimsy testimony, there were many other participants in the process. There was a judge. There was a defense lawyer. There were jurors. There was an appeal process. So the case went through a fairly rigorous, contested, overseen, refereed process.

The story of Baithe Diop has a deeply troubling side: the undeniable fact that the system is imperfect. People make errors. Well-schooled, well-trained, well-experienced lawyers and investigators will make mistakes, even in the absence of bias, though there might have been bias in the Diop case.

But there is also an inspiring aspect to this case. The letter made its way to a consummate, rigorous investigator with a photographic memory named John O'Malley. It is inspiring that a person would take the time to read a letter that wasn't addressed to him; would open his mind to believing what was in the letter; would have the wherewithal to connect the assertions to things that he personally knew from years earlier; would visit the letter's author; would personally research the case; would read the trial transcripts; and would be aggressively headstrong about the release of these convicted people, even if it meant casting aspersions on fellow investigators, fellow cops, and a fellow prosecutor's office. I'm not sure how common it is for someone to become so personally invested, or how common it is for someone who has dedicated his life to collaring bad guys and supporting fellow law enforcement officers to be just as adamant about getting someone sprung from prison. The work of John O'Malley and Margaret Garnett on Glisson's behalf enabled me to say more than once to my own office that we work just as hard and run just as fast to exonerate the innocent as we do to convict the guilty.

Often the difference between justice and its miscarriage is the quality and the character of the people charged with making life-altering judgments during the process. The first time around, Eric Glisson and company got incompetence, or worse.

The second time around, after seventeen years in prison, they got John O'Malley and Margaret Garnett. We had the same laws, the same police protocols, the same codes of ethics, the same Constitution.

The difference was that the first time people didn't take the time and the care to get the judgments right, even though it was their job to do so. The second time, John O'Malley went out of his way to make sure he got to the truth. Arguably, it wasn't O'Malley's job to fix it. But he felt it was his *duty* because he was guided by the moral imperative that you do what you can to right a wrong. In my experience, "duty" is not a word spoken as often as it should be.

Despite the portrayals in film, TV, and popular fiction, cops and prosecutors do not exist to put people in prison. They certainly exist to hold people accountable as appropriate, and to protect the public, but their job is to make sure that justice is done. Sometimes that means walking away from a case in progress or unraveling a case that's over. John O'Malley's dedication to that principle, not just in word, but in deed, has been deeply inspiring to me. I tell the story of his dedication to truth to assistant U.S. Attorneys and to cops. It's important to teach and repeat these stories in real life to real people who are still in the trenches. Criminal defense lawyers, I say with respect, do not have a monopoly on fixing miscarriages of justice or righting wrongs. The best federal prosecutors do it every day, by exercising wise discretion and, when necessary, by holding DAs to account too.

Not long after I left office, I was asked to give a guest lecture at an elite NYPD homicide training conference. I spoke to a room of cops and forensic examiners focused on solving homicides. These were exceptionally conscientious people who had all kinds of training. They were versed in ballistics, trained in fingerprint analysis, experienced in DNA evidence. All had been admitted to the program because they were among the best.

Rather than lecture them on theories or statutes, I told them just two stories. Two cautionary tales. I told them about the false accusation against Brandon Mayfield and the wrongful conviction, and later exoneration, of Eric Glisson. To my mind, that was better food for thought, the better way to grab them by the lapels, rather than reciting some formulaic checklist of things to do and not do.

There are a million ways to investigate a case. There are also a million ways to get it wrong. You can't teach all of them. What you can teach, what you can press into the minds and hearts of people who will hold the lives of other people in their hands and who, through error or neglect can destroy those lives, is a profound sense of responsibility. And duty. Also, a sense of justice, fallibility, and mission to get it right. In the end, the law doesn't do justice. People do.

And this of course is true everywhere in work and life, this attention to duty, detail, and mission. It applies to treating a patient, teaching a class, building a bridge, putting out a fire, or winning a war. There is no worthy endeavor where it doesn't apply. It is fundamental and, sadly, in short supply. The world calls out for people who care enough to be exacting and rigorous, even when no one is looking, diligent enough to breathe in the work they do, embracing and owning the responsibility, because people are counting on them.

There is one more inspiring aspect to the Glisson case.

Cathy Watkins was one of the five other people wrongly imprisoned for the murder of Baithe Diop. She was convicted largely on the basis of a sketchy layperson voice identification of the person who called the cab. A taxi dispatcher testified that

Watkins's voice matched that of the woman who ordered the fateful ride during which Diop was killed. It was thin stuff, but the prosecutors argued it and the jury bought it.

Watkins did her time at Bedford Hills Maximum Security Prison. An innocent woman, she had nothing to repent for and no need for rehabilitation. Nonetheless, she approached prison life as an opportunity for self-improvement and redemption. She took classes as an inmate through Marymount Manhattan College. Because she could take only a few courses per semester, it took her eleven long years to earn her bachelor's degree in sociology. But she earned it.

What's more, she performed so well in her studies that in 2009, after fourteen unnecessary years in prison and at the ripe age of forty-one, Watkins was named class speaker and valedictorian. She attended her own graduation ceremony behind the cold and confining walls of her prison. She and her fellow graduates all wore prison uniforms under their gowns. What message did this woman—wrongly convicted, wrongly imprisoned, whose every earnest plea of innocence had fallen on deaf ears—choose to deliver that day? She decided, improbably, to preach optimism, possibility, and hope.

This is what she said: "Even though these walls can restrict our physical movement, they cannot restrict our imagination nor our connection to the outside world."

This is what else she said: "One person can make a difference. Let that difference start with you."

And three years after Cathy Watkins's impossibly hopeful prison-yard speech, a Bronx-born stranger named John O'Malley proved her right.

Curiosity and Query:
Asking Basic Questions

In the world of criminal law, asking innumerable questions helps avoid embarrassment, errors, and miscarriages of justice. A case is more likely to be harmed by suppressed questions than by suppressed evidence. This is true in all important endeavors involving truth.

Deep understanding of any subject or set of facts requires active inquiry. That in turn requires asking questions. Every kind of question—searching questions, uncomfortable questions, broad questions, narrow questions, long-shot questions, repetitive questions, hypothetical questions. Many questions should be asked twice, perhaps even a third time, and rephrased each time to make sure the question was really understood and to make sure you understood the answer.

Smart questions are good; dumb questions are even better. There is no such thing as a dumb question, the saying goes, but the shorthand is useful here. So-called dumb questions are often foundational; they tend to get to the basics, to the bottom line. Dumb questions uncover superficial reasoning, reveal bad logic, and expose fake experts. The world is populated, even in rarefied workplaces, with bullshit artists. People are forever using acronyms they can't expand, spouting jargon they can't translate, trafficking in concepts they don't grasp. They parrot shallow talking points and slogans and other people's recollections. When you take at face value everything said to you—even from supposed subject matter experts opining with great confidence—you are at risk of perpetuating everyone's superficial understanding of the matter at hand. There is no shame in asking basic questions, in virtually any context. In fact, it is essential to your personal understanding of any issue. Too often, people like to play in the treetops before working at the roots. That is a mistake in any job and in life generally.

I don't know the right number of questions a person should ask in any particular context. But what I do know is this: find the person in the new job who asks the fewest questions, and there's your problem. One veteran in my office gave this advice to newly minted supervisors: "People are going to come into your office and ask some crazy stuff. They're not the ones you need to worry about. It's the guy you haven't seen in six weeks."

It's not that these people, the ones who don't ask questions, are not smart. The AUSAs in SDNY are the cream of the crop. They are among the best-educated, most credentialed, highest-achieving young lawyers in the country. Many clerk for the Supreme Court and are at the top of their class at the most prestigious law schools. Even as U.S. Attorney, I was intimidated by some of the résumés I saw. The office is so selective and the job so coveted that we had effectively a 100 percent acceptance rate; of the almost two hundred people I personally called to extend an offer, all but two accepted on the spot, *on the phone*.

So why the concern?

Smart people don't like to look dumb. And it is, for many AUSAs, a new experience not to know how to do something. Law school and a short stint in private practice leave most of them woefully unprepared to become line prosecutors; it is the steepest learning curve any of them will ever experience, and their decisions now have consequences for real people. They are not preparing for exams; they are thrust into a complex reality. My people were immensely resourceful, blessed with good judgment and expert researching skills. They were used to being able to find the answer to any question, usually in a text somewhere. But many answers don't come from books, of course, particularly in matters of discretion. Some dilemmas have multiple good answers, and some have none. You don't learn art or acting or judgment from a book. (Yes, I am aware of the irony of my writing a book about how you can't learn judgment from a book.)

I can still remember the steely look of one of my early supervisors when I or others asked basic questions. Years later I still remember the chill of inadequacy I felt. But I didn't let it stop me. I just took my inquiries elsewhere and asked incessant, annoying questions. And usually got the answers I needed.

If you are smart and successful and prideful about your habitual preparedness, asking what may appear to be a dumb question of a supervisor or colleague must feel like going to your office window and stepping out on the ledge, to experience the vertigo of being unmasked as an idiot. It is the nightmare of the lifelong know-it-all. I was spared this particular agita because as a young lawyer and prosecutor I pretty much always felt dumb. It was my baseline self-appraisal. I felt as if I were *always* perched on a precarious ledge of ignorance and failure, and so every stupid question I asked and that someone deigned to answer helped move me *away* from the ledge, *away* from the precipice, edging me an inch closer to the window and safety.

I asked a lot of questions, maybe too many. Every kind of question—Where do you sit in court? Do you address the court as "Judge" or "Your Honor"? Do you always test for fingerprints on a gun? What's the best witness order? What's the best system to keep track of your docket? Who should take notes during a witness interview? How copiously? What to do when a witness lies? How to handle a judge's mistake? And on and on.

My questions predated my first day on the job. I became obsessed, for example, with learning procedure before I got to SDNY. I snuck into one of the Pearl Street courthouse trial rooms where Boyd Johnson was trying the Social Security fraud case of the century, and he lent me, a full week before my official start date, the internal Criminal Division manual. It was maybe a hundred loose-leaf pages, three-hole-punched, in a ratty black binder, but in my hands I felt the weight of scripture. This religious text explained, among other things, the difference between a criminal complaint and an indictment; the picayune procedures to be followed in magistrate court; which forms to bring to the grand jury; the proper way to take a guilty plea; the procedure for forfeiting bail. I read it cover to cover multiple times until I had the basics memorized.

But let us return to the utility of dumb questions. There can be significant tactical value in *playing* dumb, in having other people treat you like an uninformed child.

Let me explain with a story.

Josh Levine was my colleague and contemporary when I first started at SDNY. He is smart, unassuming, and likable. After a few years, he was promoted to the Securities Fraud Unit, and one evening over beers he told a group of us about a harrowing experience he'd had that day.

Josh was brand-new to that senior unit, and while a quick study he knew nothing about criminal securities laws, complex business transactions, and the like. In our office, you learned by doing. And by watching other people do. That day Josh was set to attend a proffer session with a potential cooperating witness in a case against David Rutkoske, the president of a securities broker-dealer. We'd charged him with a $12 million fraud through the manipulation of trading in an internet gaming company. A more senior and seasoned AUSA, David Anders, had indicted the case and was set to conduct the proffer of the would-be cooperator, Michael Niebuhr. Josh was there to watch and learn.

At the very last minute, after the interview had already begun, David had a courtroom emergency: a fugitive of his had been caught, and he had to deal with that. David was gone. But this was an important proffer; it had been scheduled a long time in advance, and the show had to go on. With Josh. Who was clueless—about the case and the law. We were aghast. This sounded like the terrible nightmare I still have: you forgot to drop that Shakespeare class in college, and now you have to take the final exam.

The securities case was not the most complex in history, but it necessitated an understanding of various aspects of securities trading in the Over-the-Counter Bulletin Board market; "lock-up" arrangements; rule 144 stock; "lifting" offers; and a host of other technical concepts. Josh is a smart and diligent guy and would eventually try the case with great skill, but at this stage, thrown into the ocean with no life vest, he felt he would drown. This was supposed to be a swimming lesson, not an Olympic event.

What did he do?

In that moment of panic, his unmasking close at hand, Josh had a flash of genius. This is what he said, with a straight face, to the aspiring cooperating witness: "Listen, you may have to testify about all of this one day to a completely clueless jury. So you're really going to have to break it down. So, as you explain the transactions today, I want you to pretend like I'm your nine-year-old nephew. Go slow and take it from the top."

Brilliant.

It was a simple gambit but one that allowed Josh at once to save face, learn the case, and simplify the testimony. It gave him the space and excuse to ask questions to his heart's delight—basic questions, ignorant questions, dumb questions, the kind anyone's nine-year-old nephew might ask. He could be confused, and he could show his confusion. He could ask the witness to repeat himself, to say it again.

Two epilogues to this story: First, when Josh finally put the cooperator on the witness stand a year later, the straightforward and simplified testimony he gave bore great resemblance to the story he told his nine-year-old-nephew stand-in.

Second, once Josh *did* become schooled in securities laws, *did* become expert and seasoned as a senior member of the unit, guess how he conducted similar interview sessions on complex matters with potential trial witnesses? He found himself resorting to the same conceit—*tell it to me like I'm your nine-year-old nephew.* It was no longer a face-saving gambit. It was a smart method to get educated, a clever and even disarming way to put his witness at ease and in the frame of mind to speak simply and understandably.

When I worked in the Senate as chief counsel for Chuck Schumer, I saw Senator Schumer do this constantly. Someone would draft a complex bill, understand all the statutory language choices, and bring it to the senator, who hadn't thought about the issue deeply in a long while. He was sometimes brilliantly childlike in his questioning. Note I didn't say childish. I said childlike. There is a reason children often ask the best and most flummoxing questions.

What parent has not had the experience of holding forth on some matter of science or history to his child, only to have said child ask a basic foundational question, so utterly exposing the shallowness of the parent's knowledge that Dad quickly looks for a toy or other distraction and moves on?

The natural angst about asking dumb questions doesn't necessarily fade over time as you climb the ladder. And it is even more dangerous for managers and supervisors to suppress questions. The manager is expected to be a subject matter expert. The manager is supposed to *know.* But the manager is also mortal.

I returned to SDNY as U.S. Attorney after a four-and-a-half-year absence. Much was familiar. I knew most of the people. I knew all the supervisors. I knew all the judges. I knew all the basics of how to investigate and try a case. I knew the culture of the place and its traditions. At the same time, everything was different. I was now the leader of a storied institution, since 1789, where I had only recently been just an assistant on the line.

I'll admit something. Here's how I felt: I felt nervous and afraid and unworthy. I was terrified that I might not live up to the tradition of that place; that I might not ultimately measure up to the job; that I would be a disappointment to the people who had supported me.

There's a hundred years of U.S. Attorney portraits up on the eighth-floor wall, and they all looked at me every morning when I walked past them to my office. And you know what I thought they were saying to me? "Don't screw it up, kid."

Even years into the job, after things had gone fairly well, I got nervous and afraid still. I thought that if I ever lost that feeling, that's the day I should step down. Now, don't get me wrong. I had (and have) plenty of self-confidence but also, on a fairly frequent basis, roaring self-doubt.

Self-doubt in moderation is animating and motivating, not paralyzing. Leaders who have purged themselves of all self-doubt will not be leaders for long and, in my view, are dangerous while in command. I learned, over time, that self-doubt is my friend, and arrogance my enemy.

So back to my start as U.S. Attorney. I felt in some ways a deeper ignorance than I felt years before as a fledgling prosecutor. This phenomenon is surely familiar to every leader. The most expert CEO, college dean, or cabinet secretary who must head a large organization cannot possibly know and understand in a deep, granular way everything about every aspect of what that institution does and produces. It is an impossibility. In fact, I have come to believe that if you meet a leader who knows a super-impressive amount of minutiae and granular detail, that leader—with the possible exception of Steve

Jobs—is likely failing at the job of leading, endlessly losing the forest for the trees that the subordinates should be tending to. Leaders need judgment more than knowledge, along with a reliable method of cross-examining those closer to the facts than they can ever be. A trustworthy method of inquiry, in the face of lesser knowledge—plus a good understanding of people—is how leaders make proper decisions. President John Kennedy did not know more about war or warheads than his generals and advisers during the Cuban missile crisis in 1962. But as the Soviets placed nuclear weapons ninety miles from Florida, he was the final decision maker. He chose a naval blockade over a more belligerent response after an assessment made through close questioning of his more experienced team, which turned out to be the correct choice. So it goes with most high-level decisions, even when nuclear annihilation is not on the horizon.

And yet as the leader, you are called upon, regularly, to make final decisions and judgment calls on matters about which you have only surface-level knowledge. You are reliant on the good counsel of other people.

I studied summaries of the significant cases from the Criminal and Civil Divisions, which ran to hundreds of pages, single-spaced. I found myself swimming in a sea of new facts and unfamiliar law. I was briefed in the first weeks on scores of cases, day after day after day. Everyone seemed so smart and so seasoned and so on top of everything that it would have been easy to smile and nod and feign full understanding of every issue presented to me.

It occurred to me that leadership is surprisingly easy to fake if you are in an environment where those around you are exceptionally smart, diligent, and honorable. You could easily adopt a strategy of detachment and deference and a pretense of understanding, and let others run the show. Where everything is a well-oiled machine, a leader can get away without doing much;

if the status quo is already excellent, it's not hard to leave well enough alone.

But that, of course, is when the institution slips, stagnates, and stops innovating, when it ceases to keep up with the times. Before I was sworn in as U.S. Attorney, I decided to consume a shelf's worth of books on leadership and management. I was hoping for some magic formula to help me do the new job well. One passage from one book struck me above all the others. It is from a slim volume called *How the Mighty Fall,* written by Jim Collins:

> *Every* institution is vulnerable, no matter how great. No matter how much you've achieved, no matter how far you've gone, no matter how much power you've garnered, you are vulnerable to decline. There is no law of nature that the most powerful will inevitably remain at the top. Anyone can fall and most eventually do.

Those words rang in my ears, every day I was in office. In fact, I quoted the passage to the entire office on the occasion of my first annual address and repeated it throughout the years. SDNY is a storied institution, many of its cases and alumni legendary. It did not need a turnaround artist, nor did it need a mere caretaker. It needed, like all institutions, engaged leadership.

So I asked my basic questions.

But how to ask them? It was one thing, as a brand-new line assistant, to ask dumb questions because people did not expect you to know much. And even then, it was hard, as I've described, to expose yourself. I was out on the ledge once more, except this time I was no longer a novice, but the presidentially appointed, Senate-confirmed U.S. Attorney.

I thought I was expected to be the smartest, the most expert, the most qualified person in the room. I realized that I was not, but it was anything but easy to expose that fact to others because

everyone who has a boss, I believe, is forever and always evaluating that boss—at least that's how it feels to the boss. When I
presided over a meeting, especially those very early ones, I felt
every eye upon me and felt that everyone was judging not only
what I knew or didn't know but how smart my lines of inquiry
might be. That is a daunting thing. I could have retreated into
a mode of nodding and feigned understanding, or I could have
waited until the junior people left the room and then pulled
aside my deputy, Boyd, my dearest and closest friend, and asked
him to educate me away from the judgmental eyes of the junior
folks. But I tried really hard not to do that, and continuing the
practice and posture I had as a green assistant, I asked my dumb
questions.

One recurring exercise was especially nerve-racking. There
were times, early on, when we would moot an opening statement before trial in a significant case and the AUSA would come
into the library with a box as a makeshift lectern at the head of
the table, the chairs filled with fellow AUSAs, paralegals, investigators, and junior staff, ready to critique the substance and
delivery of the opening statement. The most nervous person
in that room was the AUSA delivering the opening statement.
The second most nervous person, I believe, was me. Because
at the end of the delivery, everyone had formed his or her own
view, but when the assistant finished speaking, as a matter of
deference and tradition, the feedback was given in hierarchi-
cal order with the U.S. Attorney going first. And I again felt
that everyone in the room was not just evaluating the perfor-
mance of the assistant but evaluating mine as well. Was my
feedback smart? Were my questions stupid? Did I understand
the case? In those moments, it might surprise you to learn, I
was deeply aware of the aphorism "better to keep quiet and
have people think you a fool than to open your mouth and
remove all doubt."

There's a body of literature about impostor syndrome that

I've never read, but I felt like one when I assumed leadership of the office. This is not to say, by the way, that I was an insecure mess. I was not. I am given to feelings of great confidence, at times even overconfidence. It's a strange thing to balance—the burden of your ignorance against the confidence in your intelligence and judgment so that you ask your dumb questions anyway. It's a bit of a paradox at the intersection of insecurity and arrogance. But every leader of every institution stands, on a regular basis, at that intersection. Over time you become comfortable with it, and you learn fearlessness in asking the right questions of the right people. Or you fail.

Here's what I think: if you are listening hard and if your dumb questions address the heart of the matter, it's okay. They may betray ignorance, but also likely show the right focus. If you have a penchant for asking foundational questions that people think you should already know the answers to, so what? You are on the right track. Ignorance is quickly remedied. A tendency toward the tangential, the irrelevant, the collateral, is not so easily fixed. It is okay not to know things, so long as you *want* to know things, *care* to know things, and when those are the things you actually need to know. Curiosity and query are among the most important pillars of sound leadership.

Even the smartest people don't know everything. Early in my tenure, I invited the newly appointed Supreme Court justice Elena Kagan to address the office. We did the talk, as we usually did with prominent outside speakers, in the beautiful ceremonial courtroom at the U.S. Court of International Trade (CIT), across the street from One St. Andrew's Plaza. We took photos and had a small meeting with our appellate lawyers upstairs before the event. The justice was super curious and peppered me with questions, one after another. One was this: "What does the Court of International Trade do?" I couldn't believe she didn't know, as a justice of the *Supreme* Court that sits atop all the other courts. Then I swallowed, lowered my voice, and had to confess that though it was across the street and we had often used the facilities, I too had no clue, not the foggiest idea what the Court of International Trade actually did. And we both laughed. (I should note that the CIT is a wonderful body that seeks to resolve issues related to trade and customs law around the globe. Easier said than done.)

My favorite question to ask often yielded the worst possible answer I could get; the question was, *why do we do it this way?* This may be an ignorant and basic question, but an even more ignorant and shameful answer was this: "We've always done it that way." That is literally the only answer to any question that would actually make me angry. One might think it strange that I would be offended at this justification of tradition in the conservative task of law enforcement, but that answer is a barrier to innovation, a barrier to efficiency, and a potential barrier to justice.

Our entire civil fraud enforcement program arose from the simple question, "Why can't we sue banks for fraud under a statute called FIRREA?" FIRREA (Financial Institutions Reform, Recovery, and Enforcement Act), a little-invoked law aimed at punishing misconduct that "affects" a financial institution, was passed in 1989, but no one had used it to go after a bank itself; it had been employed only to pursue frauds committed by others *against* a bank. But the plain language of the statute didn't preclude a suit based on bad conduct by a bank itself, which would naturally "affect" a financial institution. In rapid succession, three federal judges agreed with us, and all over the country the Justice Department—following our lead—began using FIRREA as a tool.

Another simple question led to a complete revamping of a long-standing, and ill-conceived, policy: "Why do we resolve civil cases by letting the defendant neither admit nor deny the allegations?" We put a stop to that, and the sky did not fall.

Asking questions as a junior person leads to deeper understanding. Asking questions as a leader does the same, plus it creates, one hopes, a climate of curiosity and self-reflection, for individuals and for the institution as a whole. And it fosters a culture of thoughtfulness, curiosity, critical thinking, understanding, and challenge, rather than rote acceptance of the status quo. Because that acceptance is how the mighty fall.

The Principles of Interrogation: "Barbarism Is Not Necessary"

E veryone has seen how confessions are extracted in the movies. You beat and punch and threaten the witness. If the Armageddon clock is ticking—and even if it isn't—anything goes, and every brutal tactic quickly yields credible results. You may waterboard and torture, cut off a finger if necessary, whatever it takes to get answers.

In the real world, however, where truth matters and testosterone doesn't flow like a river in the streets, long experience teaches that patience and humanity outperform threats and brute force every time. The people who reflexively thrill to the most violent options tend to be rhetorical bullies with no experience in the field and little knowledge of history. The tried-and-true—and civilized—techniques for eliciting truth are universal. Consider the following disparate interrogation subjects: U.S. Air Force pilots downed in Germany during World War II; an operational terrorist in New York City—the Times Square bomber, Faisal Shahzad; and a terrified witness in a homicide case. All gave up secrets to skilled interrogators who, though separated by language, time, and training, are bound together by common method and principle.

As World War II engulfed the globe, battles were won or lost not only with bombs and bullets, not only with tanks and ships, but also with intelligence. Surveillance and spycraft could give an advantage to one side over the other, of course, but another deeply important source of information about the enemy could drive victory or defeat: the prisoner of war. Prisoners of war captured by one side carried secrets about the opposition, its strength, and perhaps its future plans, intentions, and strategies.

A feature of the American effort to defeat Germany was the air war, in particular a program of brutal bombing runs over German cities. Elite U.S. Air Force pilots flew thousands of missions, dropping untold deadly payloads over many parts of the European country, most famously and lethally on Dresden, where an estimated 130,000 German civilians were killed in one deadly day alone.

The Germans downed a not small number of American pilots, many of whom survived and were taken prisoner. Each of those pilots was an elite military man, and even though no individual POW might have had earth-shattering intelligence, the secrets extracted from pilot after pilot, in combination, could be fairly useful to the German cause. Meanwhile, every downed pilot was steeped in the military version of *omertà:* you keep silent, and under the law of war you need only provide name, rank, and serial number. Many remained silent. But many others, even without feeling tricked or harassed or brutalized, talked.

What makes a captured soldier talk? What makes a secret spill? History suggests that the principles of effective interrogation in unregulated wartime are not so different from the tenets of effective interrogation in peacetime criminal inquiries.

Consider that the most effective questioner for the Luftwaffe in Germany was an obscure and quiet man whose story is set forth in a remarkable book by Raymond F. Toliver called *The Interrogator: The Story of Hanns Joachim Scharff, Master Interrogator of the Luftwaffe.* Hanns Scharff had no formal training in the art and science of asking questions, having fallen into the business rather accidentally. Born in East Prussia and fluent in

English, Scharff was headed to the German front as an interpreter when he was transferred to the Luftwaffe interrogation center at Oberursel, as an interpreter for the "professional" interrogators. When both of the interrogators for whom he interpreted crashed the plane they were flying, Scharff was suddenly promoted to interrogator himself. He proved himself to be a backup quarterback for the ages.

Like many genius practitioners of an art, Scharff learned through observation and osmosis. He became known as the slyest and most effective stealer of secrets in all of Germany. His style was gentle, his manner soft. He posed as every captured pilot's greatest ally and advocate. He fed them, and he joked with them. Scharff famously took nature walks with his POWs, who strolled free and unrestrained, as long as they promised—giving only their word as collateral—that they would not try to escape. He relied on trust and rapport, impressed them with his respect and intellect, took advantage of their human need for contact and kinship. He empathized with them. And POW after POW dropped his guard with such frequency that Scharff became the stuff of legend throughout the Luftwaffe.

His genteel method, and its fruitfulness, seem shocking not only because of a prevailing macho intuition that wartime interrogation must be harsh but also because he employed it in stark contrast to the brutal tactics of another German agency of the era, the dreaded Gestapo. Indeed, Scharff shrewdly took advantage, for his own purposes, of the Gestapo's reputation for cruelty. Genuine POWs could stay at the interrogation center and then be placed in a POW camp, he would say, but *spies* had to be turned over to the Gestapo. To show yourself to be a true POW and not a spy, he would further explain, you had to reveal something more than name, rank, and serial number. Many did. Apart from this world-class good-cop/bad-cop gambit, Scharff rejected all threats and intimidation. The hypothetical backstop of the Gestapo notwithstanding,

Scharff succeeded principally on the strength of his kindness, respect, and rapport.

As with all successful endeavors involving human interaction, Scharff's approach was marked by a few basic precepts. One precept was this: "It is advantageous to study the files before bringing the prisoner into the interrogation office." It would seem obvious, but some investigators forget that painstaking homework—not just gut and guile—often carries the day. Kenny McCabe's chief strength was encyclopedic knowledge of the mobsters he pursued. Equally important was a reputation for that encyclopedic knowledge. When he questioned people, they believed they couldn't bullshit him because he knew whereof he spoke. And so they told him more. All good interrogators understand the same.

An air of all-knowing confidence, earned through preparation and self-schooling, can pry loose tightly held information. Knowledge impresses the mark and makes him more forthcoming. Every good questioner has testimonials. John O'Malley, for example, tells of the time he was questioning a gunrunner who was describing a location where firearms could be bought on Boston Road in the Bronx. O'Malley nodded and said, knowingly, "Oh, right by Mama's Fried Chicken." It was a small thing, this bit of geographical mastery, but the gunrunner was impressed, and the path to truth was a bit smoother after that.

Scharff ceaselessly employed this technique. He kept meticulously organized files on every American POW—troves of seemingly useless bits, details, and trivia about every U.S. serviceman to come through the interrogation center—and then casually dropped those crumbs of intelligence, suggesting he knew vastly more than he was letting on and at the same time disarming his tight-lipped targets.

Homework, moreover, made for a gentler (and more fruitful) encounter. As Scharff himself said, "Barbarism is not necessary. I will collect, as you may see, a stifling amount of information and evidence beforehand, and by its display along with persuasion mainly appealing to common sense, I will make him tell me things I have not heard before." *Barbarism is not necessary.* That is no small announcement from a German military man, spoken without irony, during World War II. It is, moreover, a striking statement of both method and principle. The method being painstaking work and preparation, piecing together as much detail as possible about the subject before interrogation begins, followed by rapport building and humane questioning; and the principle being the avoidance of cruelty. The principle and the method are not coincident with each other; they inform and reinforce each other. It is the method's effectiveness that renders barbarism unnecessary. And because barbarism is not necessary, barbarism is not right.

To the present day, there rages an unsettled debate about how you can (and should) get a person in custody to talk—whether prisoner of war or criminal defendant. There are people—often partisan politicians—who insist that any sort of kindness toward a target or a prisoner is weak and coddling and ineffective. Their belief in harsh interrogation techniques suggests an inversion of Scharff's statement of principle and method—the principle being that a person in custody should not be coddled and therefore the method should not be gentle. They hold an intuitive but uninformed belief that you must beat the truth out of some kinds of people because they deserve it. They conflate the principle and the method in a desire for toughness, despite the stated goal of simply wanting information. To them, the idea of humane treatment, polite questioning, or advice of rights is weak and ineffective.

Hanns Scharff is one in a long line of real-life interrogators who have exposed—by their success—this misinformed myth. Consider how hard it must have been for Luftwaffe interrogators—in the midst of war, with no higher stakes possible, knowing that some of these American pilots were responsible for the brutal carpet bombing of their cities—to acknowledge the dignity of the American military man, treat him with respect, and interrogate him humanely.

Scharff enlisted the method because it was right *and* it was effective. He understood what generations of productive interrogators know: preparation and rapport beat intimidation and violence. His mantra, which goes to the efficacy of his approach, was this: "Soft words do more than hard blows." The use of that method and its persistent effectiveness reinforced and vindicated a moral principle: even with bombs flying and people dying, humanity was still possible. The book's author put it this way: "In the midst of war, one of the most inhumane of human activities, we learn of a man who retains his humanity."

Scharff's general principles have been endorsed and ratified by every good investigator whom I have ever met, spoken to, or overseen. Beatings and bluster seldom yield sustained, truthful answering of questions. Strategy beats savagery, and patience outperforms force.

In the Southern District, we saw this in case after case after case, even in the kinds of cases where you might naturally think cooperation or confession would be out of the question. Who might you guess would be the toughest nut to crack, the most unyielding witness? You might speculate it would be the man who has planned or committed atrocities against other human beings not from greed, power, or temporary passion but out of deep-seated ideology and ingrained hatred of the West. You might identify the hardened, hate-filled terrorist, who massacres not on account of money, mental illness, or love but out of hatred and his ill-considered cause. But that guess would be wrong.

Consider the case of the so-called Times Square bomber, Faisal Shahzad, who tried to kill a lot of Americans not nine months into my tenure.

Early in the evening of May 1, 2010, a dark Nissan Pathfinder with tinted windows was parked in the middle of Times Square in New York, on Forty-fifth Street and Seventh Avenue. Ticking in that Pathfinder was a bomb made of fertilizer, propane, fireworks, and gas. It was a crude but potent bomb. The maker of that bomb intended for it to explode in the heart of Manhattan on a Saturday evening just as tens of thousands would be making their way to restaurants and Broadway shows. The bomb killed no one because it did not explode. It did not explode, because its maker had made a blessed mistake in its construction. A nearby civilian saw smoke coming out of the car and alerted police. What followed was the lockdown of Times Square, the evacuation of countless people from the area, and a fifty-three-hour manhunt. Eventually, we learned that this attempted killer, six months earlier, had said in a Tehrik-i-Taliban Pakistan video, "I've been trying to join my brothers in jihad ever since 9/11 happened."

During those fifty-three hours, AUSAs in my Terrorism Unit went without sleep, along with their counterparts at the Joint Terrorism Task Force (JTTF), every second spent chasing leads, watching surveillance videos, and checking the provenance of every last Nissan Pathfinder in New York. There were some false starts and dead ends until late Monday night, when they definitively determined that Shahzad was the wanted man. Armed FBI units surrounded Shahzad's apartment in Bridgeport, Connecticut, to take this dangerous man into custody.

My deputy at the time, Boyd Johnson, was stationed at FBI headquarters at 26 Federal Plaza. I was at One St. Andrew's Plaza, getting updates from my terrorism chiefs about the status of Shahzad's apprehension. There was a glitch. Shahzad had somehow slipped surveillance and fled his apartment. Where was he? The most wanted man in America—even though placed on a terrorist no-fly list—was sitting on an Emirates jet at John F. Kennedy International Airport about to take off for Dubai shortly before midnight on Monday. The plane had already left the gate but was dramatically stopped so Shahzad could be pulled off.

Shahzad was soon in custody, alive and in a position to speak. A momentous interrogation loomed. Did Shahzad act alone? If not, who were his co-conspirators? Who radicalized him? Who trained him? Where did the bomb materials come from? Did he know of other plots? Lots of questions awaited him, but would he answer?

The context for this interrogation is important. This was the first true operational terrorist in New York City since 9/11. Some recent history called into question standard practices and colored the decision making. The apprehension of Faisal Shahzad came just four months after the so-called underwear bomber, Umar Farouk Abdulmutallab, was taken off an airplane in Detroit on Christmas Day 2009. Abdulmutallab had been quickly read his rights—too quickly?—and arguably important intelligence gathering had been cut short. There was great sensitivity surrounding the question of if and when Shahzad would be read his rights.

We had anticipated this moment in the wake of the Abdulmutallab case and discussed just this scenario: what to do if an operational terrorist appeared in our midst. One thing we did was to carefully research the public safety exception to *Miranda*, which generally requires an advice of rights before questioning anyone in custody. The exception gives agents the ability to question a criminal suspect before giving an advice of rights without fear that incriminating statements would be suppressed in court. That exception, set forth in a 1984 Supreme Court opinion, *New York v. Quarles*, says that a suspect may be questioned at some length about plans, co-conspirators, and anything else important for public safety. For some period, to get answers to those questions, to gather information and intelligence, the law allows questioning without a *Miranda* warning.

Depending on the circumstances, the loss of use of a confession in court due to a *Miranda* violation might not matter much if there was other overwhelming evidence of guilt. When we left the conference room, the strategy was clear: no quick *Miranda*. Find out everything possible and weigh the importance of the confession in achieving a conviction in court against the need for intelligence.

That planning paid off. When Shahzad was captured and his interview by law enforcement agents was imminent, we were ready. I spoke to the head of the National Security Division in Washington about our plan and the intent to delay *Miranda,* which we considered fully lawful and appropriate in the circumstances. That official, David Kris, agreed with the plan and told me to discuss it with Attorney General Eric Holder. I called the Command Center, which was the easiest way to get hold of the attorney general. The Command Center called me back on my mobile phone, and I remember taking the call, looking out the broad wall of windows in my office, after 10:00 p.m. I said that the case against Faisal Shahzad was already strong—agents were speeding to JFK to interview him—and that we were in no hurry to Mirandize him in order to maximize the collection of information and intelligence. The attorney general endorsed this course of action.

At that moment, Shahzad sat in what's called a secondary room at the airport, guarded by Customs and Border Protection agents, while JTTF questioners were en route. An FBI supervisory special agent and an NYPD detective entered the room. Shahzad appeared calm and relaxed. This was the first thing he had said when taken into custody: "What took you so long?" It was a question, not a taunt. They offered Shahzad food and refreshments before transporting him to a location in Manhattan where the JTTF maintained its secure headquarters. According to the plan, the detective asked Shahzad a series of public safety questions. Shahzad was responsive and even-keeled. Before long, the detectve had developed a rapport with Shahzad.

Even though the plan was to question Shahzad for many hours, it was the detective's professional judgment in the room, based on his assessment of Shahzad's demeanor and state of mind—honed by years of investigative work and thousands of interviews—that he could give the fateful *Miranda* warning and Shahzad would keep talking nonetheless.

Everyone who watches TV knows *Miranda*. It might be the best-known Supreme Court case name in America. It is a simple advice of rights: you have the right to an attorney; you have the right to remain silent; and so forth. It's known by heart by most cops and agents, though often they read from a printed card to get it exactly right.

How to know when to give a *Miranda* warning to a terrorist? How to know when to slip in the advice of rights? An agent once described it this way: "If you think of the interview of a suspect as a first date, the *Miranda* warning is a bit like getting the awkward first kiss out of the way. There comes a moment when you think, 'If I kiss him now, he'll kiss me back. If I wait, it may not happen and the moment may pass.'" Sure, *Miranda* can short-circuit questioning. But the giving of rights can show kinship, deepen trust. As Hanns Scharff knew even in time of war, rapport is the most common catalyst for the spilling of secrets.

Other agents describe the art of interrogation in similar terms, as a seduction. It is about understanding the moment, they say, when you have maximum connection to the suspect and a true feel for which buttons to push, which levers to manipulate. At that moment, the detective made a judgment call, just as every agent has to make. His judgment was this: I can slip in *Miranda* now, discharge the legal obligation, preserve the admissibility of what comes next, and likely continue the flow of information.

The fear, of course (see, for example, Farouk Abdulmutallab), is that the reminder of the right to counsel will cause the suspect to invoke and shut down. But this man, Faisal Shahzad, after pledging jihad against America, after choosing to serve as an operative for a foreign terrorist organization, after deciding to wage war inside the United States, after trying to murder scores of innocents on the street in Times Square, after attempting to flee and plan more attacks and kill more Americans—after all that, what did Faisal Shahzad do? He talked. And he talked. And then he talked some more.

There was no smack, no punch, no threat. He was fed and advised of his rights. *Soft words do more than hard blows.* He talked calmly and at length, for days, revealing key details about his plans and intentions. Among other things, he admitted that he purchased all the components of the bomb; that he hoped and believed his bomb would kill forty people; and that he had planned to come back and kill more people two weeks later. Shahzad also—receiving an explicit, repetitive, daily *Miranda* warning—was questioned about associates and possible facilitators, generating so many leads that, as we told the court, they "required the participation of hundreds of agents in different cities working around the clock."

Then he promptly admitted his guilt in court, the only example of a high-profile defendant doing this in my experience as U.S. Attorney. Faisal Shahzad was arraigned two weeks later, on May 18, 2010, and pled guilty on the spot. He's now spending life in prison and deservedly so.

Beyond preparation and homework, success in interrogation often comes down to reading the moment. It requires more emotional intelligence than bravado, notwithstanding what you see in the movies or bloviated about by politicians. The debate about *Miranda*, political sensationalism aside, is not an unreasonable one, but it is vastly overblown. Like so many things in an investigation, individual judgments, made in real time and based on common sense and experience, get the job done. Notably, the official who developed a rapport with Faisal Shahzad was not a career national security FBI agent. He was a cop who cut his teeth on the streets of the city investigating drug crimes and gaining essential experience and judgment in the back-and-forth with hundreds of witnesses and suspects. So, when it was time to make a judgment, when it was time to read the moment in the most fraught interview of his career, the odds were high that he was reading the moment correctly. Formal training matters, but typically it is the education gained in the street and on the beat that makes the difference.

The point is that effective interrogation isn't learned from a textbook. It is art more than science. It requires the gifts of empathy and human understanding. This is not to say that tougher interrogation methods never yield fruit. They may sometimes be necessary, but everyone should be forever skeptical of blowhards who reflexively claim that only harsh techniques can produce information or truth. You should be especially skeptical of those people if they have never questioned a human being in real life. This is the view of professional FBI investigators, cops, DEA agents, and federal prosecutors. I trust their judgment more than that of any ivory-tower author or political player who has never once seen firsthand what makes a bad person talk.

Faisal Shahzad, by the way, is far from the only terrorist who went from one minute wanting to kill innocent people to the next minute giving law enforcement a road map to his activities and a catalog of his co-conspirators. David Headley, who was prosecuted by the U.S. Attorney's Office in the Northern District of Illinois, was responsible for and participated in the 2008 Mumbai terrorist attack, which left 164 people dead, including six Americans. Once again, agents read the moment, and within thirty minutes of being advised of his *Miranda* rights, Headley, according to the prosecutors' sentencing memorandum, "provided extensive details about Lashkar-e-Taiba, including its organizational structure; leadership and other personnel; recruiting; fundraising; training; planning of attacks and potential targets." Other examples abound. It's the norm, not the exception.

Why do terrorists talk? What condition—combined with an interrogator's skill—causes someone like Faisal Shahzad or David Headley to reveal, upon capture, virtually everything about himself, his plans, his intentions, without having it beaten out of him? I've wondered about this a lot over the years because it seems counterintuitive. I've asked a lot of agents at the FBI why they think it happens.

This is about as good an explanation as I've heard, and it's the attitude questioners are smart to exploit: Terrorists want their stories told and known. They want, moreover, to be the authors of their own stories, and they want to be the heroes of their stories. The point of terrorism is to strike fear and to attract publicity for political ends. The ambition is to become the stuff of legend. Terrorists loathe anonymity. It's the same reason they film martyrdom videos, the same reason they use press and propaganda to spread their ill-conceived gospel and to entice future recruits. They are starved for their fifteen minutes too. In some cases, it may not be more complicated than that.

There is perhaps another reason. It's a deep desire on the part of people, even heinous criminals, to be understood, for others to comprehend why they did what they did, and people who commit shocking crimes, particularly out of ideology, are no exception to that fundamental psychic principle. The good news for investigators is that this predilection toward wanting to be understood is an entry point not only for holding those people accountable but also for discovering the scope of a terrorist cell or the identities of other people who would do us harm.

———

Of course there are advocates for harsh interrogation techniques, up to and including torture. These are people for whom barbarism is necessary not just to puff up their own sense of strength—personally or publicly—but because they believe barbarism is effective. The historical record shows otherwise.

Take, for example, the case of Abu Zubaydah, who was captured after 9/11 and incorrectly identified as one of al-Qaeda's top leaders. Zubaydah was injured, captured, and detained after a raid in Pakistan in 2002. In CIA custody, he was waterboarded at least eighty-three times; sleep deprived; confined in two-and-a-half-foot-by-two-and-a-half-foot boxes for twenty-nine hours; confined in a coffin-sized box for 266 hours; slammed repeatedly into a wall; shackled in stress positions; exposed to cold temperatures and loud sounds. At one point, CIA interrogators believed they had killed him. Zubaydah ultimately revealed information about the identity of Khalid Sheikh Mohammed (the organizer behind 9/11) and José Padilla, an American citizen convicted of conspiring to bomb the United States (whose own experience with interrogation has also been a subject of fierce debate).

Sounds great, except for one thing. That useful information was attained *before* Zubaydah's torture, during rapport-building interrogations with FBI agents. It was late March, and Zubaydah had just been captured. At the time, Ali Soufan was an FBI special agent, an expert interrogator, and one of only eight Arabic speakers in the whole bureau. He flew with another agent to an undisclosed location to speak to Zubaydah.

He found an injured but defiant Zubaydah in the small room set aside for questioning. Soufan's first question was simple: "What is your name?" Zubaydah responded, "Daoud." This was a lie. Soufan looked at Zubaydah, smiled, and said, "How about I just call you Hani?" Hani was the nickname that Zubaydah's mother had given him as a child. Zubaydah, visibly shocked, said, "Okay." That devastating, humanizing detail made a difference. For the next hour, Zubaydah talked, revealing critical, actionable intelligence to Soufan.

As Soufan would later testify before Congress, the success of the FBI's interrogation technique requires research. Preparation matters. "The interrogator," he said, channeling Scharff, "has to do his or her homework and become an expert in every detail known to the intelligence community about the detainee. The interrogator then uses that knowledge to impress upon the detainee that everything about him is known and that any lie will be easily caught."

As later documented in the Senate Select Committee on Intelligence's 6,700-page study, known as the *Report on Torture,* the CIA's detention and harsh interrogation program between 2001 and 2009 was not effective. Barbarism was neither necessary nor helpful. The committee's very first finding stated this: "The CIA's use of its enhanced interrogation techniques was not an effective means of acquiring intelligence or gaining cooperation from detainees."

Not only is torture unnecessary to extract valuable information, but it can result in basic injustice: false confessions. When the United States invaded Iraq in 2003, the administration justified the invasion on evidence from an unnamed source that Iraq was providing weapons to al-Qaeda operatives.

This source was Ibn al-Sheikh al-Libi. Al-Libi, who ran Osama bin Laden's terrorist training camp in Afghanistan, was captured in 2001. At the time, he was the highest-ranking member of al-Qaeda in American captivity. The FBI and the CIA both questioned al-Libi, and while one of the FBI officers reminded his agents to read al-Libi his rights and treat him respectfully with the goal of building rapport, the CIA agents believed they weren't getting accurate information. So the CIA reportedly rendered al-Libi to Egypt, where he was beaten, confined in small boxes, and treated to a "mock burial." He finally told his interrogators what they wanted to hear about the connections between al-Qaeda and Iraq. But al-Libi's confessions were apparently false. In 2004, when al-Libi returned to FBI custody, he recanted them. "They were killing me," al-Libi would later tell the FBI. "I had to tell them something."

The best evidence shows that nothing useful comes from torture.

You never know what human connection, what twinge of conscience will open the spigot.

A homicide had gone unsolved for many months. The case was cold. Police had looked at it, made no headway, and brought in the Feds.

There was an obvious suspect, but it was premature to charge him. There was no definitive proof. Agents went at it with what they had. They reviewed phone records. They interviewed people and chased other leads as well. They tried to flip people they believed were involved in the drug dispute believed to underlie the murder, but to no avail.

At some point, the case agent, a detective, realized there was another potential witness. The detective didn't rush to approach the witness. He followed the Hanns Scharff maxim: *it is advantageous to study the files before bringing the prisoner into the interrogation office.* The witness wasn't a prisoner, but the principle was the same. The detective found out everything he could about him. He found out about his cars, scrutinized his phone records, learned about his family, researched his friends, talked to his neighbors, followed him to his job. He soaked up everything that he could because he knew that the moment of the first approach—if handled right—could produce a watershed. If handled wrong, another dead end.

Finally, we decided to approach the witness. The detective did a routine traffic stop, spoke to him in Spanish, and asked him to come to the police station. He followed the traditional approach, building rapport with his witness. The witness figured out very quickly what this was about; it had been weighing on him for months.

The detective was as nice as possible, talked about the witness's family, talked about his wife, talked about God. He knew from his research that the witness was a deeply religious man, one who might understand the pain of the family of the murder victim. Sometimes a witness's faith is the foothold the investigator needs.

The witness began to cry. Something had broken. Wretched tears poured out of him. Would this moment of emotion and catharsis cause any sought-after secrets to pour forth as well? After a while, through bleary eyes, the witness finally turned to look at his interrogator and made an unexpected request. "Dame una biblia," he said. *Get me a Bible.*

This was a first.

There ensued a mad scramble to unearth a Bible at the police station. This involved a lot of flailing up and down hallways, yelling, "I need a fucking Bible!" Finally, one of the maintenance guys who worked there volunteered his small black Bible. It was presented to the weeping witness, who clutched it close, with both hands, and then told officers everything he knew about the crime. And the case was solved.

A veteran FBI agent once put it to me this way: "There's always some button you have on someone. Find it. You have to find it." This is what they all say. You can always find that bit of humanity if you look hard enough and if you think hard enough. Find that moment of connection, not that lever of fear. The more human you are, the more obvious your mark's soft spot becomes.

Most criminals or witnesses confess not because they are intimidated by the gun or the badge. The opposite is true; as one detective says, his uniform is an obstacle to getting the truth. Good officers focus on getting the witness or target to forget about the gun and the badge, to relate to them as people, not perps. Relatedly, Jimmy Motto, one of the best veteran SDNY investigators, once told me that in the midst of ongoing debates about compulsory videotaping of interrogations, he was worried about such a requirement. Because jurors might be turned off by tough tactics? No—because they might mistake the smart tactic of building rapport with a violent criminal as coddling. He was worried cops would look too nice, not too harsh.

In interrogation, you don't blunder forth. A real-time interrogation is an act of massive improvisation preceded, when possible, by painstaking preparation. You go in and you go with the flow once you're there, but you don't show up cold. Even criminals and their enablers may follow some kind of moral compass. Not like yours or mine perhaps, but—on this side of the sociopathic divide at least—they are still human beings. Their humanity may be hidden or fleeting, but it is there. Human beings have buttons, and the prepared, empathetic investigator learns how to push them.

After unspeakable bloodshed on all sides, the Allies claimed victory in World War II. The Germans surrendered unconditionally and in disgrace. The American POWs were released. But what of the master interrogator Hanns Scharff? What became of him?

With the war's end, the legend of the humane Luftwaffe interrogator traveled across the Atlantic, carried on the lips of the American POWs he questioned. The returning pilots spread the word of their "gentleman" questioner. The U.S. Air Force invited Scharff to give speeches to American military audiences about his interrogation methods. Many of his teachings were incorporated into U.S. military curriculums, including at the

Pentagon. More recently, starting in 2009, the FBI-led High-Value Detainee Interrogation Group spent $10 million researching effective interrogation techniques, specifically studying Scharff's work. Seven decades after Scharff charmed American prisoners of war held in Germany, the U.S. government concluded that Scharff knew better—that his techniques yielded more accurate and actionable information than methods bordering on torture.

Scharff, as I mentioned, had no formal training in the work he did for the Luftwaffe. His instruction had been in textile design. And so in 1950, after his significant wartime detour as an improbably excellent interrogator for Nazi Germany, Scharff returned to his roots. He became a mosaic artist. Welcomed by his erstwhile adversary, the United States, he settled in sunny California and made a very successful go of it, becoming internationally recognized, his art exhibited far and wide.

Scharff's most famous and enduring work is still on display in America. If you have ever been to Walt Disney World in Florida, you have likely seen it. As you pass from the amusement park's Main Street into Fantasyland and you stroll through the corridor of a castle, there along the high walls you will observe five enormous and beautiful mosaics, made up of more than a million pieces of Italian glass rendered in five hundred different colors.

Those mosaics depict, in Scharff's meticulous hand, the story of Cinderella.

Hanns Joachim Scharff died in 1992, in Bear Valley Springs, California—an American mosaic artist, ever beloved by the captives whose secrets he stole.

Snitches: The Moral Quicksand of Cooperating Witnesses

The screen door slams. It is probably summer 2007. We're at home in Bethesda, Maryland, where we are living while I'm working in the U.S. Senate. In marches six-year-old Maya, determined. Following on her heels is four-year-old Jaden. He is crying and screaming, "Maya, no! Maya, no!" Jaden has clearly done something naughty, and Maya is bent on reporting her baby brother's crime. Maya enters the kitchen, hands on hips. My wife, Dalya, and I look at her. As Maya begins to speak, Jaden becomes hysterical, tries to muzzle her. I've rarely seen him so upset. As a prosecutor by nature and training, I usually embrace reports of misconduct. In that moment, however, my response is not welcoming. Dalya and I hush Maya and try to calm down Jaden. Then we ask several questions. *Is anyone hurt? Is anything broken?* Maya shakes her head no. *Jaden, are you sorry?* He nods his head yes.

And then we do something neither of them expects. We say we don't want to know what happened. Jaden stops crying. Maya looks incredulous and might have perfected her eye roll right then and there. But that is that, and they both go back outside.

Why did we stop our daughter from reporting on Jaden? I suppose we were trying to spare our son some trauma, but there was something else too, a lesson. Tattling is not attractive. It is a betrayal. No one likes a snitch. People who snitch on those close to them make us uncomfortable, make us recoil a bit. There is baked into our DNA an aversion—a moral distaste even—for this kind of informant, even though such turncoats are the bread and butter of countless criminal investigations.

This investigative tool—the criminal turned government witness—captures the public imagination unlike any other. The snitch, the rat, the Judas. Also known as the cooperator.

Prosecutors like to think that the integrity of the prosecution is not ever on trial. In fact, we say it all the time: "The government is not on trial here." And yet *of course it always is*. The truth is simple: The criminal justice system in any society necessarily implies a moral code. Law and morality are not coextensive, but to a significant degree what a society chooses to punish is a proxy for what it deems unacceptable, reprehensible, or immoral. Moreover, the *way* that a society chooses to enforce its laws, the practices it sanctions, the powers it grants, the tools it approves, also reveals the community's moral thinking. In the risky gray zone of cooperators, that is especially true.

Hollywood makes movies about informers who turn on their former colleagues. The mobster Henry Hill is immortalized in *Goodfellas;* the fraudster Jordan Belfort, in *The Wolf of Wall Street*. This is not surprising. Tracing the arc from criminal to cooperator is irresistible drama. There is the thrilling mix of danger, betrayal, transformation. And there is, I suspect, something else. There is complexity. Cooperators occupy a troubling twilight zone. They assist cops and, as a result, may literally get away with murder. They operate as double agents against the people closest to them. It is a bit fantastical and murky, this partnership between criminal and lawman, lurking at opposite ends of the legal spectrum. It requires a reciprocal leap of faith and forces a bond in which each side is counting on, and putting its faith and trust in, the other—one hoping for strong support in favor of leniency, the other striving for a conviction and professional success. It is the most unholy alliance in the whole business of justice, and it is as commonplace as a judge's gavel.

Commonplace doesn't mean risk-free. Quite the opposite. Cooperating might save you from prison, but it could also put you in the morgue. Countless people lie six feet under because of their actual or suspected cooperation with prosecutors. When I was a line assistant, my colleagues David Rody and David Anders sought the death penalty in a case where a suspected cooperator, Edwin Santiago, was lured to an apartment, hog-tied, tortured, strangled, and burned to death. I saw the gruesome pictures of the victim, and they haunt me still. A medical examiner later testified that Santiago's body was so badly mangled, it was impossible to determine the color of his eyes.

The cooperator willing to take risks provides a bonanza to law enforcement. Clothed in the credibility of the insider, a cooperating witness can tell the story of a particular crime or an entire crime family. He can put the last nail in the coffin of an untouchable.

Look at the Mafia. Sammy "the Bull" Gravano brought down the Gambino crime family. Joseph Massino brought down the Bonannos. Look at corporate scandals. Andy Fastow helped bring down Enron's CEO. Scott Sullivan brought down World-Com's. Several cooperators brought down the Galleon Group's chief executive in the largest insider-trading case in a generation. It was cooperator testimony that sank more than a dozen of Bernard Madoff's co-conspirators. Every criminal gang of note ever dismantled was decimated by a former gang leader or associate saving his own skin. Criminal enterprises and corrupt companies are investigated by outsiders like the FBI, but they are typically undone from within.

Everyone with information about, or access to, criminals is a potential cooperator. Some are surprising. People flip on their business colleagues, on their best friends, on their siblings and spouses, even on their own parents and children. Some people's penchant for self-protection knows no bounds.

Cooperating witnesses can beat science. Famed cyclist Lance Armstrong won the Tour de France seven times. During that time period, he submitted to 150 drug tests. He never failed a single one. What did him in? Cooperating witnesses—eleven of his former teammates—who came forward to blow the whistle. Floyd Landis, the first of Armstrong's teammates to confess to doping, in 2010, who later outed Armstrong for the same, actually compared Armstrong's cycling team to a mob family.

Cooperators are magic and menace both. Wiretaps can be ambiguous, incomplete, or unattainable. Cooperators, however, are in the room for the off-line conversations, the secret meetings; they can translate jargon and coded talk. They can wear wires, steer conversations, lead you to bodies.

There are risks to the prosecutor too. Cooperators can be your ticket but also your greatest baggage. They can lie, make things up, repulse the jury. That's why you must painstakingly corroborate what they say even while you question and challenge all of it. The truthfulness of the testimony must be vetted, every stitch of it corroborated. If the cooperator says it was a rainy day, we pull the weather report. We have all been fed the cautionary tales of cooperator self-dealing and double-crossing. Some of us have experienced it firsthand.

Cooperating witnesses have long presented a legal, moral, and ethical thicket. I don't remember, as a general matter, reflecting too much on the overall fairness of using accomplice testimony to convict criminals. It's just what we did. I *did* think a lot about tactics and optics in particular cases. For example, it is a bad idea to put on a cooperating witness to testify against someone lower on the food chain. You want to cooperate up, not down. Basic fairness counsels that you don't put on the kingpin to nail the courier, because the big fish—the more culpable fish—shouldn't get a lighter sentence for selling the little guy up the river. I'm convinced my first acquittal came because our star cooperating witness was an arrogant jerk and much more distasteful than the low-level lackey who was on trial on immigration fraud charges. The jury couldn't stand the cooperator; they acquitted the defendant, despite a ton of evidence.

Every defense lawyer, of course, uses the government's cooperator as a cudgel against the case. It is a natural weakness when the linchpin of your case is also your Achilles' heel. The defense lawyer can stand before the jury, point to the witness box, urge jurors to recall the scumbag cooperating witnesses, and thunder about their dishonesty, rant about their depravity, expound on how they sold their soul to rat out someone else.

The prosecutor then has the job of winning the jury back, rebutting the argument that the whole case should be thrown out and all evidence disbelieved because the government put a "rat" on the stand. To do that, you turn your weakness into a strength and try to turn the tables.

My office used a riff like this:

"Look, ladies and gentlemen of the jury, you have every right to scrutinize the cooperator's testimony because the judge will tell you that *you* decide the credibility of the witnesses. It is up to you to decide whether a witness is telling the truth or not, and you are especially supposed to scrutinize the testimony of the cooperating witness in this case because he is testifying in exchange for hoped leniency. We are not asking you to like Mr. Cooperator. We're asking you to decide whether you *believe* Mr. Cooperator. We did not choose that witness. We would have preferred to bring rabbis, nuns, priests, and Girl Scouts to the witness stand. But they wouldn't have known anything about the crime. Your common sense tells you that the people who would know about the crime, the people who would be in a position to tell you what really happened, the people who could tell you what was in the mind of the defendant, are his *partners* in crime. So, in a very real sense, ladies and gentlemen, *we* didn't pick that witness; the *defendant* did when he chose to commit a crime with Mr. Cooperator. So, yes, scrutinize the testimony carefully, but think to yourself how it's corroborated by all the other evidence." And so on and so forth.

The defense prays that a jury does not find the witness testimony corroborated or finds the use of the "rat" so distasteful that they acquit. Sometimes that prayer is answered; usually it isn't.

Prosecutors don't dwell on general moral considerations. But in a very real sense when the rubber meets the road in the courtroom, what is lingering in the air as twelve ordinary Americans sit in judgment of another person is a decidedly moral question: Is it right for the government to do it this way? Is it right for the government to make a deal with the devil to get another devil? When we begin a relationship with a cooperator during our period of inquiry before we go to trial, we mostly ask this question: Which devil is the jury more likely to believe?

How is a cooperator born? Some targets don't need persuading; they race into the office to get in the leniency queue. Others won't flip when approached by an FBI agent, but will sing when they feel the cold steel of cuffs on their wrists; others resist even after being charged and capitulate only as the trial draws near. Still others, tight-lipped to the end, quietly plead guilty or go to trial, defiant, and do their time without opening their mouth. Many, of course, may have nothing to offer, no substantial assistance to give. One might question the fairness of a system that typically rewards cooperation in direct proportion to how much criminal activity and involvement someone has, whereas the hapless, marginal transgressor with no kingpins to expose has no chance at leniency through cooperation.

The strategy for flipping someone is not so different from the strategy of smart interrogation. Histrionics and drama are not necessary, and probably counterproductive. The best agents and prosecutors don't threaten or browbeat. They use a tone that is firm and matter-of-fact.

The decision to cooperate is fundamentally a cost-benefit analysis, so agents and prosecutors emphasize the costs and risks borne by the defendant: *Our case is strong. You are toast. If you want to help yourself, the time is now.* Pretty straightforward.

One of my favorite detectives, Kenny Robbins, would walk into the room and place, if available, a picture of the defendant's family on the table, then walk out. A short while later, he would reappear. There was no pleading or imploring. A simple choice was presented. In his stump speech to drug defendants, Kenny would starkly recast for them the meaning of manliness: "You have a decision to make. You can say I'm a *man*, and so I'm gonna keep quiet. Or, you can say I'm a man, and I want to see my kids someday." No theatrics, no banging on the table, no yelling. Kenny used soft and simple words, but it was no soft sell. If so inclined, Kenny would mention family inflection points to bring the point home. "You can choose to say I'm a man, and I want to be there for my daughter's sweet sixteen or my son's graduation or my sister's wedding or my dad's sixtieth. It's up to you." And he would wait. Of course, he would also remind them, "Keep in mind there are other defendants in this case, and the first one that gets us a few rungs up the ladder gets the cooperation agreement." This is always a real-life prisoner's dilemma.

The decision to cooperate, for any target, is fateful and often—though not always—excruciating. Leaving your life is difficult, even if it is a criminal life. Some mix of fear, loyalty, stoicism, risk aversion, and personal code of honor informs each choice. It is difficult to predict whether any particular target will flip—whether gangster, gang member, businessman, or personal lawyer to the president of the United States. In 2018, the president's former campaign chairman, Paul Manafort, insisted on his innocence in the lead-up to two criminal trials, got convicted on eight counts in the first, then pled guilty and flipped before the second trial. Then he lied to prosecutors and his cooperation agreement was ripped up. Quite the merry-go-round.

Some roll like a wagon wheel; others never budge.

For real people, the decision to cooperate represents something more than a mere bargain in exchange for a shot at liberty. As I mentioned, it could invite mortal danger. But it could also mean forsaking family, abandoning friends, severing all past relationships. It could mean forever living under a false identity in the Witness Security Program, always looking over your shoulder.

It is hard.

Mathew Martoma was a portfolio manager at the hedge fund SAC Capital. He made $276 million in illegal profits for SAC. At the news conference where I announced the charges, a reporter asked whether I hoped Martoma would flip. "From your lips to God's ears," I thought. He went to trial, got convicted, caught a nine-year sentence, and never opened his mouth.

Every element of the law is dependent on the fateful choices of unpredictable and imperfect human beings, from the cops to the lawyers to the judges to the cooperators. It is the human factor that makes every attempt to deliver justice uncertain.

Some of the hardest crimes to crack without a cooperator are those committed not by gangsters and fraudsters but by members of law enforcement. Among law enforcement people, the tendency toward *omertà,* or silence, is sometimes stronger than it is with La Cosa Nostra. Let me give you an example. A sickly Rikers Island inmate named Ronald Spear was beaten to death a week before Christmas in 2012. We believed that a correction officer named Brian Coll was responsible for the brutal homicide, but as often happens after such incidents, every officer toed the same line and told the same story: the inmate came at Officer Coll with a cane, and Coll knocked Spear to the ground in an act of self-defense. To us it looked like a pack of lies, and we assigned one of our most focused investigators, Steve Braccini, to the case. Braccini is ruddy-faced and youthful-looking, the son of Italian immigrants. He was a longtime NYPD cop who spent a generation in the Cold Case Apprehension Homicide Squad before joining our office.

Flipping people is all about reading them, about doing your homework, as Scharff taught. Braccini says, "Homework is incredibly important. Their background, past incidents, and especially homework about their families. Someone came from a broken home? That gives you an opening. Someone was abused as a child? That gives you an opening. Someone was raised by his grandma? That gives you an opening. But you have to know the openings to take advantage of them."

Braccini did his homework in the Spear case and focused intently on a particular officer who was at the scene, one who had participated in the suspected cover-up: Anthony Torres. Braccini learned that Officer Torres was a military guy, a veteran who had served in Fort Lewis, Washington, and spent six months on a peacekeeping mission in the Middle East. He had fought for his country and was honorably discharged as a private first class. Not only that, but he was a volunteer firefighter in Port Chester. Braccini learned Torres's colleagues at the firehouse were very fond of him. Here's the other thing Braccini knew: Torres's own hand had been injured shielding the inmate Ronald Spear from the fatal kicks from Coll's heavy work boots. Braccini concluded that Torres was not an irredeemable person, that he must have a conscience. Braccini told me, "He's one of those guys—God, Country, Family." The upshot of that? "He's the guy you gotta flip."

One morning Braccini and two FBI agents went to Torres's

home in New Rochelle, New York, at 5:30 to make their pitch. Torres was already gone. So Braccini called him, identified himself, and said, "I want to talk." Torres knew immediately what they wanted to speak about but said he was busy. He'd been fired from Rikers and now had a delivery job. Braccini instructed Torres to meet them at the Coach Diner in Port Chester. When they met, Braccini steered him to the last booth in the back. He intentionally boxed in Torres on one side, while the two FBI agents sat across from them. I remember Braccini telling me about the diner flip at the time, and it struck me how important Braccini felt it was for him to be physically close—not to intimidate, he said, "but with some guys you want to be at arm's length and with other guys you want to be up real close." With Torres, he wanted to be close, in touching distance. To build rapport, Braccini started with Torres's military service, then his family.

He could tell Torres wanted to talk, unburden himself. At some point, Braccini let slip that he had been a union delegate. This was a significant and smart moment of connection. It was Braccini's way of saying I get it, I understand the pressure law enforcement members feel, through their unions, to back up their peers in any controversial use of force, pressure to keep their mouths shut. It was a pivotal moment. Braccini—through a combination of empathy, commiseration, understanding, and appeal to conscience—broke the dam. An hour into the conversation, this tough correction officer, firefighter, and military veteran began to cry. He sobbed so hard that the staff at the diner became alarmed and suggested they would call the police. Braccini had to inform them that they were the police.

Ultimately, Torres agreed to cooperate, to plead guilty to obstruction of justice, and gave utterly damning testimony about how Brian Coll murdered an infirm, restrained, nonresisting inmate in his charge. When asked at trial why he finally chose to come clean, Torres said this: "I was tired of lying. My conscience was getting to me. Every day knowing what really happened just took its toll and I just wanted to accept responsibility for what I did." Braccini had read him well.

Sometimes the decision to flip, to do in your own partners in crime, is not an attack of conscience but comes in response to betrayal. Henry Hill walked himself into the Organized Crime Strike Force to cooperate only after he grew certain that he was going to be whacked by his own Lucchese mentor, Jimmy Burke. In 2018, President Trump's personal lawyer, Michael Cohen, came into the crosshairs of Special Counsel Robert Mueller's office and SDNY. He had vocally sworn loyalty to the president, but after a time he reportedly felt unsupported and even betrayed by him. And so he turned on his powerful benefactor. Cohen's reversal was dramatic and breathtakingly reported because of his proximity to elected power, but his decision is echoed through the annals of law enforcement, in story after story, where real people waver between resolve and anger and back again.

Take the case of Michael DiLeonardo, a.k.a. Mikey Scars. He was a captain in the Gambino crime family, inducted the same day as John Gotti Jr. He was dead loyal. During his years as a captain, Scars had collected hundreds of thousands of dollars through the Gambino family's extortion racket. He had passed along his share—nearly $250,000—to his superiors in the Gambino family, hoping to collect the cash later. When he was arrested in 2002 for racketeering, murder, and loan-sharking, he tried to retrieve his cut. Gotti and other members of the crime family, however, refused, falsely claiming that he had "skimmed the cash."

Scars was heartbroken. This was money for his girlfriend and their two-year-old son. A fellow inmate suggested they were taking advantage of his loyalty. "You know why they're doing this

to you? It's because they know you're never going to be a rat."
That sounded plausible. It made him mad. And it made him talk.

The decision to cooperate, to serve up your fellows, can be searing but also impermanent. After electing to cooperate, Scars was released from jail for a two-week period, during which time he became increasingly uncomfortable about testifying against his former partners. Scars had a change of heart.

He felt sick about flipping, so sick that one night Scars woke up around 3:00 a.m. and decided that he wanted to "die with honor." He thought about hara-kiri and the Roman tradition of stepping into a bath and slitting one's wrists. He went downstairs and opened bottles of Zoloft and Ambien. His final thoughts—prior to swallowing the pills—were about Gotti. Scars, a man who had fueled the Gambino criminal enterprise for thirty years, who rose through the ranks to become a captain in the family, who became a made man on the same day as John Gotti Jr., who participated in extortion, labor racketeering, and murder plots, this man wanted to die with "honor." He didn't die. His girlfriend, Madeline, found him and saved him.

Four months later, after a period of recovery and placement in total segregation, Scars recommitted to cooperating. Upon painful reflection, he realized that his loyalty and his future belonged with his son and real family, not his mob family. He resumed his regular visits to our office for lengthy debriefings about his life of crime.

When I was serving on the ninth floor at One St. Andrew's Plaza in the early 2000s, those Scars debriefings—the proffer sessions—were the stuff of legend. Sure, Scars was spilling the beans on scores of Gambino members and associates, leading the prosecutors Joon Kim and Michael McGovern and Special Agent Ted Otto, day by day, through the gory details of extortions, robberies, and murders. But every time he proffered in one of the two conference rooms on nine, the rest of us on the floor always knew it because we were met with an olfactory reminder during the lunch break. Because he was freed from the more serious security restrictions of the Metropolitan Correctional Center (MCC), Scars's girlfriend, Madeline, was permitted to bring him the food he cherished. She didn't bring peanut butter and jelly. Every day she brought an old-school Italian *spread*. Fresh pastas, meats, sausage and peppers, packed with love into catering tins covered with foil. She brought fresh Parmesan cheese, like the kind you see at fancy Italian food stores, where they shave or cut pieces from a cheese wheel. Except Madeline brought the whole wheel. The smell of garlic wafted into the grungy government hallways. Compared with the fare at the MCC, this was Michelin-star stuff. (After each proffer, Madeline would leave the leftovers in the conference room. What happened to those leftovers is classified.)

Years later when prosecutor Elie Honig and Agent Otto would visit Scars to prepare for one of the dozen-plus trials where he gave testimony, Otto would first go to Scars's favorite bakery in Bensonhurst and buy a box of cannoli. Otto then carried the cannoli to wherever they were meeting with Scars, arranging for appropriate refrigeration techniques as necessary to keep the goods fresh.

It was a small gustatory kindness that went a long way. It kept Scars talking and it kept him happy. The way to a cooperator's heart, sometimes, is through his stomach. When I worked Asian organized crime cases, authentic dishes brought in from neighboring Chinatown would put a smile on cooperators' faces. For others, even ordinary pizza could bring an incarcerated witness to tears.

As DEA special agent Jimmy Soiles once told me, "It's a sign of respect to bring people the food they miss, the food they crave." He believes ethnic food made the difference in flipping one of the most important cooperators of his career.

In the 1980s, Soiles was an undercover agent in a sweeping international heroin investigation. One target, Samir, showed up at a pre-Christmas drug meet with Soiles, delivering seven kilos of heroin into Soiles's waiting hands. Samir was Jordanian but had spent considerable time in Lebanon. Samir was held at Metropolitan Detention Center (MDC) in Brooklyn. Soiles is a Greek American with a healthy appetite. As he puts it, "Greeks understand the power of food." He also really wanted to roll Samir, who he thought could be a huge asset as a cooperator.

Soiles came up with a plan that made his colleagues think he was crazy. Three times a week, he had Samir pulled from the MDC and brought to a holding room off a corridor at the Eastern District of New York, where the case was pending. Soiles would visit him at lunchtime, but not before stopping at a Middle Eastern food truck to pick up a shawarma sandwich or kabob platter, one for each of them, extra hot sauce. He would arrive to see Samir sitting there quietly, parked in front of his jail-issued sandwich: bologna and cheese with mustard on white bread.

Soiles thought to himself, "Bologna and cheese wasn't gonna cut it." Soiles put the shawarma in front of Samir, desperate for him to smell it. Soiles would eat his own shawarma and make some calls. Samir would sit stoically, eyeing Soiles and resisting temptation, touching neither the shawarma nor the bologna sandwich. Then Soiles would leave. Three times a week he did this, week after week.

One day, Samir finally broke his silence. He looked up at Soiles and said, "What do you want from me?"

Soiles responded, "I want information that will lead to arrests and the seizure of narcotics."

Samir asked to make a phone call. Then, for the first time, he ate his shawarma. Soiles knew it was over. Samir went on to become one of the DEA's most productive cooperators of all time; he helped charge dozens of international drug traffickers. Patience, kindness, and ethnic food can pay rich dividends.

Soiles says he knew he could get to Samir through his culture. "I didn't know if it was gonna work, but I sure as hell knew it was better than bologna and cheese on white bread." His buddies thought he was crazy, but he was right.

Cooperation has a special wrinkle and higher hurdle in SDNY.

It would seem self-evident that you accuse people of crimes that you can prove. It would seem the height of injustice to level allegations against a person if you don't have independent, verifiable proof. That only seems right and smart. There was and is, however, one exception to that rule in my old office.

There is a category of people routinely charged with crimes that cannot be independently proven; where there is little or no corroboration; where the statute of limitations might even have expired; and where no part of the crime happened in the Southern District of New York. They are charged nonetheless— with murders, robberies, shootings, drug deals, and more that we could never have independently proven. You might ask, who are these poor bastards, these unlucky, mistreated, railroaded defendants?

In fact, they are not poor bastards at all. They are the luckiest people in the federal criminal justice system. They are lottery winners, every last one of them. We have already talked about them. These are the Southern District's cooperating witnesses.

Let me explain. Under our practice, in order to become a signed-up cooperator, you have to admit and acknowledge every bit of criminal conduct you had ever committed in your life whether it had been uncovered or not, whether it was recent or not, whether anyone else in the world knew about it or not. This sounds like a tall order, and it is.

The reasons for the policy are partly tactical. There is the wish to present a clean, reformed, repentant witness—not the proverbial shifty "rat" with selective memory and selective testimony. We want to offer someone who had so turned the corner that he now admitted crimes freely, prepared to suffer the consequences for criminal conduct that had been *volunteered* to us. The effect in court was palpable. Every time I examined a witness who admitted guilt for crimes that we hadn't known about at the time of the arrest, I could practically hear the moral surprise from the jury box.

As I said, this is a tall order. It will not surprise you to learn that at the beginning the average defendant looks at you as if you were crazy, looks at the investigators as if they were crazy, thinking, "Why on earth would I tell you something that you don't know?" And some never did come clean, though many did.

John O'Malley would start in on a potential cooperator with characteristic bluntness: "Okay, now I need to know everything you've done from the time you took a nickel out of your mother's purse when you were five years old." One time he said that to a guy arrested for a single robbery, a gigantic six-foot three-inch member of the highly violent Bloods gang. He sported tattoos and a lengthy rap sheet, but this was his first robbery arrest, and he was caught dead to rights. After O'Malley directed him to come clean on everything, the defendant insisted he'd only done the one robbery. Ever. O'Malley stood up and said, "We're done. Meeting's over." He got up and left. That was that.

Truth is central. You can't build a case, or deliver justice, on *mostly* truth. Truth has to be total. The witness oath, after all, requires not just "the truth" but the "whole truth" and "nothing but the truth, so help me God." Partial truths, dubious excuses, clever denials—these do not inspire faith that the process will lead to a just result. So you push, push, push for the truth. And you guard against lies like a World Cup goalie in a sudden-death penalty shoot-out.

Two weeks later, the Blood's lawyer called and said his client wanted to apologize to Mr. O'Malley for lying to him. He in fact apologized. He also confessed ultimately to two hundred robberies. That happened every day in conference rooms in our office.

We followed this tough policy largely to enhance the credibility of our cooperators, to mitigate the perception of a sweetheart deal, and to show the acceptance of responsibility. A witness who had told us things that we didn't know was someone whose forthrightness and candor were both remarkable and admirable. The practice, moreover, seemed just in the broad scheme of things. Lay bare your crimes so the judge can know the scope of your conduct and weigh it in sentencing. As an extreme form of transparency and acceptance of responsibility, it was upright.

But in this aspect, the process of signing up a cooperating witness and compelling the acceptance of accusations that we might not otherwise prove also unfolded as moral allegory. For the defendant, the shift was often cathartic. It is the closest, I think, we come in criminal law to a formalized process of redemption and atonement. In a sense, we are saying it is not enough to admit only some crimes. If you want to go forward in the world and live again among your family and friends as a respected and reformed and rehabilitated person, it is not enough to admit what we already know. Freedom and absolution require more.

You must confess all your sins.

SDNY investigator Billy Ralat would tell people, "You can't change the past, but you can get that bowling ball off your chest." I once saw, firsthand, Billy perform a bowling ball exorcism. We were prosecuting homicide defendant Freddy Abad, and one of the people charged in the murder conspiracy chose to cooperate. This potential cooperator, Rubio, had no problem at all, like many, explaining the details of the crime with which he was charged. But there was one issue nagging at us given our full-confession policy: we had heard from another source that Rubio had another body; that is, he had killed someone and gotten away with it. Mind you, we didn't have a victim's name. Nor did we have the precise location or the precise date.

One afternoon in a conference room on the seventh floor at One St. Andrew's Plaza, Billy and I and another AUSA, Bill Johnson, questioned Rubio about the other killing. We had built up a rapport with him over time. Billy's tone was not harsh but firm and imploring. Billy gave up some of the details of what we knew, gave the impression he knew more than we did. It wasn't straight-up deception but a tactical bluff. Billy was onto something, and once he was onto something, he took it where it needed to go. I can't remember how much time elapsed, but through a combination of persistence and cajolery and not a small amount of kindness in the questioning, Rubio, in a burst of emotion, confessed to shooting a man in the head in the back of a white van as he had been instructed to and then dumping the body. I could feel my heart beating in my throat when that happened. Rubio went on to testify and helped to convict Freddy Abad at trial. Abad was sentenced to life in prison; after testifying, Rubio was given time served, which amounted to just about six years in federal prison, with another three years pending on an unrelated fifteen-year state charge.

Did Rubio get a free pass? Well, he didn't get off scot-free; he helped permanently lock up an even worse guy; and that relatively light sentence—in the overall scheme of things— furthered an important incentive structure for cooperation generally. Our system has decided it wants murderers to flip on other murderers, and as in all things you don't expect people to give something for nothing. It is transactional. It is utilitarian. It is also justice.

Detective Kenny Robbins likes to describe the complete about-face of a narcotics defendant he once collared. Mr. O. was a Colombian heroin trafficker who grew up with "legit cartel guys" and fell into the life. He flipped virtually the moment he was arrested, came clean on everything, gave up all his associates, superiors, and drug routes. He confessed all his sins. Then he worked overtime to redeem himself, dedicated to making things right. He had so much information the DEA nicknamed him the Goose. As in the Golden Goose. Even after his official cooperation was over, he continued as a paid informant, because he remained plugged into that world. The DEA eventually set him up in his own travel agency, where the Goose would overhear drug talk and report it. All told, he helped bring in almost forty traffickers and facilitated the seizure of millions of dollars in drug proceeds. Fifteen years on, Kenny still receives a Merry Christmas and Happy New Year message from the Goose.

What did the Goose do with all that informant money the DEA paid him over the years? He put his daughter through Princeton.

There is an oft-overlooked benefit to our strict policy on cooperation: the exoneration of innocent people. Think back to Eric Glisson, Cathy Watkins, and their four hapless co-defendants. Recall that the only reason John O'Malley had the feeling of déjà vu when he read Eric Glisson's letter one fateful afternoon was that some years earlier he had taken Gilbert Vega and Jose Rodriguez down this difficult, tortuous, teeth-pulling exercise of truth and complete confession.

Some years later—and as John O'Malley and other investigators in my office would tell you—the practice of debriefing people who flipped created both a mental and an actual database of previously unknown perpetrators. On the one hand, crimes previously unsolved could be closed, including homicides. And on the other hand, we also discovered, as we did in the Glisson case, the wrong people had gone to prison because the real perpetrator had sat in our conference room and admitted to it. In fact, SDNY investigators and agents regularly ask this potent question: Do you know anyone who got locked up who shouldn't have? Many did. By O'Malley's count, the office exonerated thirteen people, all on the backs of cooperators who came fully clean about their own crimes. It surprises me still that most prosecutors don't follow our unforgiving practice; to me it is a failure of effort, of imagination, and perhaps of justice.

Most of the moral concern about cooperation is focused on whether the cooperator gets too much benefit in the bargain. Kill a guy, squeal on someone else, go free. That's the typical moral headache. And so it seems almost a silly question to ask, given the benefit of extraordinary leniency that can flow from cooperation, but let's ask it anyway: Is the cooperation arrangement fair to the *cooperator*? Is it *just* to use people as a means to an end, in such a transactional and utilitarian way? Does such a system deny the cooperating defendant his inherent worth and dignity, treating him merely as a device—and often a fungible one—for some perceived public good, pursued after a cold-eyed cost-benefit analysis by the prosecutor? After all, the cooperating defendant is relegated to a cog, a lever in the machinery of justice, flipped to the "on" position for trial purposes. Various moral philosophers, Immanuel Kant among them, would not approve.

But herein lies an irony. The very moment that the government uses a man as a means to an end, enlists one criminal to nab another, the moment that the Faustian bargain is struck, marks the beginning of the humanizing of the cooperator. Before the flip, the names typed in the indictment's caption on the other side of the "United States"—on the other side of the *v*—are often faceless, disembodied defendants.

After the flip, there is usually endless debriefing of the defendant, countless proffer sessions. And something happens, day after day after day, sitting in a windowless room, hours at a time.

You get to know each other. You go through the history of his life, not just his crime. You hear about his associates, about his friends. You hear about his family. You hear about the neighborhood where he grew up, about the beatings that he took from his father—if he knew his father. You learn how far he went in school, what disciplinary problems he had. You learn about his mental health; you ask about his drug history; you find out which members of his family, in whatever neighborhood they grew up, were stabbed or robbed or beaten or shot.

You may bond over shawarma or pasta or sausage and peppers.

This defendant, whom you were going to break your back to convict and send to prison, now becomes real and complex and three-dimensional—becomes human. You, for the first time, become aware of a complete person.

You may realize he is more than the crimes he has committed, just as every person is more than the worst thing he or she has ever done.

There's another dynamic at play here, of course. This person has, overnight, ceased being your adversary. This person might have killed, maimed, beaten, robbed, ripped off other humans; when he was your adversary, you would have stopped at nothing within the bounds of the law to hold him accountable. But now, not only is he no longer your adversary; he's your ally. He is your comrade in the quest for accountability for those who remain your adversaries. He is your key to getting the job done. And it's not just any job; it's the job of delivering justice by solving a crime, upholding the rule of law, doing right by the victims of crimes. It is *righteous*.

The newly flipped witness becomes your compatriot in the struggle to succeed in your mission, also the ambition to succeed. It can be hard to square your mental view of this person when you first brought the case compared with when he is ready to testify on behalf of the government. Sometimes bonds develop, and you have to remind yourself that this person might have switched sides but still did awful things. He may not be a good guy, but he's good enough to be with the good guys now, good enough to trust.

This is the point of maximum danger.

Elie Honig, who was one of my chiefs of the Organized Crime Unit, flipped countless mobsters. When he became more senior, he gave the introductory lecture on the use of cooperating witnesses. During his extensive PowerPoint presentation, he would issue a stark but simple admonition: "You may not fall in love with your cooperator." There are rules and rituals of detachment we encouraged: don't use first names, don't divulge personal information, keep your distance. These were best practices and should have been followed, but I confess they were often honored in the breach. People let their guard down. It is human nature.

Cooperators, like birds, can go south. Take Sammy the Bull. After a controversially light five-year sentence notwithstanding nineteen murders, Gravano entered the Witness Security Program. By the late 1990s, Gravano had begun operating an Ecstasy ring in Arizona, moving twenty thousand pills a week; that bought him a fresh twenty-year prison term. But for every Sammy the Bull, you hope there are many more like the Goose.

Cooperator stories are legion, enough to fill this book and several sequels. I end with two that especially struck me from my time as U.S. Attorney.

The first involves Noah Freeman and Donald Longueuil. They had both worked as money managers at SAC Capital, the massive hedge fund led by Steve Cohen. They were not only co-workers but also close friends. They had similar backgrounds and interests, with diplomas from Boston-area schools, North-eastern and Harvard, respectively. They met after college through their shared love of ice-skating. They competed together, skied together, and traveled together, and when Noah's fiancée ended their engagement, it was Don who made sure his friend got out of bed in the morning. When Noah began dating another woman, who was a friend of Don's fiancée, the athletic couples bonded over a love of biking and triathlons. The two friends did many things together. One thing they did jointly was break the law by trading on inside information.

On the night of November 19, 2010, to our everlasting annoy-ance, *The Wall Street Journal* breathlessly reported that my office was investigating insider trading on a massive scale and that scores of arrests were on the horizon. On that night, I feared, as did the career prosecutors and FBI agents, that significant evidence was being destroyed and would never see the light of day. That would mean that a lot of important work would go out the window. And guilty people would not be arrestable.

Meanwhile, our investigation ground on, and the team put together a case against Freeman. One December morning, B. J. Kang, an intense and taciturn Korean American FBI agent, approached Freeman in the parking lot of the all-girls Win-sor School, where Noah decided to teach after leaving life as a trader. Freeman immediately recognized Kang's square jaw and impassive face from news photos taken during other arrests. Kang had become something of the FBI's grim reaper in those days, the tip of the spear on the most high-profile insider-trading cases, methodically rolling up cooperator after cooperator. Free-man was no exception. Now, as the retired stock trader saw his fate approach him, he offered no resistance. He said to Kang, "I knew this day was coming." In fact, Freeman was so prepared he had already hired a lawyer. Freeman didn't need to be pitched, didn't need a Kenny Robbins–style speech. He'd just had a baby daughter, and for him the calculation was easy: under no circumstances could he do time. Prison and parenthood were utterly incompatible. He would flip. So Freeman was permitted to remain free, and the approach was kept secret.

A short time later, Freeman and his lawyer came into One St. Andrew's to proffer and to discuss his cooperation. Often people have limits as to what they are willing to do. Noah Freeman— baby girl in mind—appeared to have none. In fact, he would not just plead guilty, he would not just testify, he would not just give up everyone's crimes at trial, he would cooperate *proactively*. And he would do it eagerly. He would wear a wire. And, shockingly, he would wire up against his best friend and best man, Donald Longueuil.

And so on December 20, 2010, Freeman was welcomed into the home of his unsuspecting best man. Longueuil, fully trusting his friend, ruined himself. He described, volubly, how he had destroyed critical evidence on the night of the *Journal* article, how he took two pairs of pliers to obliterate the flash drive where he kept inside information. He described to Freeman how he "ripped it apart right there . . . pulled the external drives apart . . . put them into four separate little baggies, and then at 2:00 a.m. . . . on a Friday night . . . put this stuff inside [his] black North Face jacket . . . and threw the shit in the back of like random garbage trucks, different garbage trucks . . . four different garbage trucks."

But for the availability of a miniature recording device and Noah Freeman's inclination toward self-preservation, Longueuil would have gotten away with insider trading and obstruction of justice. Instead, he pled guilty and was sentenced to thirty months in prison.

Cooperation is a part of law enforcement life and rarely raises eyebrows among law enforcement types, except perhaps to signal elation if the case would otherwise have been tough to crack. But there was something shocking about Freeman's blitheness. He was so quick to do it. *Too* quick. The prosecutors on the case, David Leibowitz and Avi Weitzman, almost couldn't believe it. Both had flipped many, many people, Avi especially, having come from an organized crime background in the office. But the quick and cold-eyed, cold-blooded calculation by Freeman was extraordinary, breathtaking even. It defied the norms of human behavior. It is an interesting thing to be an experienced prosecutor, a bit jaded perhaps, to believe you've seen it all, to not bat an eye at either the crime or the cover-up in this matter (happens all the time, yawn), but to be floored by a decision that helped the case. What kind of person flips on his best friend, *and so easily*? What is the right moral judgment here?

We exploited the betrayal, as we always do, but it was unsettling. Is it possible to find immensely helpful cooperation more distasteful than the crime and the cover-up? Apparently, it is. I think about it still.

The story of the second case continues to vex me for different reasons.

By 2011, we were on a public corruption juggernaut. We had continued and expanded on what my predecessor, Mike Garcia, had spearheaded before me: a sharp focus on investigating and prosecuting elected officials in city and state government. The New York State legislature was particularly corrupt. During that time period, if you were an incumbent state senator, you were more likely to be indicted than defeated at the polls.

This corruption matters. State legislators, believe it or not, are important. In New York, each senator represents more than 300,000 people; each assemblyman, almost 130,000. Senators confirm appointments of state officials and court judges. State lawmakers determine our budget. They decide how much money goes to children's education, to public safety, to transportation, to health, and to public welfare. They decide what constitutes a crime and how it should be punished. And they draw the boundaries of the electoral districts in which you live, work, and vote. So it was dispiriting that the public's increasing sense of disillusionment with their government had reached unprecedented proportions.

Public corruption crimes were, to me and to many people, especially galling and destructive. When elected officials commit crimes related to their office, it is a double transgression: they have violated not only the law but also their oath. It makes a weary public even more cynical, more jaded, more disillusioned. It casts a shadow on the bodies they serve and on honest colleagues, who will be viewed with greater suspicion by everyone. Good government is about honest democracy. It is about the will of the people, not the self-aggrandizement of politicians. Ultimately, it is about the social contract itself and what its terms should be.

One afternoon in 2011, I received an unexpected call from the Bronx district attorney, Rob Johnson, who was well aware of our anticorruption efforts. He confided that his office had indicted, under seal, a sitting New York State assemblyman, a Democrat, named Nelson Castro. He was charged with perjury for lying in connection with forged petitions and fraudulent voter registrations. They had tried, without success, to put him to use as a cooperating witness but couldn't get anything going. Johnson said, "Given all the tentacles you have into corruption in the state legislature, could we work together to make something happen?" We connected our public corruption teams with each other. Before long, we had a plan to use Castro proactively to expose corruption by having him arrange meetings with businessmen seeking favors from fellow politicians; he was eager and willing, because he wanted to work off the trouble he had gotten into with the Bronx DA. He was even willing to wear a wire, which was no small thing. It was not lost on me that the deterrent effect in the assembly when it became known there was a wired-up colleague in their midst was potentially massive. If a politician believes that other politicians may be working with the FBI, may be the eyes and ears of law enforcement, he may think twice about committing a crime.

It turns out that Castro had dealings with several dirty Russian businessmen who wanted influence with members of the assembly. While in office, Castro recorded meetings with these four businessmen whose corrupt plan was to open a number of adult day-care centers in the Bronx, but they were so greedy that they wanted to avoid competition and have the legislature bar any competing adult day-care centers from opening. They wanted neighborhood monopolies. The businessmen paid cash bribes in exchange for permits, clientele, and introduction of the protective legislation. As I said later in announcing charges, "It is a fairly neat trick to hatch a scheme that offends core principles of both democracy and capitalism, simultaneously." During the course of the investigation, the same corrupt Russian businessmen also made contact with another sitting state assemblyman, Eric Stevenson, for the same purpose; Stevenson eagerly did their bidding for cash bribes, ultimately accepting over $22,000 in kickbacks.

But we were rapidly approaching a dilemma. The entire state assembly was up for reelection in November 2012. And here we were, in the fall of 2012, with Assemblyman Nelson Castro's guilty plea still sealed, his wearing a wire still secret, his cooperation still unknown. As the election neared, we had a decision to make. Do we compel Nelson Castro's resignation to allow a non-corrupt officeholder to take his place? Or do we continue the secret investigation? It was not an easy question to answer. The case was not ready. To stop now or to unseal the charges against Castro could spook the Russians and halt the collection of damning evidence. It would also warn the other assemblyman, Eric Stevenson. Also, apart from the case we were developing against the Russians, Nelson Castro was attempting to help us investigate other individuals, and those investigations were at a very early stage. We didn't know whether they would pan out, but we didn't want to shoot ourselves in the foot before we had to. If we did nothing, we would be arguably complicit in the reelection of a corrupt figure who we knew would not finish out his term.

It nagged at me then, and it nags at me now. In myriad situations involving secret cooperating witnesses, this is standard operating procedure. The doctor or the businessperson or the teacher who has flipped and elects to wear a wire presents himself or herself falsely to the world. And we don't bat an eye. And we permit them to continue in their jobs in medicine or business or teaching (or drug dealing) so that we can get the result we want and nab other criminals in the familiar Faustian bargain. So, in a sense, you could ask, what was the big deal?

But it *was* a big deal because this was no ordinary professional. Castro had been elected by the people of his district. Castro swore an oath to uphold his office. And the incumbent Castro was now going to sweep back into office on a false premise of integrity and honesty that we were not puncturing because we had other fish to fry. We let the plan stand. As it happens, the other investigations did not pan out. But the Russians did get Stevenson to introduce, on February 20, 2013—three months after the election—the moratorium legislation they coveted, in the form of Bill No. A05139. This was slam-dunk evidence. They, and Assemblyman Stevenson, were arrested on April 4, 2013, and our secret cooperator, Assemblyman Castro, resigned that day as well, with 80 percent of his term remaining.

So, did we defraud the public or do a public service?

I've been asked about this decision many times. I think it is a fair criticism to say we should have pulled the plug. Maybe that would have been justice, not necessarily criminal justice, but overall justice—including fairness and transparency in the electoral process. But the idea—given the epidemic of corruption—of permitting another compromised politician like Assemblyman Eric Stevenson to remain unaccountable while we took down Nelson Castro weighed heavily in favor of continuing the secret operation. And so we continued it, and for some period of time Castro's constituents were—because of us—deprived of a clean and honest representative. It may be that we treated him too much like an ordinary cooperator. Based on the seriousness of the corruption problem at the time, it raises the question: Is it appropriate to take more dramatic steps if the problem you perceive is extraordinary? We obviously took the view that the bigger the problem—in this case, pervasive corruption—the more aggressive and unorthodox we were prepared to be. Maybe that was wrong. Maybe that was right.

It's an important question to ask, and we deliberated hard because of it. Truth be told, I would be more bothered today if we had pulled the plug, which is not to say I'm unbothered that we proceeded.

In delicate matters of law enforcement and the exercise of discretion, even hindsight is not twenty-twenty.

The cooperator relationship and dynamic is complicated. No book prepares you for the complexity of it, especially in the area of violent crime. Harvard doesn't teach you how to speak to a Blood or a Crip. It is a universe that is utterly outside the experience of virtually every elite federal prosecutor I hired.

It's worth admitting something else. If you lived a sheltered life, became a law enforcement straight arrow, who maybe once got in trouble because your dorm party in college got loud, it can be exhilarating to talk, face-to-face, with a real-life criminal, a real-life gangster. It is a window into a world that ordinary people never get. The first time I sat in a room with a member of the mob, I couldn't believe it. It was surreal. It was also fascinating. More than *Goodfellas* and *The Godfather* combined, times ten.

And when your thoughts turn to the thrill of it—that this

is a fascinating person, this colorful guy who killed people or extorted people—do you need to check yourself? Remind yourself that this isn't a Scorsese film and worry that enjoying the rapport with a violent criminal is unseemly?

What other questions are worth asking yourself? Is it cool? Cool to learn the slang, the methods, the rituals, to hear about the brutality of life on the street? It is, frankly.

Can you be fascinated and repulsed at the same time? Probably yes, though those are feelings hard to keep in equipoise. Is it just part of seeing a three-dimensional person?

Is it a coincidence that mob prosecutors love mob movies, which often glorify the Mafia more than law enforcement? What does that say? What does that mean? Is there a prurient interest in all of this?

Could Kenny McCabe have been one of the greatest mob investigators of all time without harboring a deep fascination with the ways of the underworld? Probably not.

But maybe it doesn't matter, so long as you stay focused on the mission, keep up your guard, maintain your skepticism, so long as fascination doesn't bleed into fetish. So long as you keep both eyes trained on the ultimate destination, which is justice. The road to justice is not always easy or even pure. Along the way, there are distractions and detours, trade-offs and Hobson's choices. Nowhere are these hurdles and pitfalls more pronounced than in the morally murky world of flipped witnesses. Any powerful weapon or tool—cooperators included—carries danger and risk. It is not surprising, then, that it takes steel and nerve and delicate judgment to navigate that road.

Continuity and Change:
Justice Through Innovation

D oing justice sometimes requires more than diligence and dedication. It requires, on occasion, a spark of creativity or innovation, a novel approach or rethinking of business as usual.

I have no scientific or technical ability to speak of. I don't know how to fix a car, build a computer, or cure a disease. I still don't understand how a plane can possibly fly. That makes me like most people. Like everyone else, I marvel at technological leaps, but I'm amazed also by simple ideas with real consequences, because they seem within a mortal's reach. In many ways, I am more impressed by the everyday advancements made by passionate and thoughtful people who do their jobs with care and focus—the ones who are not in research and development but who bring us the kinds of modest innovations that make you wonder, "Why didn't I think of that?" Just as modest mistakes, in aggregation, can work tragic miscarriages of justice, modest innovations and improvements multiplied by each other over time can drive significant change.

I mentioned earlier one of my favorite books about business and leadership, *How the Mighty Fall*. I took to heart a particular lesson—that continued success, even in a successful or storied institution like the SDNY, requires continuity *and* change. Continuity of values, of excellence, of the natural focus on terrorism and financial crime; but also change, when needed, in priorities, in technique, in strategy. If you merely tread water, the current will over time take you far from the shore. This is true for every kind of business or organization, including a prosecutor's office.

Change and innovation do not come easily to conservative institutions. "Think outside the box" is the kind of exhortation you expect to find in morning pep talks at Silicon Valley start-ups or glossy business magazines for aspiring entrepreneurs. It is not a slogan of investigative agencies.   .

This is not surprising.

Apart from the clergy, there is perhaps no profession more staid than the law and no subset of lawyers more culturally conservative than prosecutors. Law enforcers have to be meticulous rule followers and scrupulous students of precedent, rightly handcuffed by statutes and codes of conduct, not to mention conscience and the Constitution. That is quite the confining cube. Attempts to think outside the box, then, can feel like the intellectual equivalent of trying to breathe in outer space. Habit, training, and personality conspire not only to choke creativity and innovation but also to foster active aversion to change—of any kind.

Once while I was U.S. Attorney I gave a speech at a cutting-edge tech company in Palo Alto, California. SDNY was the first office to contract with that tech firm to help analyze troves of digital data we gathered in complex cases, and the CEO invited me to speak to the workforce at HobbitCon. The crowd of software engineers was young—very young—and clad mostly in T-shirts, jeans, and shorts. My lame concession to Silicon Valley casual was a patterned shirt under my conservative blue suit and no tie. Looking at the empty stage as the technician miked me up, I asked about the missing podium. "We don't use podiums," he said. Next I spotted not one but two enormous beach balls being tossed about in the audience, on either side of the huge room, each periodically floating downward before being punched back into the air. The Federal Law Enforcement

Officers Association this was not. I jokingly asked the technician what the likelihood was that one of the beach balls would hit me in the face. He paused, seemed to perform a calculation, and said, "Once you begin speaking, I would say no more than fifteen percent."

With those odds, sans podium and sans tie, I unbuttoned my jacket, stuffed my notes back in my pocket, and climbed onstage. Among other things, I spoke about the yawning culture gap between government and the tech industry, superficially evidenced by sartorial differences but more seriously revealed by government's generally backward attitude toward technology. By far the biggest laugh came when I explained that long after the rest of the world had moved on to iPhones and Microsoft Word, the Department of Justice still clung to BlackBerrys and WordPerfect. The laughter was loud, sustained, and telling.

Mindless adherence to old ways of doing things is, I think, worthy of mockery. Tradition is good and useful and grounding. But lazy habit and knee-jerk hostility to change are not tradition; they are an intellectual straitjacket. In every walk of life, people get caught up doing things the same way for the same reasons without pausing to examine the possibility of a better way. That's true of how people commute to work. It's true of how people prepare breakfast. It's true of how people make pitches to clients. There's always the human tendency toward habit and complacency.

Even in the most staid environments and professions, however, innovation matters. This does not mean wholesale, reckless, or radical reinvention. Gains are often more about common sense than genius, about applying a drop of imagination to a problem at hand. Some of the best innovations are simple and obvious in retrospect. Sometimes a valuable innovation is simply employing a trusted tool or technique from one field to another. This principle applies not just to tech start-ups but to every workplace from food companies to clothing retailers to investigative agencies. The atom bomb might have required the Manhattan Project, but small improvements, reforms, and innovations are within the reach of any person—in any line of work—who is open to new thinking.

Let's start with a frivolous example outside law enforcement that I've always loved. As a kid, I put ketchup on my burger. I still do. Like everyone else on the Jersey shore, my own Indian immigrant family used Heinz 57 sauce. We used it to coat Mom's high-fat, masala-flavored hamburgers (whose tastiness was particularly impressive given that Mom never even ate beef until she came to America as an adult). Drawing an appropriate dollop for your hamburger patty was, back then, very hit-and-miss. Oh, the daunting physics of ketchup extraction from the Heinz bottles of yesteryear.

People of a certain age will remember this. You would turn the ketchup bottle upside down, thwack the bottom, which was now the top, and . . . nothing. Then you would grip the container at an acute angle to your plate and give it another frustrated smack—dead on the raised "57" on the side of the glass bottle. Again nothing. Or worse, big globs of ketchup would overshoot your meal by a good two inches. God forbid your ketchup bottle was only a quarter full. The cumulative effect of gravity on the stored upright bottle and the viscosity of its contents meant your burger could go cold before it could be garnished.

This was not great for the ketchup cartel. What to do? Heinz, for one, spewed outright propaganda. In the 1970s, the leading purveyor of ketchup in America made some marketing executives rich through a years-long campaign to turn this tragic design flaw—the slow-dispensing ketchup bottle—into a *virtue*. In a series of television ads, played against the backdrop of a Carly Simon song, "Anticipation"—"Anticipation is making me wait"—the company actually extolled its glacial ketchup flow. Salivating actors wait patiently to season fries and hamburgers, with taglines like "The taste that's worth the wait" and "slowww-www good." In one commercial, the announcer intones, "Think how good it's gonna taste . . . when it finally gets there." He's talking about the ketchup. Imagine that ad campaign for a restaurant with horrid service. Or an airline with a late arrival problem: "Think how good Aruba is gonna be . . . when you finally get there."

To be clear, ketchup was not a crisis in America, nor was it my greatest childhood lament. But I do have a memory of realizing the problem had been solved many years later, long after the introduction of plastic bottles, with simplicity and elegance. I was at a cookout somewhere. Sun shining, birds chirping, burgers grilling. Lo and behold, some ketchup visionary had figured out how to fix the problem.

What was that innovation?

Someone simply put the lid on the bottom. That's it. Now your ketchup flowed as you wished—no whacking, no wait. It's the same radical principle now applied to shampoo and conditioner bottles. The striking part, to me, is that the improvement required no trailblazing scientific discovery, no space-age polymer, no new chemical compound. Once plastic came into wide use, anyone could have thought to place the lid on the bottom. Gravity was fairly well understood by this point. Undoubtedly, there were clever families in the 1970s who, on their own initiative and for this reason, maintained their ketchup bottles in the fridge upside down. They were not physicists.

It may not rival nuclear fusion, but the case of the ketchup bottle teaches an important lesson. Improvement came because someone decided to think differently, thought to engage in a perspective shift. Someone literally thought to turn orthodoxy on its head.

Common sense and cleverness go a long way, even in the most mundane settings and circumstances. There's a simple story of crime prevention I read about many years ago that has always stuck in my mind. A high-end clothing store was experiencing repeated robberies. The thieves would come at night and trip the alarm, but they were able to sweep up armfuls of expensive garments from the racks and be long gone with substantial loot by the time the cops appeared. This happened again and again. The robbers were too quick, the cops too slow. Then a store employee had an idea—just alternate the direction of the clothing hangers. The first hanger facing forward, the second hanger facing backward, and so on. This would make it impossible for the thieves to quickly grab armloads of garments in one fell swoop. They'd have to pluck one at a time. Sure enough, when the neighborhood robbers next showed up to steal, they were caught red-handed, still greedily trying to get their haul up—one hanger at a time—as the police arrived. Again, no rocket science here. Nothing was invented or even reinvented. Any ordinary person, thinking a little bit outside the box, could have dreamed up that plan.

That's why I love it.

I don't know how to inspire ordinary smart people to engineer a faster microprocessor, build a bigger rocket, or colonize another planet. But what I can do is ask them to question the way they do things, to apply old tools in novel ways, to brainstorm, to think anew. True inventors are special, I suppose, but the rest of us can be inventive too. Everyone can, from time to time, turn orthodoxy on its head.

Criminal investigations are no different in this way from any other professional endeavor. They require skill, expertise, dedication, and focus but also periodically a dose of innovation. Law enforcement is a conservative enterprise by nature and by design, but that doesn't mean it doesn't benefit from entrepreneurial jolts too. And there are examples of such jolts. They are not earth-shattering. But that, as I have been trying to suggest, is the point.

Wiretaps have long been an effective means of investigating crime. Court-authorized wiretaps have been the bread and butter of narcotics and organized crime investigations for generations—not only in the Southern District of New York, but everywhere. Before I became U.S. Attorney, someone in SDNY had a novel thought.

Why not employ wiretaps to investigate suspected insider trading? Voilà! Innovation. Often, thinking outside the box is merely a matter of applying a trusted tool, technique, or principle to another area. That's all this was. The application of the wiretap statute to insider trading could have been tried many years earlier, but as with the upside-down ketchup bottle, it doesn't seem to have occurred to anyone. That's especially surprising because at the heart of every insider-trading crime is an illicit communication—the tip of material-nonpublic information from one person to another, and through generations of insider-trading cases one of the hardest things to prove was the existence of that tip.

Barriers to innovative thinking include risk of opposition and rejection. People fight for the status quo and against change. In criminal enforcement, every innovation that makes it easier to charge people with, and convict people of, criminal violations has a naturally occurring adversary—the defense bar. As a general legal matter, any argument that wiretaps should not be used in insider-trading cases was meritless. Insider trading is a species of securities fraud and has for decades been a permissible basis for a wiretap.

But sure enough, when my office "innovated" in this way, defense lawyers cried foul and fought it in the courts. They lost at every juncture. We were treated to a semi-comical paradox in the arguments of frustrated defense lawyers over the use of wiretaps. On the same day—October 4, 2010—two different prominent defense lawyers made the opposite points on the same issue. One was arguing to a judge that a wiretap should be suppressed in an insider-trading case given that the government could not show the necessity of the tap because all sorts of less compelling evidence sufficed. Meanwhile, *at almost literally the same time,* another well-known lawyer was arguing to a jury—equally strenuously—that they had to acquit his client in an insider-trading case because even though there was a cooperating witness, without an intercepted electronic communication like a "tape recording," the government had not met its burden of proof. Both arguments failed.

In these cases, no new statute was passed, nothing was invented. It was a simple commonsense reorientation; the innovation was lying in plain sight. Innovation may not necessitate particular genius, but it does require a deliberate focus on reevaluating how something has been done in order to solve a problem or improve a process. It requires pausing, reflecting, reorienting, and thinking, is there a new way to do this?

There was an especially glaring loophole in New York State law when I was U.S. Attorney as we were prosecuting numerous legislators for public corruption. As I testified at an open hearing, "A galling injustice that sticks in the craw of every thinking New Yorker is the almost inviolable right of even the most corrupt elected official—even after being convicted by a jury and jailed by a judge—to draw a publicly funded pension until his dying day." This right—enshrined by the legislature itself—defied logic and justice. And we thought it should succumb to a commonsense principle: convicted politicians should not grow old comfortably cushioned by a pension paid for by the very people they betrayed in office.

But this didn't have to be the end of the story. Rich Zabel, my deputy, came up with a clever—and just—legal antidote to this glaring miscarriage. What state law didn't permit, we could accomplish legally through federal criminal forfeiture law: first, we would seek fines from corrupt officials that accounted for their future pensions; second, we would consider forfeiture actions to satisfy criminal judgments; and third, our office would claw back pension interest accrued while the politicians were engaging in illegal activity. The principle was just and the strategy was lawful. Every legal challenge failed. Rich saw a way to solve the problem that no one had seen before.

Here's another example. For a long while now, a scourge of the internet has been these sites on what's called the Dark Web where you can find essentially open markets to buy and sell weapons, narcotics, child pornography, and other nasty stuff. Identifying people who are engaging in criminal activity behind the cloak of online anonymity is deeply challenging. When I came into office, our point person on all things cyber was a mild-mannered AUSA named Tom Brown. He was devoted to cyber issues long before it became all the rage. His quiet passion drove many of our best cases.

Tom did a lot of work with Chris Stangl, who was the supervisor of CY-2, a cyber-crime squad in the FBI New York. They solved many cyber crimes together. One was a hack of Citibank that involved at least one bad guy in Russia putting sniffer software on an ATM processing network in Texas, resulting in the theft of 300,000 accounts. The stolen account data was distributed by at least one other bad guy to cashers around the world, either directly or through brokers.

The FBI located one broker living in Tallinn, the capital of Estonia. In connection with the broker's arrest, Tom and Chris traveled there to coordinate with the Estonians and start the SDNY/Estonia relationship—yes, we build relationships directly with foreign countries where possible. Tom and Chris would frequently meet for brainstorming sessions (usually at bars) about how to build bigger and better cases. In Tallinn, they found themselves at the Ice Bar in Old Town. While sipping Viru Valge brand Estonian vodka from tumblers made of ice at the small bar, Tom and Chris discussed the usual difficulties involved in identifying cyber criminals. Indeed, it had taken months of painstaking work to pinpoint the Estonian broker.

What if they could short-circuit the identification problem and work proactively rather than reactively? The epiphany was to build an undercover internet forum—a website where criminals could gather, buy and sell stolen information, and generally conspire, sort of like an online speakeasy. "Build it and they will come" was the idea. Instead of having to wait for criminals to act and then try to identify them, we would allow them to come to us and then use the website to identify them and shut them down.

The operation, dubbed Card Shop, was a success. We stopped several hundred million dollars in fraud by identifying stolen credit card information that was trafficked over the site, and prosecuted twenty-four criminals from multiple countries around the world.

All of this happened because two people decided to take a step back and see how they could solve a difficult problem. There is nothing new or novel about an FBI sting. It has been used in corruption cases, mob cases, gang cases, drug cases, and even terrorism cases, but nothing of this type or scale had ever been ventured in the cyber area, and there's no reason why that should have been true.

If you were a liberal arts major in college, you would not stroll into work one day, sit at your cubicle, and expect to invent the adhesive that made the Post-it a completely indispensable office supply for a billion people, not to mention 3M's runaway moneymaker. But every day presents an opportunity to rethink habits, policies, and procedures, which if reexamined through the prism of common sense can be revamped to enhance the quality of life or the bottom line or even public safety.

Final story:

Innovation doesn't require a Ph.D., but people with doctorates have good ideas too. Toward the end of my time as U.S. Attorney, we made an unusual investigator hire in the form of Kurt Hafer. Our typical investigator tended to be a former cop schooled in street-level investigations from time doing homicide or gang or mob work for twenty years before joining our office—people like John O'Malley and Kenny McCabe.

Kurt Hafer was not like that. Skinny to the point of worry, Kurt had a freckled face, a sprout of red hair, and the look of someone leery of guns but at ease with paper cuts. He had a degree in physics from California Polytechnic and a Ph.D. in biomedical physics from UCLA. We hired him away from the U.S. Department of Energy, where he had specialized in investigating ways that the department was being ripped off. At the time, the Energy Department had a budget of some $32.5 billion and hundreds of contracts with private sector companies—some of whom engaged in double billing and other kinds of fraud.

What Kurt lacked in street experience, he made up for in intellect, initiative, creativity, and hard work. Given his background and his facility with math and financial issues, we assigned him to the securities fraud unit on the fifth floor.

He immediately went to work.

One project Kurt gave to himself was generating more leads on insider-trading cases from suspicious activity reports that financial institutions are required to file. A suspicious activity report is an important lifeblood of generating leads in connection with money laundering, securities fraud, and every kind of financial misconduct. A suspicious activity report, or SAR, is required by law to be filed by financial institutions in a central repository when they believe someone has engaged in, well, suspicious activity.

Some banks file more; some file less. Some financial institutions are very detailed in the suspicious activity reports that they fill out. Some are bare-bones. Some file because they want merely to discharge the obligation, to check the box. Some do it because they are actually trying to get something investigated. The problem is that all these reports end up streaming into a vast, undifferentiated ocean.

Kurt was suspicious of the suspicious activity reviews.

His intuition was that we should have been generating more leads on insider trading than we were. Something must be wrong with the key-word search. The sample yield had to be underpopulated, and he worried how much wheat was being cut out along with the chaff. So, Kurt decided to take a step back and dispense with the search term function altogether. He went old school, rejecting the digital for the analog. He sat down and literally reviewed, by hand and with his own eyes, SAR after SAR after SAR. He began by looking at just one top investment bank and read from beginning to end, SAR after SAR, to get a feel for how these things were written. He set aside two hundred hours over the first two or three weeks of each month in his new job.

What he saw both surprised and disappointed him. To any halfway intelligent person reading some of these SARs, alarm bells should have sounded. Kurt kept seeing SARs showing that there was stock purchased, stock sold, profit made, and an intervening stock-moving event—all the makings of a textbook insider-trading case.

The problem was that no one was reading those incriminating SARs because the key-word searches were too narrow and specific. Kurt asked himself why these gems were not being screened in and discovered this was for two reasons. First, even though the missed SARs clearly showed suspicion of insider-trading activity, the magic phrase "insider trading" often had not been typed into the form. This was a failure of training at the financial institutions but also a failure of imagination by the people employing such a limited key-word search. Second, in many instances the person filling out the SAR had no clue what the dollar amount of the gain was and simply entered zero. Therefore, if an investigator screened with a minimum-dollar threshold, an incriminating zero-dollar SAR would also fall through the cracks.

This was an easy fix, though it appeared no one until Kurt had thought to do it. Kurt refined the key-word searches, made them more expansive. He also continued from time to time to do old-world and full-text reviews of SARs. Guess what happened? Credible insider-trading leads generated in-house at SDNY doubled or tripled.

Sometimes innovation requires a step backward when technology makes us less rather than more effective. Innovation—whether in relation to how a company makes a product or how an agent investigates a case—means constantly reevaluating and reassessing technology and the capacity for human error or lack of imagination. It also means resisting shortcuts, laziness, and complacency.

What Kurt discovered was that a popular and once-effective tool was outmoded. It was not getting the job done. The irony is that once upon a time the use of search terms to find the bad guys in a vast sea of clues was itself the innovation. But that innovation had stagnated. Today's innovation, if not updated and tended to, becomes tomorrow's obsolescence. That is true of cars, computers, and smartphones. It is also true of investigative techniques. Sometimes justice is served by turning orthodoxy on its head.

PART II

Accusation

Introduction

So your inquiry has come to an end. It was hard and perhaps painstaking. You hope it was open-minded and fair. The truth, as best as possible, has been investigated. Now comes the next and distinct phase of the justice process. Presumably, you investigated because there was smoke. Did you find fire? And did you find enough proof to blame someone for that fire? As Dostoyevsky wrote in *Crime and Punishment,* "A hundred suspicions don't make a proof." The fundamental question for people on the cusp of making an allegation—once the inquiry is complete—is this: When do you pull the trigger, and when do you walk away?

This is not always so straightforward and simple.

Sometimes you walk away because no one did anything wrong, because the evidence gathered exonerates the target. Or you walk away because the transgression is minor and it's not worth the time and energy. It's beneath the state's wrath. Or someone did do something awful, but your inquiry didn't yield enough proof to meet the relevant demanding standard, beyond a reasonable doubt, for example. Or someone did something scandalous and harmful, but it was an accident or happened too long ago and the law doesn't recognize the crime, for that reason or other reasons. Or it *is* a violation, but you conclude that no one else has ever been charged with a crime in similar circumstances. Fairness likely dictates that you walk away in that scenario too, unless there's a compelling reason to break precedent.

These situations arise every day, in every jurisdiction. How to navigate this thicket in a principled and just way? That is what the next pages explore.

The first precondition to making a just decision in this accusation phase is a commitment to deliberation and against any predetermined outcome. You take the evidence gathered—the bank records and recordings and the witness interviews—and you sift through them, ponder them. You consider alternative and innocent explanations for damning events. You contemplate alternative interpretations of words spoken or emails sent. You entertain the possibility of innocent coincidence and investigator bias. Remember Brandon Mayfield? People over-interpreted a series of facts about him, found innocent Spanish-language documents incriminating, and relied on wholly incidental facts like his conversion to Islam to justify incorrect first conclusions about a fingerprint match. That kind of inattention is fatal to justice.

So you check your facts, you check your reasoning, you check your bias. You challenge your understandings and conclusions. You ask others to poke holes too. In fact, when investigations were overt, I routinely took meetings with defense counsel, heard them out, pressed them for innocent explanations of guilty-looking behavior and more exonerating analyses of applicable law. Sometimes we avoided error (and injustice) because these defense advocates showed us how we were wrong. (Mere strenuous denials of wrongdoing, I should point out, are insufficient to make us go away.)

This kind of deliberation—and pause—is fundamental to justice. To charge a human being with a crime is to shatter that person's life. It is also to upend the lives of those close to that person. A criminal defendant, even if acquitted or cleared on appeal, will never be the same again. It is not enough to receive, eventually, a fair trial in a court of law; by then, one may be ostracized, bankrupt, unemployed, or unemployable. And so the decision to charge in the first place must be as just and fair as possible. The same is true, incidentally, for a news outlet deciding to publish serious allegations about a public official or private citizen; the bell is near impossible to un-ring.

Beware the trigger-happy prosecutor or cop. Prosecutors aren't cowboys or gunslingers. It is vital to keep always, front of mind, what this moment means, this moment of decision about the way forward—not only for the institution making the charge, but also for the target and for public faith.

The individual and institutional psychology of this moment is worth addressing. Accusations are not automated; they are not prescribed by computer or algorithm. Justice, as I keep repeating, is done by human beings. Decisions about what to do (or not do) with the fruits of a good-faith inquiry are made by real people who are not omniscient, who are often flawed or biased, and who are always operating in imperfect systems and bureaucracies.

I would often talk about it this way with my most junior prosecutors: I likened being a prosecutor to a car with a very powerful engine, capable of going at great (and dangerous) speeds. For a car to get you somewhere (safely), you need two things. You need the accelerator. But you also need brakes. You need to step on the accelerator, because we have to get where we're going: wrongdoers need accountability, victims need vindication, society needs order. So we have to use the accelerator. But sometimes we need to brake—take stock, reconsider, question our analysis. Braking saves lives too.

While you should beware the prosecutor who is trigger-happy, worry also about the one who is gun-shy, the one with a lead foot on the brake. They can undermine justice and accountability with the opposite bent. For some people, it is hard to pull the trigger on decisions of consequence. Accusing is the ultimate confrontation, whether in the criminal justice system, the workplace, or anywhere else. We are generally loath to confront, especially when the consequences are grave. We are taught, as children, not even to point at people. It's rude. It has consequences.

Some people will be tempted to indulge in endless investigation. There's always someone who can be interviewed a second time, or a third. There's always more research to be done, always another rock to turn over. Perhaps people delay because the preliminary nature of an "inquiry" is something of a safe haven. Investigations and inquiries can be quiet; suspicions can be hazy and held close. As far as the wider world is concerned, the possibility of some actual allegation is mere hypothetical, the stuff of rumor. Until Special Counsel Robert Mueller actually charged Trump's national security adviser Michael Flynn or former campaign chairman Paul Manafort, despite intense speculation, no one knew if it would really happen. There is no gauntlet until it is thrown down.

Accusations, on the other hand, are concrete. They are specific, stark, and public. They are written declarations of war. That can be scary, especially in hard or close cases. The decision to make a public accusation, particularly in the prosecution context, is momentous. And there are people, of a certain constitution, who sometimes in the name of thoroughness delay that moment unduly. If you're in the business of investigative reporting or internal compliance at a company or, of course, law enforcement, you have to have the fortitude to make the call. There is always more investigating to be done. Actions have consequences, of course, but inaction has consequences too. If it ever falls upon you to investigate something with an eye toward exposing some conduct, you have to be the kind of person who is capable of pulling the trigger, and at the right time.

What goes on behind the scenes to separate smoke from fire and accidents from arson is important to understand. Sometimes, cases seem to cry out for prosecution but are so purely circumstantial that hesitation is natural.

Here is an example to set the stage for the following pages. In 2008, *The New York Times* uncovered what looked like massive and appalling fraud at the Long Island Rail Road (LIRR). Rail employees were claiming that they had debilitating conditions and injuries in order to obtain disability pension benefits. Upon being approved for early pensions, available at age fifty, many employees would remain physically active, golfing or playing tennis as if it were going out of style. The rate at which LIRR workers applied for occupational disability benefits was staggering; in fiscal year 2007, it was twelve times the rate at a similar railroad such as Metro-North, which also operates trains into New York City. Between 2001 and 2007, 753 LIRR workers claimed disabilities from arthritis and rheumatism, whereas Metro-North had only 32. On the one hand, that discrepancy alone reeked of fraud. Three doctors had approved thousands of claims, and the obvious working theory was that the doctors were involved in blatant deceit.

On the other hand, the hard evidence of fraud was circumstantial and statistical. It is tough to prove that ailments such as back, shoulder, or joint pain are made up. There is no X-ray or MRI or blood test to confirm or rule out such self-reported afflictions. Diagnoses and prognoses must be made based on subjective patient self-reporting.

There was, nonetheless, a mountain of viscerally provocative evidence that many of these pension recipients, after claiming debilitating conditions that prevented low-key desk work, participated in extremely taxing athletic activities. Here are just a few brazen examples, exposed by *The New York Times* in its lengthy investigative report:

- One retiree—Gregory Noone—complained of severe pain when he tried to grab things with his hands. He got an early disability pension. Soon after, in 2008, Noone played golf 140 times in nine months. Apparently, despite his stated condition, he either could grip the clubs in his bag with ease or was the most masochistic golfer in amateur history.

• Another retiree—Sharon Falloon—claimed that it was painful to walk and stand. She got her early pension. Not long after, she was videotaped at a gym taking a step aerobics class for forty-five minutes.

• Yet another retiree—Frederick Catalano—alleged that he could neither stand nor sit without experiencing extreme pain. Within months of retirement, Catalano earned a black belt in jujitsu.

All of this looked like sheer abuse.

The investigation documented example after example of this kind of thing. Was it time to make an accusation, charge the lot of them, including the rubber-stamping doctors?

Well, not so fast. Notwithstanding the immediate and miraculous athletic prowess of so many disabled pensioners, this was not a slam dunk. After evaluating the evidence and the likelihood of success of a fraud case, notwithstanding its breathtaking scope, our friendly rivals across the river at the Eastern District of New York declined to pursue it. They walked away. Given the circumstantial nature of the case, this was not necessarily an irresponsible decision. But we decided to take our own deep dive.

One of the railway's oversight agencies, the U.S. Railroad Retirement Board, though increasingly wary and suspicious, had blessed all of the payments. And that other bit of eye-popping statistical proof—that LIRR disability rates in 2007 were, inexplicably, twelve times those of Metro-North? That fact, we determined as a legal matter, might not even be admissible at trial, because a judge could find it prejudicial and legally irrelevant.

On top of that, there were no telltale documents showing a conspiracy; there was no wiretap; there was no confession, just mildly incriminating but inconclusive statements to the FBI by two doctors. The ripest and most impactful targets were these doctors (not the individual scheming pensioners) who would have the ready—if implausible—defense that they simply relied on the testimonials of their patients.

Here's what else was missing: there was no strong cooperating witness who could outline the scheme for us (and a jury). That is what we needed. And so that is what we set about to get. We began by charging individual pensioners.

This was a concern not about innocence but about proof. That is an important distinction. Pursuing the case required some leap of faith. I asked the team one late afternoon, after seeing memos summarizing the evidence and its circumstantial and statistical nature, "Why don't you hum a few bars of the summation?" so I could understand how this proof was going to be presented—not to a magistrate judge or grand jury, which was just an intermediate hurdle, but to an ultimate trial jury, where the burden is proof beyond a reasonable doubt.

We concluded that there was such overwhelming common-sense evidence that LIRR doctors and workers had perpetrated a years-long, billion-dollar scam on the transportation authority that even if the trial-quality evidence was short of a smoking gun, we had enough to charge, with fingers crossed that people would flip and strengthen the case.

The team built a powerful seventy-four-page criminal complaint, marshaling the facts, detailing the athletic prowess of supposedly disabled retirees. We aggressively charged to get people to flip. They did. By the time we were done, we had charged thirty-two individuals, and all pled guilty or were convicted at trial. Also we had begun to reform a hopelessly broken pension system.

The point of sharing the LIRR story is not to boast about this great blow for justice made possible by our aggressiveness. It is to demonstrate how tough these decisions can be—these tough calls that are not capable of scientific precision.

What follows is an exploration of this distinct phase on the journey to justice. Here I try to explore and explain the always fraught decision to accuse someone of something, knowing that it will be an earthquake for that person and a test for your own office, and the equally consequential decision to walk away. You will hear about the importance of culture in a prosecutor's office, about taking care not to create insidious pressure to bring a prosecution, which can lead to injustice.

You will also read about the difficulty of making judgments in real time about who poses an actual threat, with imperfect information but a responsibility to protect the public from harm. How long can you wait, and how much evidence do you need, when a hapless would-be terrorist makes jihadist threats or when a husband openly discusses harming his wife? What is the difference between fantasy and conspiracy? On what side do you err? On what side would you want us to err, when lives are on the line but the proof is not yet overwhelming? As you read these stories, ask what you would do.

Other times people complain bitterly when prosecutors do what they must often do, consistent with the facts, law, and conscience—which is to walk away. When harm is suffered, when a house burns down, when an innocent is shot, when a driver kills a pedestrian, or when an economy collapses, there is a natural thirst for scalps. Sometimes this is consistent with justice, but sometimes it is not, whatever anyone says. It's easier to explain why you did something than why you didn't. That's true in many contexts. But in the business of justice, it's a special dilemma: When is it fair and proper to walk away? You'll read about the reasoning regarding petty crimes, the dangerousness of zero-tolerance enforcement, judgments about resources, and why some cases can't be brought, no matter how much anger or thirst for justice.

Finally, culture is important. I spent much of my time focused on the culture of my own office, SDNY. I obsessed over it. Taking a page from my predecessors, I seized every opportunity to spread a certain gospel—that justice was more important than victory, the right thing always more important than the expedient thing. I'm proud of the culture I inherited and I hope I sustained—a culture of such diligence and attention that John O'Malley would work so hard to exonerate six innocents. But culture is important everywhere, in all institutions. There was more criminal smoke in some places than others. Why? To my mind, it was culture, and I've included my thoughts on how bad cultures at institutions can lead to costly and threatening investigations, which result in damaging accusations.

The Grinding Machinery

Investigations, once begun, take on a life of their own. They develop a kind of momentum, even when the destination is far from clear or certain. Once an inquiry is opened, all sorts of things are set in motion: personnel are assigned, shifts are set, lists are made. A process begins. Often, an investigative plan is developed and even written down or typed up. Agents fan out; they serve subpoenas, surveil locations, search records, tap phones, approach witnesses. They may scorch the earth. That frenzy of activity is not just sound and fury. It signifies something. It is the concrete, outward manifestation of an urgent search for truth and accountability; it is the groaning real-world machinery of the justice process.

But what often accompanies all this investigative action and forward motion is a dangerous psychological momentum. Because while all this activity is going on, whether the leads are panning out or usable evidence is materializing, something else is happening too. *Investments* are being made. And *expectations* are being set.

Law enforcement agencies are like Wall Street in one way. They want a return on their investment. It's only natural. Human beings want their efforts to amount to something; we desperately want something to show for all our work. No one wants to be Sisyphus. A farmer may love tending to his crops, but he lives for the harvest.

Law enforcement agents, however, are not Wall Street investors (or farmers). Profit and justice are different. Justice often must suffer the loss of substantial investment because that is what justice itself demands. When a backbreaking investigation does not yield enough evidence of a crime, when it turns out that a miscreant has come up to the criminal line but not put a thieving toe over it, when everyone thinks the target probably did the deed but doubts linger, when the law in its idiocy or a court in its naïveté has exempted from prosecution bad conduct that reasonable people loathe and want to punish, there is only one choice: to walk away. Walking away can be deeply and viscerally unsatisfying. But if all the raised expectations and personal investments and sunk costs sweep people toward an unjust charging decision, that is a miscarriage.

There are plenty of outside accelerants pushing forward this inherent psychological momentum. When bad things happen, politicians, the press, and the public look for scalps and scapegoats. These are all contagions that can infect a fair inquiry. The fair-minded investigator stays pure and infection-free by going about her business, head down, in a metaphorical hazmat suit, immune to external pressures. Imbecilic mob chants of "lock her up!" or "lock him up!" fall on deaf ears.

Outside forces aside, there is sometimes an internal source of pressure that is also dangerous and inexcusable. That occurs when leaders of an institution—even inadvertently—create pressure to produce a particular result. They do this by forgetting, as I sometimes did, to make clear that they are prepared to accept that there may be no pot of gold at the end of the rainbow and that this is okay. Because profit and justice are different.

In the winter of 2015, we were in the throes of investigating the potential corruption of two of the three most powerful political leaders in New York State: the Democratic assembly

Speaker, Sheldon Silver, and the Republican senate majority leader, Dean Skelos. These were important cases; these were high-profile men; and public corruption was an acute problem in New York. Naturally, the leadership of the office, myself included, paid these cases a lot of mind. From the perspective of the line prosecutors, some of the attention was welcome, but a lot of it probably wasn't.

Unfortunately for them, my corruption prosecutors were conveniently clustered at the opposite end of the hallway from my own office on the eighth floor, making supervisory harassment especially easy. During certain periods, I would wander, almost daily, into one of their offices. Sometimes my volley of questions was general: What's the latest? How's it looking? What witnesses do you have lined up? Other times more granular: When is Dr. Taub coming in for his first proffer? Do we have backup for Silver's clinic grant from the Department of Health? When are we renewing the wiretap on Adam Skelos's phone? These questions, which came not only from me but also from the deputy U.S. Attorney, Rich Zabel, and then Criminal Division chief, Joon Kim, were intended to do more than just satisfy our curiosity. They were also meant to convey interest, support, and urgency. We also pestered the intrepid SDNY investigators who spearheaded the investigations, John Barry and Bob Ryan. It was important to be thorough but also expeditious because clouds were hanging over two men who had been popularly elected by the people of the state. For this reason, as with all public corruption cases, there was a special need for speed, to either put up or shut up. That was in the public interest, in the office's interest, and in the targets' interest, which, perhaps surprisingly to some, is an important consideration.

But even good-faith questions about the progress of an investigation, if asked with sufficient intensity (and frequency), can build a subtle pressure toward a particular outcome. Such a dynamic can convey that the leadership will be disappointed with anything less than a criminal charge whether the case is weak or not, whether the case is just or not. That kind of pressure, if not defused, can undermine both fair process and a just result. Leaders can't be blind to that.

One evening, I heard secondhand from Rich Zabel that one of the corruption prosecutors had said, "I'm worried Preet will be pissed if we can't make the case." That was a full-stop moment. It might have been a passing remark, but to Rich (and to me) it was a wake-up call, because we realized that our well-meaning but endless badgering might be creating a pressure cooker.

Now I became less concerned about the cases than about the morale and psyche of the teams. Passing remark or not, I was deeply bothered that at least one AUSA might have been worried about disappointing me rather than exclusively focused on finding the truth and making the fairest recommendation, whatever that might be.

Rich and I decided to clear the air. I called a meeting the next day in the eighth-floor library and convened both the Silver and the Skelos teams, along with their supervisors. It was rare to call an all-hands gathering so abruptly. Both teams filed in—Andrew Goldstein, Howard Master, Carrie Cohen, and Jamie McDonald on Silver; Tatiana Martins, Rahul Mukhi, Jason Masimore, and Tom McKay on Skelos. When we had a quorum, I walked the few steps from my office into the windowless, book-lined library. That small library was stopped in time, same law books on the same shelves, same flag in the same corner, for at least a few decades. I had added one functional ornament a couple of years earlier—a round clock mounted on the far wall directly in my line of vision so I could know when to end meetings that dragged on too long.

I sat as usual at the head of the long wooden table in the center, the teams arrayed on either side. I glanced at that clock now. It was past 5:00 p.m., quitting time for so many people but very early in the workday for these prosecutors, especially during those investigations. I'm sure I made a joke or two because that's how I started almost every meeting. And then I launched into it. I said something like this:

"I want to make sure that everyone understands something. I'm really proud of all of you. I hired most of you, and I did that because I trust you and I respect your judgment. We only stand for one thing in this place, and that is to do the right thing. And I ask a lot of questions about these cases because I care about them, because we can't get it wrong, and because whatever we do will have consequences for the state of New York. And on people's faith in government. And on the reputation of this office. But I want to make something very clear: I want you to be aggressive, thorough, and complete. And if on either case you guys tell me there's not a proper charge to bring, I'm going to be just as proud of you and just as proud of this office as I would be if you recommended bringing charges. So I don't want you to ever think that I or Rich or Joon or Dan is looking for a particular result. That's not what we do here. That's not what I want you to do. I'm sure you know that. I hope you know that. But I wanted to have this meeting to remove any doubt. We have the luxury in this office of being able to spend time, energy, and effort aggressively pursuing investigations of the most powerful people in the state and in the country because we think no one's above the law. But as one of my predecessors used to say, 'You judge an office not just by the cases it brings but also by the cases it doesn't bring.' And if it's not right to bring a case, we won't bring it."

I closed by saying, "I don't want you to worry about this or me for one second." I saw mild relief on at least two faces. Meeting adjourned.

We ended up filing charges against both Silver and Skelos. Both went to trial and were found guilty within eleven days of each other. Months later, the U.S. Supreme Court changed the law of what constitutes "official action," and both convictions were reversed; both men were retried after I left office and convicted again on all charges.

Some months after Senator Skelos was convicted, one of the prosecutors in the case, Jason Masimore, asked to meet with me. His email said nothing about what he wanted to discuss, but I knew. It was the same type of email I had received dozens of times. ("Hi, Preet. Do you have a few minutes for me to stop by?") The language was usually general, even cryptic, but that email always meant only one thing: someone had decided to leave the office, was coming to let me know, was asking to say a personal farewell. Often I was expecting it; sometimes I was surprised. I was always a little sad. Sometimes for me, but always sad for them because I knew this might be the best job they would ever have.

Jason came in and sat down on the low couch against the front wall of my office. I walked over from my desk to one of the leather chairs. I thanked him for his service. I said I was sorry to see him go because I was. We reminisced a bit about the trial. We joked about what I thought was his finest moment as a prosecutor when he quoted from a Shel Silverstein poem called "Gorilla" in his devastating rebuttal summation in the Skelos case, described later in this book. Before leaving, Jason said, "Preet, I just want to say one more thing." Then he brought up the meeting in the library from many months earlier. "That was a really important meeting. And I think about that meeting, and I just want you to know the day I was most proud to be part of this office was not the day we convicted Dean Skelos. It was the day we had that meeting when you reminded us that our job was only to do the right thing. No matter how we came out on charging."

There's often another factor at play when it comes to any inquiry concerned with wrongdoing. To be sure, every criminal investigation is about learning what happened, about finding the truth. But every step and phase is also colored by a moral agenda—the drive to hold someone accountable for a law transgressed or a harm done. When it looks as if a bank has cheated a client or a product has injured a customer or a politician has abused his power, the strong human inclination is to want to hold someone to account, even though ultimately the law may not recognize the crime or the provable facts may not support alleging one.

A criminal investigation is different from, say, a medical inquiry in this way. Medical mysteries (unless of the medical examiner variety) are value neutral. Someone is sick. The doctor wants to know, what is responsible? Is it viral? Is it bacterial? The effort at medical diagnosis is generally not accompanied by any moral agenda. No one says they want to hold the virus or the bacteria accountable. There is no blameworthiness and hence no prospect of punishment. A disease doesn't get sent to prison. Doctors want only to incapacitate it, render it harmless. Cancer may be a scourge, but it is not evil in the moral sense, any more than a bolt of lightning can be evil.

In a criminal investigation, where some harm or bad conduct is evident, a moral agenda hangs like a cloud. Or maybe it's less like a cloud and more like a voice in the investigator's head—an imperative to "get the bad guy, get the bad guy." On the one hand, this voice can drive you to work your fingers to the bone, to leave no stone unturned so the result is not just the truth but also ultimate justice. That's a good thing. But, on the other hand, if people are not careful, that voice can put a thumb on the scale, undermine neutrality, and cause a rush to judgment. Think of the Central Park Five. Think of Cathy Watkins and Eric Glisson. I could fill this book with many more examples.

Punishment and accountability are a critical part of justice, but at the investigative stage, entertaining visions of eventual reckoning puts the cart dangerously before the horse. Not all misdeeds are crimes because the law is finicky that way. Also, not all initial suspects are guilty because sometimes things are not what they seem. The fair-minded investigator or prosecutor has to keep this foremost in mind and has to operate in an open-minded environment where rush to judgment is anathema and walking away always remains an option, no matter how much investment has been made.

God Forbid

Here's a dirty secret: sometimes the decision to accuse someone is not based exclusively on past conduct. Obviously, the proof you bring to bear in support of your accusation has to be retrospective, has to be based on what has actually *happened,* and has to be sufficient. But in real life, especially if your mission is to protect rather than just punish, the decision to charge (and when) is inevitably tied to an assessment of potential future harm. This is why prosecutors will spend lots of time and effort building a case based on a minor statute against, say, a mob figure or a suspected terrorist. Because it's easier. Think Al Capone and income tax evasion. Some prognostication is necessary, but it's a tricky business. As the physicist Niels Bohr once said, "Prediction is very difficult, especially about the future."

This fortune-teller dynamic arises in countless contexts. The decision to terminate someone from a job, for example, should reasonably be grounded on an identifiable, concrete, past transgression. But realistically, it will likely also be influenced by a prediction about whether that person will do it again and by the company's appetite for that risk. In most cases, the decision to make an accusation is discretionary, and so future harm must properly be in the calculus.

Think of every tragic story you have read of a child in a foster home beaten to death by a guardian, or a wife killed by a violent husband, and it later comes to light that there had been warning signs, 911 calls, even protective orders.

On February 14, 2018, a nineteen-year-old previously expelled from a high school in Parkland, Florida, massacred seventeen students and teachers in their school, making it one of the worst mass shootings in U.S. history. A month prior to that, he stated on social media that his goal was to become a "professional school shooter." That social media post did not constitute a crime. No one arrested him. But did his post express a fantasy or an intent to murder? The answer is now tragically well-known.

It is an article of faith that we hold people accountable for their actions, not their thoughts. But even that truism has its limits. Pure thoughts, in a vacuum, are not capable of detection, much less prosecution. But expressed thoughts—when they get written down or communicated to others in any way—are no longer secret and untouchable. They may reflect malicious intent and, combined with concrete actions, may very well constitute a crime.

In fact, the federal criminal law of conspiracy is actually defined as an agreement between two or more people who have a meeting of the *minds* to break a particular law. It requires no action, just an expressed thought accepted and agreed to by another person. Society (and Congress) decided that this kind of "thought" is not only regrettable and dangerous; it is also indictable and punishable as a crime.

So, how to juggle the risk of harm in any case with the fact that the harm has not yet been visited upon anyone? This dilemma arises increasingly in terror threats. Take, for example, the controversial prosecution of James Cromitie by my office. On the one hand, there was evidence of a harrowing plot to blow up a synagogue in Riverdale. In 2008, Cromitie, our lead defendant, told Shahed Hussain—an FBI informant posing as a Pakistani businessman—that he was willing to do "something to America." Hussain later expressed an interest in joining Jaish-e-Mohammed, a foreign terror organization. In November,

Cromitie, referencing an attack at a synagogue, stated, "I hate those motherfuckers, those Jewish bastards." And he suggested he wanted to destroy a synagogue.

By late April 2009, Cromitie and his future co-defendants—David Williams IV, Onta Williams, and Laguerre Payen—had agreed to bomb a Riverdale synagogue and "shoot down" military planes in Newburgh. The group obtained what they thought were three IEDs with C-4 plastic explosive material and a Stinger surface-to-air guided missile from Hussain. Two days later, the defendants planted the fake bombs at two locations in Riverdale.

Now, this was not the most astute gang the world has ever known. Sophisticated terrorists these were not. All of the men were struggling with poverty. None of the defendants had any particular experience or expertise in bombs or weaponry. The plan was—from beginning to end—coordinated and supervised by the FBI. It was a sting, after all. No one was ever in actual danger. Despite the group's alleged commitment to Islam, Cromitie once had to ask the others if they knew about the Kaaba—the mosque building in Mecca that Muslims are supposed to face during daily prayer. Onta Williams was a drug dealer. Payen was a suspected schizophrenic (he kept bottles of his own urine in his home), who also thought visiting Florida required a passport. They might not have been the smartest terrorists, but they appeared bent on committing an act of terror.

Judge Colleen McMahon was critical of the sting: "Only the government could have made a terrorist out of Mr. Cromitie, a man whose buffoonery is positively Shakespearean in its scope." Referring to the crime, Judge McMahon stated that "the government instigated it, planned it and brought it to fruition." When she sentenced all four "buffoons" to twenty-five years in prison because of the statutory mandatory minimum, she called them "thugs for hire, pure and simple."

Should we prosecute seemingly harmless but ill-meaning

half-wits who make clear they want to kill Americans but don't show the hallmarks of competence? Recent lessons in New York, in London, in Paris, and in other places teach that even an ill-equipped person with ill intentions, if armed with a car or a knife rather than a cache of weapons, can terrorize and kill lots of people. It takes no planning, no special expertise, no particular competence. It just takes ill will and a few seconds to swerve into a crowd or to stab a commuter on a train. That's not a hypothetical. That's arguably what happened on Halloween in lower Manhattan, when Sayfullo Saipov—a twenty-nine-year-old terrorist from Uzbekistan—drove his rental truck over a crowded bike path near the World Trade Center in 2017. Saipov killed eight people and injured twelve, making this the worst terrorist attack in New York since 9/11. My former colleagues have sought the death penalty against him.

Law enforcement people are trained to hear that "God forbid" voice: God forbid this person does something. God forbid we take no action and this trash-talking misanthrope kills someone. God forbid this is a Tsarnaev brother and three people get blown up at the Boston Marathon. *God forbid.*

When the possibility of harm is afoot, prosecutors are aggressive. Who knows which threats are real and which are puffery? There is a reason that every "threat" to the president—however half-baked and implausible—buys a visit from the Secret Service. Not necessarily to make an arrest, but to make an inquiry, to show up at a doorstep and assess the threat, to disrupt or take stock. Most "threats" to the president do not result in an accusation, though virtually all result in some investigation and a visit. Sometimes that makes sense to do even when the target is not the president.

Once, the presiding judge in a case became controversial. That judge—Katherine Forrest—presided over the trial of Ross Ulbricht, the operator of Silk Road, a billion-dollar online black market for drugs, weapons, and other contraband. After Ulbricht was convicted of seven felony charges, Judge Forrest sentenced him to life in prison and ordered him to pay over $183 million in restitution. During and after his trial, Judge Forrest became the victim of abuse and harassment. She was "doxed," meaning that her Social Security number was anonymously posted on a Dark Web site called 8chan. Judge Forrest's personal address was put online, and her critics called for SWAT teams or anthrax to be sent to her residence.

In addition, against that backdrop she received another series of threats from readers commenting on Reason.com, a libertarian media website. At the same time, her husband and her chambers received ominous communications; she (and we) became legitimately concerned about her safety. In October 2014—prior to Ulbricht's conviction—a user called on a drug cartel to "murder this lady [Judge Forrest] and her entire family." On May 31 and June 1, 2015, a string of threats was made by online commentators: "it's judges like these that should be taken out back and shot"; "send her through the wood chipper"; and "shoot them [her] out front, on the steps of the courthouse."

Prosecutors in my office took aggressive action. They subpoenaed the records of six *Reason* users who had posted threatening statements. They sought a boilerplate gag order—always intended to be temporary—so that *Reason* could not prematurely and publicly discuss the subpoena before law enforcement could run down the leads, to determine whether there was any actual threat. Pretty routine and responsible, even if Judge Forrest was not the president of the United States. The value of murderous speech, by the way, is not high. For this I earned the endless antipathy of the libertarian periodical. We were accused of "government bullying" and violating the First Amendment right to freedom of speech—or, in one critic's words, having a "horrific, chilling effect on free speech." The line between hyperbole and plausibility is hard to discern, and in some lines of work you don't want to take any chances.

The demarcations between thought and action are not so clear. This is the nature of threat assessment: At what point should responsible people take action when feeling their way in that hazy twilight zone where a person has articulated and planned but not yet acted? Here is how we handled these questions in a set of macabre cases.

Skip this section if you are faint of heart.

Kathleen Mangan and Gilberto Valle were young and married, living in Queens, New York, with their infant daughter. Like many marriages, theirs was not perfect, and over time the frequency of intimate relations had dwindled to a level that was upsetting to Mangan. When one day she dared to raise the issue, Valle offered a blunt critique: Mangan just wasn't "kinky." She gamely offered to play along: "What do you want? Fuzzy handcuffs?" Valle responded, "No, that's not kinky enough."

Things did not improve. Valle rarely came to bed, night after night preferring to park in front of his laptop computer screen until the wee hours. Finally, incensed and suspecting infidelity, Mangan installed software to spy on her husband's late-night cyber activities.

One morning in October 2012, while Valle was still sleeping, Mangan drifted to the living room to see what secrets her spyware had unearthed. She sat at the desk, logged on to the laptop, and with a fast-beating heart checked the results. She quickly realized that Valle was not in fact cheating on her. But this was cold comfort.

The truth she discovered was far worse.

As she scrolled through screen shots and secret emails, Mangan couldn't believe her eyes. What she saw shocked her so deeply that she resolved, in that instant, to flee her shared home, for good. She ran to the park across the street, called her father, a retired cop in Vegas, who told her to get the computer and rush to the airport. He would have a plane ticket waiting. After a tense exchange with her awakened husband, Mangan departed without even packing, clutching her eighteen-month-old daughter in her arms. In her panicked rush to leave, she left behind her baby's toys, stroller, and pretty much everything else.

What was it that Mangan saw when she inspected the laptop? What was her terrifying, life-altering discovery?

Among other things, she saw gruesome pictures appetizing only to people of a certain grotesque culinary taste. She saw photographs depicting feet detached from bodies and a dead, naked woman covered in blood, roasting on a spit. Her husband, it seemed, was an aspiring cannibal. Valle had been obsessively visiting websites like Dark Fetish Network, a hive for every kind of depraved and violent sexual fantasy. It was a virtual meeting place where people shared pictures—and plans—relating to abduction, rape, mutilation, and cannibalism. Valle was a regular participant in these "fantasies."

Mangan's terror was fueled not just by the pictures. She also saw a series of chats on the site and discovered a clandestine email account that Valle was using. Mangan read explicit discussions between Valle and other men about the kidnapping, rape, torture, murder—and eating—of real-life women.

Most shocking of all, Mangan saw emails written by her own husband, salivating at the thought of torturing, killing, and cannibalizing *her*.

Kathleen Mangan would later testify about discovering her husband's violent plans: "I was going to be tied up by my feet and my throat slit and they would have fun watching the blood gush out of me because I was young and if I cried—he—if she cries, don't listen to her don't give her mercy. And Gil [Valle] just said, it's OK, we will just gag her."

Here is more testimony from Mangan about what she learned regarding other potential victims:

"Lorna and Kim were supposed to be raped in front of each other to heighten the terror. Andrea was going to be burned alive. [Valle] talked about devising an apparatus so that the girls could be on the spit longer and then taking them down in 30-minute shifts so that they could live longer and be tortured longer. They talked about how to put them on the spit. They decided to make an apparatus, it was better because then the girl would be alive and fully aware of her terror, according to them, which was the fun part, according to them, and like how to drive a spit through their womb. Over and over again, just kept saying that the suffering was for his enjoyment, that he wanted to make it last as long as possible, that he had no remorse."

It is hard to read. Now imagine that this man is your spouse, the father of your infant, and that he is, incidentally, an active New York City police officer, with a shield and a gun. Gilberto Valle was a cop in the 26th Precinct in Manhattan.

Imagine that the chats are about people you know. Consider Valle's conversation with Michael Van Hise about Kathleen's former colleague Alisa. Valle, using the name "Hal M," described how he would "abduct her right out of her apartment, stuff her into a large piece of luggage after tying up her hands and feet." He made plans to rape her with Van Hise, adding that he would "leave her clothes on," to give Van Hise the "pleasure of unwrapping [his] gift." After considering Van Hise's offer to hang Alisa together, Valle responded, "Its [sic] up to you. She is all yours. I really don't mind if she experiences pain and suffering. I will sleep like a baby."

When Kathleen arrived in Las Vegas, she made a report to the FBI. That lead was passed to Special Agent Anthony Foto in the New York field office, and a young prosecutor in my office, Hadassa Waxman, caught the case. For the next several years, Hadassa and Foto, along with prosecutors Brooke Cucinella, Randall Jackson, and others, would be immersed in this world of fetishism, fantasy, and potential conspiracy to kidnap and kill.

At the outset, we had to make a decision whether to investigate or not. No one had been assaulted. No one had been threatened. No one had been kidnapped, and no one had been eaten. Dark Fetish Network was a self-described fantasy site and arguably just a place to go for people who had the most fringe appetites and desires. Surely, they were not all felons, at least not anywhere that the First Amendment was operative.

Someone later summed up the quandary of the case this way: "Some fantasies remain fantasies. Some fantasies graduate." This is essentially what we set about to discover: Had this fantasy graduated?

Three considerations became important. First, Valle was not fantasizing about hypothetical people or out-of-reach celebrities. His rape and murder talk was about particular women, personally known to him and whose locations he researched improperly from the NYPD database that he could access as a cop. Second, his "fantasies" were a far cry from credit card fraud or embezzlement or check kiting. He was discussing heinous crimes that in the federal system could subject him to the death penalty. Finally, Valle was not some asocial shut-in, trolling around in his parents' basement. He was an armed and active-duty NYPD officer, and he was having repeated hair-raising conversations about killing and eating particular human beings.

We opened the case.

The FBI quickly set about trying to find out whether the fantasy had graduated. In a short time, they believed it had. Valle was in regular contact with other people appearing to plan gruesomely violent acts, and he had taken real steps:

- He performed various how-to searches on the internet, such as "how to chloroform a girl" and "how to fit someone in an oven."
- He spent hours plotting the abduction of Kimberly Sauer, a woman he had known from college, and created a computer file with an unimaginative but telling title: "Abducting and Cooking Kimberly: A Blueprint."
- He visited that target, Kimberly, in Maryland.

- He appeared to stalk a woman friend of his wife's in the school where she taught.
- He shared photos and specific details (including age, weight, height, personal information) about women he personally knew.
- He exploited the NYPD database, in violation of police rules, to perform searches and gain personal information on potential victims whom he in fact referred to as "victims."
- He affirmed that he was "for real" with multiple people he chatted with online.
- He and another man negotiated an actual price of $4,000 to kidnap Alicia Friscia, an amount later upped to $5,000.
- And he reviewed recipes for human flesh. (Yes, there are actual recipes for human flesh available on the internet, not all of which recommend fava beans and Chianti as accompaniments.)

Valle, moreover, was not musing in a vacuum. He was chatting with three other real people about his plans—Moody Blues, Michael Van Hise, and Aly Khan.

What would you have done with this evidence? If we charged conspiracy that day, who would have had the more righteous position, the prosecution or the defense?

Still, we did not arrest. We decided to keep a close eye on Valle while continuing to dig. We believed that he had already crossed the line into criminality. But more would be better. More is always better. Whatever your own view of whether Valle had already crossed that criminal line, he certainly seemed ready, willing, and able. He was ripe, we thought, for a nudge from an undercover agent. If an undercover FBI agent didn't become the catalyst, someone else—like one of his Dark Fetish buddies— very well might, creating an uncontrolled and uncontrollable situation. The FBI routinely puts undercovers into dynamic situations because we want to be the provocateur; we want to be the cause so we can control it and so we can prevent actual harm.

The tactical plan was to introduce an undercover officer to test how far Valle was prepared to go. Next we would introduce bait—that is, a potential victim that he and his cannibal buddies could set their sights on. We also wanted wiretap evidence, maybe also have Mangan wear a body wire and approach her husband. With eyes and ears on him, we would both protect the public and help build the airtight case that this was unquestionably criminal conduct.

We never got the chance.

Sometimes, as we've seen, targets have plans of their own. The Internal Affairs Bureau at the NYPD advised us that Valle had abruptly put in for a ten-day vacation. Surveillance would be hard to keep up. Also, Valle was showing signs of depression. A depressed Valle was a dangerous Valle. There was serious concern about where he might go and what he might do. We had to make a quick call. Was it time to charge?

On the continuum of when you decide to pull the trigger and make an accusation, it is possible to act too soon. But you are always balancing that against the fear of erring in the other direction and letting harm happen because you waited too long. Every institution has to know its mission and has to determine, even with imperfect information and lack of omniscience, how to act and when.

We decided to grab him on conspiracy to kidnap. Because our investigation was cut short, no wiretap was up and no sting was in place. We didn't have him going to the store and procuring actual materials. We didn't have him buying ingredients for the chloroform he researched. We had him talking about cutting women, but there were no knives. We had him talking about hanging women, but there was no rope. We grabbed him anyway.

As you can imagine, the specter of a "cannibal" cop within the ranks of the NYPD was irresistible to the New York tabloids. For days, their covers featured the mug of Gilberto Valle, who frankly looked more like a teddy bear than like Hannibal Lecter.

Valle was represented ably by the federal defenders, and the case went to trial.

At trial, the jury seemed riveted and also disgusted by the depravity of the principal evidence. The jury deliberated for about sixteen hours and convicted Valle. That to us felt reasonable, responsible, and right.

But the story doesn't end there. The trial judge took under advisement the standard motion for acquittal that defendants make at the end of every federal trial, rarely granted and usually swiftly denied. It felt odd to us that months went by without a ruling. Finally, after more than fifteen months, during which time Valle remained in custody, the judge vacated the conviction for conspiracy to kidnap. Everyone was taken by surprise: we were, Kathleen Mangan was, and members of the jury too. One juror later said, "When the verdict was overturned by the judge, I felt betrayed."

In the judge's view, the fantasy had simply not graduated. There was too much nebulous discussion, too little action, too much moving of the dates, too little distinction between reality and fantasy, and he ruled that no reasonable jury could have found Valle guilty of conspiracy.

Among other things, the judge pointed to example after example where a supposed plan was made to perform an abduction, the day passed, and nothing happened. Despite very colorful talk, there was no giant oven; there was no pulley apparatus. The judge set Gilberto Valle free. We were pretty hot about it, so we appealed the decision, and we lost again.

Valle nevertheless lost his job at the NYPD. But he kept busy. After being freed, he wrote a memoir, signed a contract to write a novel about cannibals, and was interviewed sympathetically and at length in a documentary film.

I've thought a lot about the Valle case. In every simulation I've done in my head, notwithstanding the judge's later decision to clear him, I'm firm we did the right thing. In fact I believe it would have been irresponsible not to file charges. I don't know how many prosecutors, when presented with the facts before us, would not have proceeded. We took great pains in our own deliberation to separate the grotesqueness of the conversations from the gravity of the articulated intentions.

On the other hand, do I think that Valle's release is one of the great miscarriages of justice? In fact, I don't. I think it was wrong. I don't agree with the judge. I think our charges were fair. And I would do it all over again. But I can believe all those things and also appreciate the complexity of the debate over what is fantasy and what is not. The question of whether to accuse or not accuse can be difficult, especially when your hand is forced, as ours was.

It is of course not permissible to prosecute people merely for their thoughts. But it doesn't solve any conundrum or intelligently take into account reality to just blithely recite like a mantra, "Don't prosecute thought crimes."

It happens to be true that there were thousands of subscribers to Dark Fetish Network. You won't be surprised to learn that we didn't arrest all of them. It is possible that on a self-described fantasy site there are many mere fantasists, but it is also likely that a core of people will act or have acted. How to find *them*? More worryingly, what about the people who are still in fantasy school but whose fantasies may graduate. How to monitor *them*?

It is also true that in a fair criminal justice system, the defendant is not required to prove the negative. The defendant should not be required to prove that he would not take some future action, but those responsible for keeping the public safe might justifiably act with greater aggressiveness and haste when the potential harm is greater.

As I said earlier, there were three factors we focused on: that Valle was fantasizing about actual, not hypothetical, people; that he was fantasizing about things that would be capital crimes, not small offenses; that he was an officer with a gun, not some harmless shut-in. Should that have been relevant to the decision to accuse before we had the ability to put in place wiretaps or a sting operation?

That's an interesting question. And if we changed some of the details, then what would the answer be?

What if it were a civilian who was on an internet site, chatting generally about embezzling money from his employer. Would we have acted with what we had? Probably not. To what degree is it fair or just to bring a charge more quickly because of the nature of the crime (depending on your perspective) being merely fantasized about or actually plotted? Where on the continuum of conduct do you intervene? Not every murderous fantasy leads to fatality, and not every fatality begins with a fetish. How to know where the boundaries are?

Arguably, if you were aroused by the thought of strangling someone, maybe you will be aroused even more by *actually* strangling someone. One person who believed this to be true was Kathleen Mangan, Gilberto Valle's then wife. Kathleen would later text Valle, "I think part of you wants me back, but the other part of you wants to kill me. I don't know which Gil is real. I'm afraid I don't know you at all." How much weight was her view owed?

We made the decision we made, prosecuted the case we had, and Valle is a free man nonetheless.

Depravity is not guilt, but perhaps it eases the decision to charge.

But the story doesn't end there either.

You may be wondering what happened to the three men with whom Valle was chatting (and allegedly conspiring). Were they mere fantasists too?

One of them, Aly Khan, disappeared in Pakistan.

Another, a nurse named Dale Bolinger, a.k.a. Moody Blues, was later convicted of the non-fantasy crime of attempting to rape a minor and sentenced to nine years' imprisonment in the U.K.

The third was Michael Van Hise, the sole American among the trio. After initially being on edge because of Valle's highly publicized arrest, he resumed his grotesque online talk with others about kidnapping, rape, and murder. As a result, he presented to us the opportunity to do all those things we did not have the luxury of time to do with Gilberto Valle. We did a wiretap. We searched more emails. We inserted an undercover who engaged our targets in online chats on Dark Fetish Network.

We began monitoring a new threesome who talked and acted a lot like the later-acquitted Gilberto Valle. Apart from Van Hise, they were Richard Meltz, former chief of police at the U.S. Department of Veterans Affairs in Bedford, Massachusetts; and Christopher Asch, a former librarian at Stuyvesant High School in New York who had previously been fired for inappropriate touching of boys. We now had a full-blown investigation of Van Hise, Asch, and Meltz.

Ultimately, as we had hoped to do with Valle, the first FBI undercover dangled as bait a "victim" for them to kidnap, rape, and murder. In that role, the FBI cast a young, tall, blond FBI agent whom the first undercover described as "hot" and with a "tight ass." A number of meetings were arranged. At a March 13 meeting, undercover agents met Asch to discuss the kidnapping of this victim. To this meeting Asch brought more than his thoughts. He showed up with a white bag containing maps of New York, a list of gun shows in Pennsylvania, a document titled "Construction Materials" listing various tools needed for kidnapping, and readings on sexual torture devices. Also in the bag were a leather whip, clamps, leather straps, a vise wrench, handcuffs, syringes, and doxepin hydrochloride (an antipsychotic often used to put people to sleep). On April 14 at the direction of Meltz, Asch purchased an actual Taser gun. The next day, when the targets came to do surveillance of their "victim," Asch again brought a bag. This one contained bleach, rubbing alcohol, vinyl, leather and latex gloves, vise grips, duct tape, rope, a dental retractor, a speculum, and the aforementioned Taser.

He also brought skewers.

Now we had not just talk but tools. We grabbed all three and charged them with kidnapping conspiracy before the same judge who would later set Valle free. How did these men fare? Meltz pled guilty and was sentenced to ten years. Van Hise and Asch were both convicted at trial. This time when the same arguments about fantasy and thought crimes were advocated with great zealousness to Judge Paul Gardephe, he was unimpressed. He refused to junk the convictions. The judge said, "While the alleged conspiracy in Valle was rooted in lies and demonstrable fantasy, the Van Hise / Asch / Meltz conspiracy was rooted in reality," and then the judge listed various differences. In the second case, there were actual meetings. While in the Valle case, there were none. He referred continually to the fantastical elements in the Valle case to distinguish it.

Asch was sentenced to prison for fifteen years, Van Hise to seven years.

Every accused person must be convicted on particularized evidence. That is a bedrock principle. There's no such thing in the law as guilt by association, nor should there be. But given the proof not only about Valle himself but also about one of the people he was allegedly conspiring most closely with, Van Hise, we were hardly barking up the wrong tree.

Timing can be everything. If given the chance, would Valle have taken further action, as Van Hise did? We will never know. At least, I certainly hope not.

Walking Away

If prosecutors did everything within their lawful and constitutional authority, we would be living in a hellscape. Discretion, judgment, wisdom, and restraint matter too. Legal and constitutional authority is not the end of the argument; it's the beginning. There can be wisdom and justice in staying one's hand. Discretion is an empty concept if not exercised. Duty counsels not just use of power but fairness and proportionality. This of course is true for all leaders, because any leader who exercises technically permissible authority to the fullest extent would be an autocrat.

The hardest decision to make can be the one to walk away. But that is what justice sometimes requires. And this can take more strength than blundering forth. Let's look at some examples.

First, there are the low-level offenses.

My good friend Anne Milgram, former attorney general of New Jersey, was once a young prosecutor in the Manhattan DA's Office. Back in those days, in order to take the New York City subway, you needed a token—a metal coin—and sometimes the token would get stuck in the slot at the turnstile. From time to time, subterranean scammers would take advantage of this design flaw and try to pilfer them. There were two methods, both gross: either use a straw or, even more impressively, literally put your mouth on the slot and suck up the token. This was

Anne's lawyerly analysis of the charging decision in those cases: "If you're willing to do it, you should get to keep it." There's logic to that, but those cases were required to be prosecuted anyway.

Some will no doubt stridently support every such low-grade prosecution, and there's an argument for that too. Most famously, that school of thinking is referred to as the broken windows theory of policing, which focuses on charging traditionally lower level crimes that, in excess, can contribute to a level of social disorder and community disruption. I get that, and at certain times and in certain places, in the right context, it can make sense. But we can take it too far. Even as MetroCards have replaced the subway token, turnstile jumping continues, but the Manhattan DA's Office announced in 2018 it would no longer prosecute such cases. That was a good decision in my book. It is unlikely that there will be a huge increase in the turnstile-jumping crime rate.

When I was a junior prosecutor, a colleague of mine set about charging a man for escaping from prison. As I can't remember his name, let's call the escapee Harry. Here are the basic facts: Harry was incarcerated in a federal correctional facility after being lawfully arrested and duly convicted of a felony. One day he escaped from the prison. His escape was willful, and he was caught. There was no question about Harry's state of mind. He was not on furlough, and no one *accidentally* finds himself outside the prison to which he has been assigned. Harry had no legal defense. That's about as open-and-shut as a case gets. Escape from prison ordinarily is, and ordinarily should be, considered a very serious crime, and so my colleague dutifully proceeded to indict the case.

Now let's consider a fuller rendering of the facts: The facility from which Harry escaped was the Federal Correctional Institution at Otisville. Otisville is not Alcatraz; it is not Sing Sing. Otisville is a medium-security facility. The prison store is also a delicatessen and serves gefilte fish. There is an adjacent minimum-security camp, and this is where Harry was housed. Sometimes, as was true here, security is decidedly lax.

The open-and-shut case arrived on my colleague's desk with incontrovertible evidence that Harry had escaped. Only he wasn't really trying to escape. Not for good anyway. Poor Harry, who had been within the confines of Otisville for some period of time, snuck out of prison to satisfy the oldest of human needs. He slipped out for sex. With his wife. He was gone for just a few hours, and that very same night *he tried to sneak back in.* That's right. After being home free—and after having achieved his conjugal purpose, successfully, we hope—he came back. That's when the ever-alert guards at Otisville caught him, as he was creeping back *onto* the premises under cover of nightfall.

The legal analysis was simple bordering on self-evident. There was a clear statute. There was irrefutable proof. Indict him. I suppose the argument against the mitigating facts was this: if you steal $20 from a cash register and then later return it, you're not off the hook. Presumably, that was the principle we were applying in deciding to charge Harry.

But guess what? The grand jury wasn't having it. The grand jury, in its wisdom, refused to indict this particular ham sandwich. I didn't think this then, but I do think it now: good for them.

There's a valid argument that you want to deter escape. I handled some more serious escape cases myself as a prosecutor. But it seems in retrospect that this was the kind of case where the infraction could have been addressed through some punishment related to the conditions of confinement, withdrawal of privileges, not necessarily adding a felony conviction to a person who literally just strolled out of the prison compound, completely undetected, and then returned. This was not El Chapo or a character from *The Shawshank Redemption* digging a tunnel underneath the property to make his big getaway. Sometimes it's fair and just for prosecutors to give someone a break.

Justice is not served by prosecuting everything to the fullest extent, even when we're talking about transgressions against the "rules" we set in everyday life. Not everything needs to be, as the saying goes, made into a federal case. All of us exercise such discretion all the time. Depending on the circumstances, we may forgive a white lie, a friend's tardiness, a forgotten birthday, or a rude remark. Like benevolent traffic cops, we let people off with warnings all the time. Too much leniency in life, as in law, can undercut respect for rules and decorum, but Javert-like strict liability for every conceivable infraction is insidious too.

What to do about low-level offenses generally? There were categories of cases that, as a matter of policy, we did not pursue. And I think correctly. For example, even though a federal statute criminalizes the mere possession of narcotics, we virtually never charged that. In part, this was because we believed it was not worth our time and effort, not worth clogging up the courts for nonviolent and petty offenses.

We might arrest five serious narcotics traffickers caught on a wiretap, and at the time of the arrest there would happen to be a sixth person present who was not involved in the conspiracy but who was holding several grams of cocaine for personal use. While we would have been completely within our rights under the law to charge the hapless sixth person, we would most likely let him go, without referring him to the DA. Why? Because his crime is mere possession and it is an issue of prosecutorial resources. But in exercising our discretion at times like this, we were clearly making a larger judgment call too.

Another example: from time to time, we had cases involving the worst kind of person you'll ever come across, a sex trafficker. These are not what you think of as traditional vice prosecutions. They are aimed at violent criminals who are coercing, victimizing, and enslaving other people into the sex business. We didn't charge the so-called prostitutes with crimes, because we viewed them as victims. Even though prostitution is a crime routinely charged by DAs, we didn't refer them there either. What's more, people who are patronizing the brothel, in certain circumstances, can also be charged federally: the so-called johns. But likewise, we made a policy decision not to charge those people or refer them to the local prosecutor.

Back in 2008, before I took office, tremendous controversy arose when the then governor of New York, Eliot Spitzer, was caught arranging for women to travel interstate to engage in prostitution with him. SDNY filed criminal charges against people who ran the prostitution ring known as the Emperors Club VIP. The office launched an investigation into whether Spitzer misused campaign or other public funds to pay prostitutes. No such evidence was found. The question then was what to do with Spitzer, given that he was technically guilty of criminal conduct in connection with the prostitution offenses.

But as I said, there was a longtime policy of not charging "johns." Should that be upended because a sitting governor was in the crosshairs? Then U.S. Attorney Michael Garcia ultimately decided it shouldn't and issued this public explanation:

> In light of the policy of the Department of Justice with respect to prostitution offenses and the longstanding practice of this Office, as well as Mr. Spitzer's acceptance of responsibility for his conduct [which included his resignation from office], we have concluded that the public interest would not be further advanced by filing criminal charges in this matter.

Some didn't like this decision and wanted Spitzer to be locked up. I wasn't U.S. Attorney then and I don't know every fact, but the decision to walk away in that case seems just and right, in the circumstances.

The reason often given for not prosecuting certain kinds of cases is "lack of resources." And while it is true that the cost of diverting law enforcement labor to low-grade crimes can be substantial and this is a legitimate basis to decline, the resource argument can obscure a moral and ethical judgment. Exercise of discretion is a bulwark against over-criminalization. It is both a recognition of (and an imperfect fix for) the laziness of legislatures who pass broad statutes, ratcheting criminal sanctions ever upward. So, basing decisions on resource allocation, in a way, masks more substantive judgment calls and avoids a debate about values. A decision not to go after turnstile jumpers is more than just about resources; it is also a considered judgment about racial unfairness and disproportionate punishment for certain communities. A policy of not prosecuting sex workers but only traffickers may also reflect a suspension of moral judgment about the conduct of the former group.

Now, there is a flip side to all of this. Sometimes authorities rely on rule-of-law arguments to justify *not* exercising discretion, to convey the impression that their hands are tied, that the law inexorably demands the particular harsh action when, of course, discretion is always available. The rule-of-law mantra may mask a judgment call, a value-based decision, or some other policy position. In the past year or so, a firestorm has erupted over the separation of families arriving, mostly from Central America, at the U.S. southern border in the hope of asylum. We repeatedly hear the familiar slogan: it is the rule of law. Suddenly Congress's penchant for over-breadth and over-criminalization—here, making the mere act of crossing the border a misdemeanor—is a sacred command that must be followed inexorably, without exception.

They say there is no choice, no way out of criminally prosecuting every single trespasser, separating every parent from every child, though according to news reports, few members of Congress expressed support for these family separations. The rule-of-law justification in this instance, then, is an expression of an odd phenomenon: the government has exercised its discretion to *suspend* its exercise of discretion. This is, I believe, an abdication of responsibility to be ethical enforcers of the law. And please understand, the law leaves plenty of room for ethical interpretation and action (or lack of action).

Immigration offenses have long been a point of controversy, even in non-border districts like SDNY.

When I started in the office, we were prosecuting people just for the crime of illegal reentry—coming back to the United States after being deported—whether or not they had committed any new crime or had been deported for an aggravated felony. At some point, SDNY changed the criteria on this matter: We would spend the time and energy to prosecute only people who illegally returned and had *also* previously committed an aggravated crime. But this didn't come from D.C. or Congress; SDNY fashioned this policy because it was fair and judicious. And how would we justify it? Limited resources. These defendants—often facing little to no jail time but nonetheless ineligible for bail because of their lack of immigration status—would do time in custody during the pendency of the case (at significant government expense), get time served, and then be deported. Not prosecuting them meant they could instead proceed straight to deportation.

Broad policy decisions—letting drug users, sex workers, turnstile jumpers go—are one thing. One can have a principled debate about a category of crime, weigh the pros and cons, consider the costs and risks, then make a policy call. The more complicated and difficult decisions involve individual cases, rather than broad tranches of crime, where sometimes the right decision, notwithstanding an available statute and sufficient evidence, is just to let it go. To let it go, by the way, does not mean that the particular infraction goes unpunished. For these purposes, we are talking about the criminal law and about staying our hand with respect to indicting someone, convicting him, putting a mark on his permanent record, branding him a felon for life. Criminal prosecution is the bluntest and severest of tools available. In many, many cases, there are other less onerous ways to punish people, including fines and workplace discipline. I have been a prosecutor, and I can say unabashedly that prosecution cannot solve every social, political, or even public safety problem. It just can't.

Do you walk away from a case simply because you're unlikely to win? That is a difficult and profound question. The written guidance for the Justice Department is that you bring a charge if you are more likely than not to obtain a conviction.

Frankly, that is a questionable blanket policy. That's not always justice. If the person is guilty as sin but some of the evidentiary stars are aligned against you, I don't think walking away can be justified. The decision to charge has to be separated from the likelihood of success in a meaningful way. They are distinct inquiries, and specific circumstances matter. An undue focus on winning (or saving face) corrodes the mission, distorts decision making, and undermines just process.

With respect to the decision to charge, you have to separate out the likelihood of success from the *fairness* of making a charge. You have to consider the question of *whether* to charge and *rightness* of charging.

What's needed is a two-pronged analysis—belief in guilt and the likelihood of success. The federal prosecutor must absolutely believe in the guilt of the potential defendant, based on actual law and knowable facts. At this stage, I am not talking about provable facts or even admissible evidence. I am saying that based on what you know to be true, even before you get to what you can properly get before the jury, do you firmly believe the person did it? That is a must; it is not sufficient, but it is necessary. That means that even if you have a winnable case but you have a legitimate qualm about guilt, you *cannot* proceed. Period. It also means, on the other side of the coin, that if an otherwise solid case has now become a long shot because your four credible witnesses are in the wind, you *should* proceed. To some, a prosecutor's decision to bring a case is based solely on what he can prove in court. I don't think that's quite right. If fifty witnesses tell me someone is guilty of a crime, and they all die in an earthquake, it's still a righteous case and if I have a chance of convicting, I should bring it. The latter scenario arose in a way in my very first criminal trial as a line prosecutor.

It was a case against a felon charged with possession of a firearm. Under federal law, felons aren't allowed to have guns. By the time of the trial, the main witness, a heroin addict who saw the bad guy holding the gun, had fled. We couldn't find him anywhere. The only other percipient witness was Juanita, a woman with an IQ hovering at about 70 who, when these crimes happened, was under the influence of both cocaine and heroin. The odds of prevailing seemed very low. I knew from the other evidence that the defendant was guilty, but I got cold feet, bordering on frostbite.

We were so concerned about the likelihood of success—or rather, failure—that literally minutes before jury selection my trial partner and I called the Criminal Division chief. I think it was my first conversation with him since my swearing-in ceremony, and I was nervous. We said we'd like his approval to dismiss the case. It was going to be embarrassing, and we were all on display, reputations on the line.

Alan Kaufman was not considered especially hard charging or zealous. If anything, people on the line thought he could be a bit receptive to defense arguments. Given our deep concerns, we expected our request to be granted.

The chief pointedly asked two questions, which I remember still. First, do you believe the defendant is guilty? I said 100 percent, absolutely. I just lost the key witness, but guilt is not in doubt. Second, he asked, is acquittal a foregone conclusion, or is there a chance you can convict? I paused and thought about it. There was circumstantial evidence connecting the defendant to the gun and ammunition; bullets were found in a backpack that also contained the defendant's driver's license, for example. So I said yes, conviction is possible but highly unlikely. Hearing my answers, much to my dismay, Kaufman did not let us dismiss the case. We proceeded to trial. I put in the case. Juanita was exceptionally challenging, as expected, and the jury deliberated seemingly forever. They ended up hanging on one count and convicting on the other—of being a felon in possession of a bullet. He was sentenced to 108 months in prison. It was a seminal experience for me.

When terrible things happen, people want accountability. This general human desire is powerful and predates the Bible. Sometimes prosecutors are in a position to provide it, because the law and facts align, because evidence is obtainable and admissible, because the system permits it. When that happens the prosecutor's decision to bring a case is capable of being judged. The case is public, the allegations are there for all to see. People can evaluate whether the case is well made and righteous. It can be criticized, with some basis, as overly harsh or overly weak. It is an open process, and a defense lawyer and a judge and a jury will have something to say about it. On those occasions, however, when after diligent and thorough review, after assessment of the law and its limitations, prosecutors decline to bring a case, that is a much more difficult decision to evaluate.

We began to address the complexity of walking away in a prior chapter, but we need to dive deeper. Let me repeat something I said there because it is profoundly important and, without a deep commitment to this principle, justice is not possible:

> When a backbreaking investigation does not yield enough evidence of a crime, when it turns out that a miscreant has come up to the criminal line but not put a thieving toe over

it, when everyone thinks the target probably did the deed but doubts linger, when the law in its idiocy or a court in its naïveté has exempted from prosecution bad conduct that reasonable people loathe and want to punish, there is only one choice: to walk away. Walking away can be deeply and viscerally unsatisfying. But if all the raised expectations and personal investments and sunk costs sweep people toward an unjust charging decision, that is a miscarriage.

People, of course, are fallible and capable of misjudgment, cowardice, and corruption. How to know if the decision to walk away was the correct one? After all, a young black man was shot. Or a crane fell and killed someone. Or a woman lost her life savings. Or an entire economy collapsed in a financial crisis. Where are the cuffs? Where are the trials? Where is the justice? These are all fair questions—more than fair, they are essential questions—but they are often difficult to answer. It is generally impossible to prove the negative. Good-faith critics haven't seen the evidence, haven't seen the credibility of the witnesses, haven't been in the grand jury, haven't compared the precedents.

This is not to say that we must blithely trust every prosecutor's decision not to bring a case. In fact, in the pages of this book, I am implicitly critical of other prosecuting offices for not pursuing cases that *we* brought after they declined, even as I am mindful that such decisions are difficult to judge from the outside.

Of late, such criticisms are suffused with political biases. Chants of "lock her up!" or "lock him up!" tend to be predetermined by party affiliation rather than by dispassionate assessment of the evidence and the law. Millions believe Hillary Clinton should have been prosecuted; millions think the same about Donald Trump. And woe unto the feckless prosecutors who did not (or will not) oblige. It is hard to see how many of those self-certain opinions about the guilt of politicians believed to be noxious are held objectively. And it is a daunting and dangerous task for the prosecutor to try to defend any decision.

It's very hard for the FBI or the Justice Department to show convincingly the purity of the decision not to charge Hillary Clinton, especially to people who don't like her and who sniff the vague scent of corruption. If Robert Mueller and others decide not to charge or decline to make a referral on President Trump, it will be very difficult to show the purity of that decision too, even if it is pure. It's much harder to assess the quality of the decision not to do something than to do something. That is the nature of logic, the difficulty of proving a negative.

We could demand that our prosecutors explain at length their decisions to walk away, especially when the smell of smoke is strong in public nostrils, so citizens can be satisfied about the rectitude of those decisions. But prosecutors can get into deep trouble, if they talk too much about a decision not to prosecute. That's precisely what got the former FBI director Jim Comey— who spoke disparagingly and at length about Hillary Clinton even while asserting no criminal case was warranted—rebuked by the inspector general, criticized by everyone, and, depending on whom you believe, fired from his post. When you make the decision to decline—and we declined on significant people, including the mayor of New York City and the governor of New York—it becomes difficult to explain fully and transparently to the public why you didn't pull the trigger. After all, the subject has a right to fairness also, to be free from prosecutorial slander. You owe it to the system and to the guidelines of the department, as well as to the presumed innocent party you chose not to charge, to keep your mouth shut. It is a quandary. Believe me, I appreciate the impulse to talk. A decision to decline, to walk away, is not a blessing of the conduct, but in the system we have, minimalism tends to be the best practice.

The rightness of a decision *not* to act can never be judged with the same precision and logic as when action is taken—the decision to decline a job or turn down a marriage proposal, how to judge these well?

If you make the decision not to charge, in a high-profile case, how do you provide commentary in accordance with justice and fairness? On the one hand, there are lots of fair-minded people in the public who want the assurance of a grand jury report and a statement of reasons as to why a charge wasn't filed. And that's the case if it's against a politician, or a cop who shot an unarmed teen, or the CEO of a bank that arguably engaged in shady dealings during the financial crisis. In the absence of a charge, the clamor for some kind of explanation is deafening. And it is understandable.

It is natural that the public wants to know. They see incidental evidence of criminal activity and harm to victims, and they ask questions. Prosecutors are human beings. That a criminal charge is not deemed appropriate, or evidence is not sufficient to bring the case, does not mean that a prosecutor is blessing the conduct, giving the subject a clean bill of health. If you care about transparency, and you care about not unduly whitewashing bad conduct, that's an inherent dilemma. But some dilemmas are unresolvable. You can't solve for pi, and maybe you can't solve for this.

As we saw in the deviation from that practice in the Clinton email investigation, trying to justify your action—or lack of action—can lead down a bad path. If you're making comments about a case in one instance, like Hillary's emails, you will be asked why you didn't talk publicly about another matter, like the Russia case. I understand why the public wants it. I also understand why a prosecutor might be tempted to respond.

The unsatisfying, frustrating, infuriating result of silence can be widespread loss of faith in the decision. Yes, a prosecutor has a responsibility to the public. But there is also a responsibility to the concept of justice. Sometimes those two things are in conflict. And part of a prosecutor's job is to take the hits from the public when it feels cheated. I have a lot I could say about the people we did not charge, after lengthy investigations. But I won't. It is what it is.

After the financial crisis of 2008, the whole world screamed for bankers to be hauled off in handcuffs. "They ruined the economy, destroyed retirement accounts, set the country back. Lock them up." The reaction is completely understandable (and not entirely foreign to me, as someone also frustrated by the situation). People lost homes, savings, jobs, livelihoods. Many are still recovering in the aftermath. So, I also understand that any and every explanation for why there was not a slew of charges is unsatisfying. There is anger and incredulity, and I have experienced it everywhere I have gone.

I get asked about this topic frequently, and rightly so. There should be pressure on law enforcement to ensure they're making every effort to hold people and institutions accountable, but much of what happened in 2008 was not the product of a few people with clear, provable intent to rob others of their savings. Most extensive analyses of the worst economic downturn since the Great Depression acknowledge that various factors came together to form the financial equivalent of a Molotov cocktail. For a prosecutor, that makes for a murky case, especially when any hope of conviction rests on proving someone's mental state. Certainly, the heads of financial institutions did what they could to evade culpability, diffusing responsibility and wrongdoing throughout entire companies and through reliance on third-party professionals.

This is an important point: sometimes people forget that before we were prosecutors or agents, we are Americans and citizens and future pensioners ourselves. We too saw our fortunes crushed and our accounts depleted. We too were victims of greed and recklessness. We uniquely had not only every professional incentive but also a deep personal incentive, whether appropriate or not, to hold accountable anyone the law permitted. Although I led one office among many with relevant jurisdiction, I'm sure I speak for all of them when I say that if there were people to prosecute successfully, everyone would have been more than willing to do so.

Conduct can appear criminal at first blush, but upon further analysis no provable crime has been committed. That is not to say that there weren't people at very high levels who did not engage in criminal conduct. That may very well be, but in the system that we have, you can't proceed without proof of particular people engaging in particular conduct with a particular mental intent. The bar to prove intent is high. As I've said, it's often difficult enough to figure out what's in our own heads, never mind proving beyond a reasonable doubt what illicit sparks are flaring in someone else's brain. Accident is not enough. Negligence is not enough. Mistake is not enough. Even recklessness is not enough.

There were many bad practices that contributed to the financial crisis. One practice involved the reselling of mortgages. Essentially, banks would bundle up mortgages into a type of financial security—which often included mortgages with a high risk of default and might not have had much value—and then sold those packaged securities to other financial institutions. In retrospect, some of the things that banks sold look like junk (and to be sure, the sellers downplayed how junky they were). Notably, the buyers were sophisticated counter-parties themselves with access to expertise and lawyers of their own. Generally, the buyers were forewarned about the potential lack of quality of their purchase in the small print and footnotes of lengthy prospectuses. And many of the banks—even while offloading some of this mortgage liability—retained much of it as well, resulting in near collapse themselves when the market tanked.

Various financial institutions found ways to protect themselves from liability. One particular shield was a reliance on independent, third-party blessings from accountants and lawyers. It is frustrating, enraging actually, to think that professional accountants and attorneys might have blessed potentially deceitful practices, but again the criminal prosecutor's job is to prove intent on the part of the particular person.

I often frame it this way: If I took a hundred people at random and audited their tax returns, undoubtedly I would find a few who took an illegal deduction. In order to prove that was a crime, you need evidence beyond a reasonable doubt that the person specifically *intended* to defraud the IRS. One available good-faith defense is this: "I gave all my financial information to my accountant, who is an independent professional, and I told him to tell me what is allowed and what is not, and that independent accountant told me that I could take the deduction. I relied on professional, third-party advice." You may think that's dastardly or a cop-out or an unseemly get-out-of-jail-free card, but if I can't prove that the taxpayer and the accountant were in criminal cahoots, I can't prosecute.

Also—and this is controversial because we are talking about the financial crisis—consider whether you want that taxpayer prosecuted. Because the standard by which it seems some people wish for us to be able to put bank presidents in prison, if applied to average people in connection with their tax returns or their own small business practices, would subject millions to prison without proof of intent to commit crimes. You can find behavior reprehensible, careless, greedy, thoughtless, and cruel, but that's not enough to bring a case. This, of course, is a supersimplified example to explain a larger, more complex situation, but the principle remains the same.

The feeling that people with power and money are harder to

hold accountable, are more able to hurt people with impunity, is not wrong. But when we shift basic standards of proof because of singular events, there are consequences for the equal application of law and due process for *everyone*. If we decree that proof of knowledge and intent are no longer necessary because there is a certain kind of fraud that is intolerable, if the law is not carefully drawn, we risk finding ourselves in an ever more intolerable legal system, where prosecutors have even more power than they have now, where people can be imprisoned on trifling circumstantial evidence with no direct proof of their state of mind. It bears some thought.

Here's another hypothetical that roughly parallels some of the odious conduct connected to the financial crisis: Suppose one day you're cleaning out your attic and you come across an old rickety chair. You don't remember where it came from and you don't believe it has any real value, but you're having a yard sale on Sunday. You present the chair to the public as a rare antique, posting a sign with a $10,000 price tag. Someone takes the bait and pays that exorbitant price for the chair that you didn't believe was an antique. Most people would say that's fraud. Should we arrest you forthwith?

Now, let's add some facts: Suppose that the person who bought the chair was a sophisticated purchaser of antiques—just like the buyers of some of those junk securities packages. Let's assume further that the person who bought the chair brought with him a known expert in antiques who advised the buyer that this was *indeed* an antique chair. And not only was it a valuable antique chair, but it was actually worth $20,000 and therefore the $10,000 price tag that this supposed fraudster had attached to the chair was in fact a tremendous bargain. Suppose that would be the testimony of the purchaser and his expert and suppose further that they would testify that even had they known that the seller believed the chair was crap, they would have bought it anyway, at $10,000. Is it a crime now? If it is, good luck proving that to a jury. Good luck getting twelve jurors to find unanimously that the buyer was duped, or harmed. This is an oversimplification, but it is roughly the dynamic with respect to those tranches of junk mortgage-backed securities.

In the real world, for good reason, where the rule of law matters and where actual liberty is at stake, we don't have the therapeutic luxury of bringing cases whenever we're angry. We can only bring cases when the facts and the law lend support to an indictment.

These two hypotheticals are very rough analogs of the kinds of things that happened in the lead-up to the financial crisis. If someone saw fit to release to the public all the files in all the cases in all the districts where crisis-related investigations were conducted and closed—and there were many—people would have a better ability to understand and evaluate those decisions.

There are limitations to what the law can do, and either laws need to be changed or we need to examine the other components that had a hand in the collapse and decide how they can be regulated or changed as well. No one likes the fact that bad actors got away with harming many innocent people.

Lots of arguments and criticisms have been made, and I respect and appreciate the frustration. Here is what I do not respect. Some understandably bitter armchair prosecutors have heaped bile on the hundreds of career prosecutors and agents around the country who did not bring the money changers to justice. Some have suggested fear or intimidation or political motives for the perceived restraint. I'm more than willing to accept credible criticism on behalf of the law enforcement community, but the idea that self-interest or politics or fear was a factor is a silly criticism, at least at SDNY.

As for political considerations, I don't even know what they would be. The hundreds of engaged career agents and prosecutors were Democrats, Republicans, and independents. Many were completely apolitical. All suffered in the financial crisis too. They were, and are, politically and ideologically diverse. There was, moreover, no personal or political gain in going soft on banks or soft on Wall Street. Politically, toughness on Wall Street is self-evidently full of electoral reward. There is a misunderstanding on the part of the lay public about what happens to the most aggressive prosecutors, the ones who bag the biggest scalps. They are not pariahs to the private sector. They are the hottest recruits. They are the most sought after by the very industries they assailed because they had talent and success and balls. The incentive structure is the opposite of what cynics assume: the most aggressive prosecutors are not shunned; they are recruited. If you brought a hedge fund or a bank or a private equity firm to its knees, you were not an outcast; you were a superstar. My most successful prosecutors claimed the best jobs in the defense bar; my most timid ones—the ones who might have seemed afraid of going after corporate corruption aggressively—had the hardest times finding jobs, because they had done nothing to distinguish themselves. For good or ill, the market rewards aggressiveness, not timidity. So every personal, professional, and moral incentive was in favor of holding financial crisis miscreants accountable.

Fear is also a silly diagnosis. During my tenure alone, we prosecuted, among many other people, Ahmed Khalfan Ghailani (who murdered 224 people in Africa), the son-in-law of Osama bin Laden, violent Somali pirates, members of al-Shabaab, al-Qaeda in the Islamic Maghreb, paid assassins, Russian spies, Crips, Bloods, the most violent gangs in America who killed witnesses and threatened law enforcement. Also the most notorious arms dealer in the world, Viktor Bout, and every kind of mobster.

On the white-collar side, we prosecuted—without fear or favor—billionaires like Raj Rajaratnam; the Democratic Speaker of the New York State Assembly and the Republican majority leader of the New York State Senate, and retried them after the Supreme Court changed the law and the appeals court had to reverse the convictions; we prosecuted Gambinos and Genoveses. Our own law enforcement partners were not immune either: we prosecuted cops at the NYPD, correction officers at Rikers Island, FBI agents, and DEA agents too; if they had broken the law, we made them face it.

Some of our prosecutions (because they were focused on powerful people) invited severe blowback not just to the office but to me personally. I was banned from Russia thanks to Viktor Bout. Our prosecution of the Iranian gold trader Reza Zarrab earned me direct and personal rebukes from President Erdogan of Turkey, who personally pled with Vice President Joe Biden to have me fired. The prosecution of the Indian diplomat Devyani Khobragade made me, for a time, persona non grata in the country of my birth.

For the important work that they do, the men and women in SDNY—like prosecutors and investigators across the country— endure public criticism, personal attacks in and out of the courtroom, intimidation tactics, and death threats too. So, neither I nor anyone I know was too afraid to prosecute rich men in suits.

Culture

W hile we are on the subject of accusations—when they should be alleged, under what circumstances, and on what proof—it's worth pausing for a moment on a question that was posed to me quite often when I was U.S. Attorney: How do institutions avoid scrutiny, escape the ire of law enforcement, and dodge costly allegations? A thousand books will tell you that culture plays a deeply important role. I add myself to that chorus, based on years of seeing people get it both wrong and right.

In 2013, SAC Capital was a hedge fund with over $15 billion of assets under management. On July 25, 2013, my office charged four hedge funds under the SAC umbrella with insider trading. Our indictment described their insider-trading activity as "substantial, pervasive and on a scale without known precedent in the hedge fund industry."

By that point, we had already charged eight SAC employees with insider trading, including Noah Freeman, Michael Steinberg, and Mathew Martoma. Six of them had pled guilty, while two—Martoma and Steinberg—were found guilty at trial. Martoma, an SAC portfolio manager who focused on the health-care sector, illicitly earned $276 million, the largest single profit from insider trading in history.

The pervasiveness of the conduct was at the heart of our decision to accuse the funds. But there was something else. There was a clear and defiant corporate culture that ignored warning signs and red flags, that flouted norms and exalted greed, that used its compliance program as cheap window dressing.

Here's a telling example from the indictment: In 2009, SAC Capital hired an employee named Richard Lee who was tasked with overseeing a $1.25 billion "special situations" fund related to corporate restructuring, mergers, and acquisitions. Prior to Lee's hiring, an employee at his old hedge fund warned SAC that Lee was part of that fund's "insider-trading group." Because of this, the SAC legal department objected to Lee's hiring. But SAC leadership overruled these objections. Despite Lee's track record, SAC hired him as a portfolio manager in April 2009.

Lo and behold, shock of shocks, Lee immediately set about illegally gathering inside information on public companies. He worked at SAC from 2009 to 2013, with a brief break from the firm, and throughout that period he engaged in an insider-trading scheme. As an SAC portfolio manager, Lee traded securities using nonpublic information about companies such as Yahoo and 3Com Corporation. Based on his work history, this was about as foreseeable as nightfall.

Here's a problem: Business leaders speak too infrequently about integrity. They speak about power and profit and market share and the bottom line. This is all well and good—and necessary—but the watchdogs within companies and other institutions are relegated to the wings. There are compliance officers and in-house attorneys and accountants and auditors, but they hold little sway with the corporate upper echelon. On the business side, the adjective that most commonly precedes each of these titles is usually a pejorative like "pesky."

Imagine if we had our entire criminal code and regulatory structure, but no Constitution. Every institution, whether it's a country or a company, needs a charter of first principles that are everlasting—not just a hodgepodge and mishmash of bureaucratic rules and requirements that can be ignored with little or no consequence.

Getting people to listen and report and sound alarms and seek advice requires more than email reminders; it entails understanding what motivates real people in real life, people with vulnerabilities and fears and biases and every other ordinary human failing and foible that can prevent us from doing the right thing.

The funny thing is that every successful business leader understands this; no one would think that rote reminders alone can spark creativity or spur productivity or advance morale. It takes a lot more. But somehow when we get to talking about ethics and compliance, these long-term and long-known leadership lessons get short shrift, because short-term profit is the shortsighted goal.

Here is a disturbing truth: In the shadow of most massive frauds and cover-ups are lurking all manner of enablers—people who were helpful either to the perpetration of the crimes or to their concealment. Think Enron. Think WorldCom. Think Madoff. Think Theranos. Think also Penn State and Harvey Weinstein and Bill Cosby. Think of the doping scandals in baseball and cycling. Think of the sexual abuse scandals in Olympic gymnastics and in the Roman Catholic Church. People are too often afraid to confront power. They are afraid they'll be fired. Or afraid they'll be ostracized. Or lose valuable connections. Why? Because that is the culture of so many institutions. Those fears are real.

Something happens to otherwise normally functioning brains when it comes to simple ways to promote integrity. People want formulas and magic words, when what is missing is common sense. I spoke once at the New York Stock Exchange to a distinguished group of lawyers who specialized in representing boards of directors of major public companies. After my talk, a lawyer rose to ask me a question. "Mr. Bharara, what percentage of a board's time should be spent focused on ethics and compliance?" What a vague and misplaced question. There is, of course, no mathematical formula. I said some version of this: "Well, if the company has a good reputation, no issues have come to light, there hasn't been an enforcement action in years, and you have decent indication that good people are being hired and promoted, then maybe you don't have to spend so much time. On the other hand, if rumors abound of bad conduct, four agencies are investigating you, two executives have been led off in handcuffs in recent months, then you should be spending a *lot* of time focusing on ethics and compliance." That drew laughs. Common sense, for some reason, draws laughs.

Smart lawyers and businesspeople wouldn't ask such silly questions in any other business context. What percentage of time should the CEO be focused on competition? On innovation? On employee morale? Right-minded entrepreneurs know that all of it is important and that time allocation depends on the circumstances. There are no magic formulas. How much time should you spend disciplining your child? Well, that depends on the child, now, doesn't it?

In many places, there is a culture that is willing and even wanting to come up as close to the criminal line as possible, to maximize some perceived edge or profit. In a culture like that, people will invariably miscalculate and bad things will invariably follow. It's a dangerous thing to walk the line and to train other people to do it. A culture of minimalism is dangerous.

Consider the following thought experiment: Imagine a man who really wants to drink his alcohol but also really wants to avoid a drunk-driving arrest or conviction. If you're a very smart guy and you decide you want to drink and then drive afterward, I suppose you could strategize your way to close in on the DUI limit without going over it. If you're a genius and know your body mass index, your rate of imbibing, the quantity of food you've consumed and over what period of time, you might calibrate so perfectly that you come in right under the blood-alcohol limit, time and time again.

But if that's your policy and practice, how long before you get pulled over? How long before you blow the legal limit? How long before you kill someone on the highway, and how long before all the other people who went out drinking with you are following your irresponsible example and killing people on the highway?

A couple of times, after performing this spiel to a group of business students, I have been asked this question: "Mr. Bharara, you've talked about making sure you don't cross the line and that it's dangerous to wander too close to the line. So, exactly how far from the line do you recommend people stay?" It is asked as if it were a geometry problem. I say, "Oh, about three and a half feet should do the trick."

I am always a bit taken aback at these attempts to quantify ethics. I answer such questions by explaining that I disagree with the premise of the question; its orientation is unfortunate and off base; that if you are single-mindedly focused on walking the line, you are bound to end up afoul of regulators and, God forbid, criminal prosecutors. Even more dangerous perhaps, you are sending a message to every other person at the firm that line walking is a good idea. That can work for a while, but not forever. A culture of minimalism is lethal.

I'll never forget what I once heard at a law enforcement conference in London. The global head of compliance of a Fortune 50 company put it this way: "I earned a degree in psychology in college before I earned my law degree. And I have found that in this job, which is all about motivating people to act better and modifying ordinary people's behavior, I find myself relying much more on my psychology degree than on my law degree."

There is much wisdom in that insight.

Too often the compliance function seems narrowly reactive only to what regulators want and expect. Here's a news flash:

Regulators and the regulations they promulgate are not perfect. But we hear at conferences and in training materials everywhere the constant refrain: do X because that is what regulators expect; do Y because regulators will more likely be persuaded that you discharged your duty.

It's like teaching to the test.

You're forgetting about the core value of education. When you teach to the test, you're not explaining to students that what's important is the value of education and curiosity and wisdom; you're teaching them they've just got to get some answers right to get a good grade. That, to me, is failure.

Values are more about the forest than about the trees.

I once met a hedge fund general counsel and asked what he did to welcome people who came into the firm. He said very proudly that he met with every person who started and had a personal session with them so that they would be familiar with him and be comfortable coming to him. He said he takes them through a lot of the regulations and requirements, and he takes them through recent changes in securities laws.

That's terrific. But I wondered, how did he begin the talk?

Did he begin the talk with a simple and strongly delivered message? Here's what you need to understand about this place: We don't cheat and we don't steal and we don't lie. If you do, you're out, simple as that. We have zero tolerance for any of that nonsense. That message, I submit, will sit a lot longer than the ocean of minutiae that will follow.

And yet I don't know how often simple messages like that are delivered.

It is hard to be the internal police. It's akin to an internal affairs bureau at a police department. There are lessons on how to deal with the issues of culture in that analogy. Nobody likes Internal Affairs.

Ray Kelly, the former police commissioner in New York, made

it a point to confer a lot of authority, legitimacy, and respect on the head of his Internal Affairs Bureau. His successors did too, but my first direct experience was with Commissioner Kelly. Kelly was not perfect, no leader or culture is, and the NYPD had various problems, but one episode stands out in my memory.

In 2011, we had occasion to arrest eight of New York's finest for significant crimes. At the time, there was long-running friction between the NYPD and the FBI in New York. This was due in part to overlapping jurisdictions, competition over primacy in terrorism investigations, and Kelly's strong personality. Now here we were, the FBI on the cusp of arresting a crew of active and retired cops. It would be a big black eye for the police department. So as not to rub salt in the wound, I suppose, the head of the FBI at the time told me that the bureau was opposed to a press conference announcing the charges. Without thinking much, I concurred.

Then I thought about it some more, and I was troubled. These were serious crimes, involving conspiracy to distribute M16 rifles, handguns, and other stolen goods, worth over $1 million, in exchange for cash kickbacks. To me it looked like a terrible double standard. For a state senator or a gang leader or a Wall Street executive, we do news conferences, but when it comes to serious corruption at our law enforcement partner, we don't?

That seemed dead wrong. But I didn't, however, wish to stand up at the podium alone. That too would send a bad message. It already looked as if the FBI wasn't coming. That left Ray Kelly. I requested an urgent meeting. Breakfast was set for Monday, the arrests scheduled for Tuesday, October 25. We met at 8:30 a.m. at the W hotel by Wall Street, in a booth in the second-floor restaurant. The commissioner appeared intimidating as usual, as if he could break the skinny waiter in two. Kelly, for his part, was having a tough week. In addition to the SDNY case, there was a developing ticket scandal embroiling the NYPD. As we finished our eggs and bacon, Kelly said he'd let me know by noon if he would participate the next day. He called a couple of hours later and said he would join me. In the end, the FBI showed up too.

And so the next day, the head of the organization, the "CEO" of the New York Police Department, Ray Kelly, stood onstage with me, along with the head of Internal Affairs, and pulled no punches. He talked persuasively, poignantly, and powerfully about why that kind of corruption can't be tolerated at a police department. He didn't sweep these crimes under the rug. When leaders do that, people recognize it.

People determine culture.

A business student once told me during a class that he had interviewed at ten Wall Street firms the prior summer. He said only one out of the ten asked any question suggesting it cared about the student's integrity or cared about its own reputation for integrity. In an environment where people are driven largely if not entirely by making money, ethics should be relevant to the way employees are evaluated and compensated.

Imagine if, in a prosecutor's office, we promoted only the best trial lawyers with no regard for how ethical they are. Imagine I have two prosecutors in my office, one is more skilled at trials and case making, but on a couple of occasions his initial judgment on disclosure is not great. It turns out okay because that person is just a line prosecutor and there is a supervisor with better judgment, and a bad thing is avoided. In time, maybe that person could be trained, but there is at least a minor question going forward about his ethical judgment.

The other prosecutor is slightly less skillful at trying cases or writing briefs but always demonstrates impeccable ethics, candor, and judgment, and there is not even a hint of worry if she were completely autonomous.

Which prosecutor would you want me to promote? Which is the lower risk? Which is better for the long-term reputation of the office? More important, which prosecutor is better for the wise exercise of discretion and pursuit of justice? I tried always to promote the second one.

There is another problem. Everywhere we also see perverse and destructive incentivizing. Incentivizing people to do the unethical thing. We saw, for example, underwriters compensated for how many home loans they approved rather than for how many they processed. Think of how perverse that is. Why not work ethics and integrity into a compensation scheme as a valuable incentive?

Consider the astonishing recent scandal at Wells Fargo, where bank employees created up to 3.5 million fake bank accounts for existing customers without their permission or knowledge, charging them unearned fees. Why? For one thing, they didn't care about honesty and integrity of course. But also they were incentivized to do it. Employees were under immense top-down pressure to meet unrealistic sales targets and quotas in order to get their own paychecks, so they resorted to phantom accounts to please their supervisors and the company.

Culture is defining. Not just for business organizations, but for all institutions. Culture shapes universities, medical practices, movie studios, prosecutors' offices, and sports franchises. White Houses too. Some cultures are healthy, some are merely ill, and others are on their deathbeds. In all cases, it takes leadership from the top to fix ailing cultures. Too many leaders are loath to tackle the problem. Some people don't like going to the doctor, but sometimes only the doctor can put you on a path to wellness. That is true for the health of actual people, but it is also true for the long-term health of institutions.

I have found, over time, that there is never any redundancy in repeating and reinforcing the need for, and importance of, integrity in any enterprise. Simple things, in fact, bear repeating.

Whether one runs a U.S. Attorney's Office or a giant corporation or an investment bank or a university, everyone—from the mail room to the boardroom—needs to understand and feel in their bones that the institution and its leaders care about integrity. That is the best way to protect against all manner of accusations, criminal or otherwise.

Bollywood

When your chosen profession requires making public accusations for a living, you must brace for the fallout. One consequence of all that accusing is angry blowback from the accused and their supporters. Depending on the size of their bullhorn and the aggressiveness of their counsel, they might strike back hard at the prosecutors and agencies responsible. Some of this is to be expected; zealous advocacy is commonplace. But, as we will see, there comes a time to wonder—especially if the target is powerful—whether the pushback has gone from zealous self-defense to interference.

A typical, if upsetting, tactic is to question the prosecutors' motives, to allege bias and attack their good faith, because if you can discredit the prosecutor, maybe you can cast doubt on the case. Do the words "witch hunt" sound familiar? In the Nixon/Watergate days, these were dubbed "non-denial denials." They never professed innocence; they just savaged the accusers. Sometimes, distastefully, attacks take on an ethnic or racial tone. At various points over my tenure, depending on who was being prosecuted, SDNY was accused of being anti-black, anti-Latino, anti-Swiss, anti-Chinese, anti-Russian, anti-Italian, and so forth. Also, oddly, anti-Indian. On other occasions, we were accused of being anti–Wall Street, anti-Democrat, anti-Republican, anti-politician, and even anti-poker. Over time, after we had prosecuted a rainbow coalition of defendants and organizations, you would think it would have sunk in that we were just anticrime.

The best way to inoculate yourself from ugly disparagements is to keep your head down and let the frivolous criticism roll off your back. But even when criticism is colossally stupid, it can still sting. Criticism is hard to take, especially false claims of bias. I thought I had a thick skin before I became U.S. Attorney, but I was not especially self-aware in this regard. Aristotle once said, "To avoid criticism, say nothing, do nothing, be nothing." Wise words, but Aristotle didn't live in the age of social media.

The key is to learn which criticism to take to heart to make yourself better and which criticism to laugh off; which criticism is well placed and which is foolish. The point is not to be dismissive about criticism but to be discerning about it.

Accused parties often grasp at straws in lashing out. Nowhere did I feel that more than when, from time to time, our office prosecuted people who, like me, were of Indian origin. Screams of "witch hunt" in that context were a bit more awkward and hurtful because the argument had to be that not only was I making decisions based on ethnicity but I *also* was bending over backward to direct agents and prosecutors to investigate people of my own ethnic background. I am not overstating this. I suppose because of the absence of any other Indian American U.S. Attorney at the time and the relative dearth of Indian American defendants, in the minds of some it was a spectacle when my office charged someone from South Asia.

In 2009, just a few days after we arrested the billionaire hedge fund CEO Raj Rajaratnam for insider trading (along with a number of white people, I might add), *The Wall Street Journal* ran an odd story. This was the first sentence: "It seems like a courtroom drama made for Bollywood: The Sri Lankan hedge-fund kingpin being prosecuted by a fellow immigrant, the Indian-born U.S. attorney for Manhattan." That would be me.

Now imagine if a major news outlet had run a story like

that a year earlier, except about a different blockbuster case: "It seems like a made-for-Broadway drama about the biggest Ponzi schemer in history: Bernard Madoff, who is Jewish, being prosecuted by a fellow Jew, U.S. Attorney Lev Dassin. It's like something out of *Fiddler on the Roof*."

Just imagine the outcry. How long would the writer of that article have remained employed?

I am a bit taken aback at how much was made of these coincidences. My goodness, there's a South Asian defendant, and there's a South Asian prosecutor! Holy cow! You know where this happens every day? India.

By happenstance, a small subset of the insider-trading defendants we charged and convicted were of South Asian origin. Never mind that the original investigation and wiretapping of Raj Rajaratnam and his cohorts were initiated by Michael Garcia, my Latino predecessor; never mind that there was overwhelming proof of their guilt; never mind that there was disproportionate membership in hedge funds of highly educated Indian professionals. A growing chorus developed in some of the ethnic press about my self-hating penchant for prosecuting Indian Americans. They included, apart from Rajaratnam, Rajat Gupta, Anil Kumar, Samir Barai, Mathew Martoma.

I was asked about the "controversy" at functions. It irritated me every time. There came a point where career prosecutors would walk into my office and tell me the next round of potential defendants based on confidential informants, wiretaps, or other investigative techniques, and I would breathe a loud and comic sigh of relief if there was not an Indian name. Once, on the eve of announcing a round of insider-trading arrests, an AUSA turned to me abruptly and said, "By the way, Preet, you know that one of the defendants is Indian American." I was surprised because—again although it didn't matter and we were racially and ethnically blind on these things—I thought I would have spotted an Indian-origin name in the caption. I said, "Who?" The AUSA said, "Sam

Barai." I said, "Sam's not an Indian name." The AUSA added, "It's not, but that's the name he goes by."

I would try to joke about it. At one point, some reporter got juiced up enough on the issue that folks in the office actually tallied up the number of South Asian insider-trading defendants over time. It was a small fraction of our total, though I suppose disproportionate to the general population. When presented with this absurd thesis, I would try to defuse it with a joke. On one occasion, I said, "Just FYI, everyone, I do not wake up every morning, rise from my bed, fling open the windows, shake my fist at the sky, and say, 'Bring me the head of an Indian!'" At least most days I didn't do that.

On another occasion, I was asked to introduce a speaker at the annual banquet hosted by the newspaper *India Abroad* at the Pierre hotel in Manhattan. The event was, as always, full of high-profile Indian Americans, including people from the finance world. During the cocktail hour, I endured someone asking with a straight face why my office prosecutes so many South Asians. Later, as I rose to speak and looked around the room, I thought to myself, how can I poke fun at this nonsense in front of this large crowd?

So, against my better judgment, I went to the podium and began like this: "It's great to be here this evening. I'm Preet Bharara and I'm the U.S. Attorney for the Southern District of New York. It occurs to me as I look out at all of you and see so many prominent Indian Americans captive in this room, I have something important to say to all of you." I paused and then said slowly, "You have the right to remain silent." Laughter. I continued, "Anything you say can and will be used against you in a court of law." More laughter. "You have the right to an attorney. If you cannot afford an attorney—though that seems unlikely in this crowd—one will be provided for you."

By the time I was done administering the *Miranda* warning, there was a good amount of laughter in the audience.

Some individuals seemed to make it their personal mission to perpetuate this insidious narrative. Dinesh D'Souza, an author and commentator known for his extremist, insulting, and evidence-free commentary, pled guilty to charges my office brought against him in 2014 for a campaign finance violation. He knowingly reimbursed straw donors to fill the campaign coffers of a candidate for senate. Despite admitting to his wrongdoing (and his lawyer concluding on the record that he had "no defense" for his client), D'Souza continued to frame his prosecution as an act driven by my own perverse and personal desire to prosecute Indians and Indian Americans.

D'Souza didn't just call me a "Holder henchman" or a tool in the Obama administration; he also insulted my profession, my family, my appearance, and (ironically) employed Indian stereotypes along the way: "Since Preet Bharara doesn't have a strong Indian accent he may be employable as one of those tech guys who helps you fix your computer," he tweeted.

He gloated when I was fired and framed me as someone with a personal vendetta toward my own people. Even after being pardoned in 2018 by President Trump, D'Souza continued to maintain the self-hating Indian theory. The self-described "scholar" tweeted, "KARMA IS A BITCH DEPT: @PreetBharara wanted to destroy a fellow Indian American to advance his career. Then he got fired & I got pardoned." Classy fellow.

But the bubble of ethnic criticism didn't end with certain Wall Street prosecutions or the hallucinations of an ethnic propagandist. There was once a more serious and sustained crisis. Several years into my tenure, in 2013, the State Department arrested a mid-level female Indian diplomat, Devyani Khobragade, for visa fraud in connection with lies about what she would pay her domestic worker. She had agreed under penalty of perjury and other legal sanctions to pay her Indian domestic worker $9.75 per hour. The evidence showed that Khobragade paid Sangeeta Richard less than *$1.00* an hour and violated a multitude of other

fair labor practices in the United States. SDNY agreed to prosecute the case, at the State Department's explicit request.

It was not the crime of the century but a serious offense
nonetheless and a burgeoning problem among the diplomatic
corps in the United States. That's why the State Department
opened the case; that's why the State Department investigated
it; that's why the career agents in the State Department asked
career prosecutors in my office to approve criminal charges.

Khobragade was afforded a number of courtesies during the
course of her arrest, because of her diplomatic status, but she
was strip-searched per regular procedure by the U.S. Marshals
Service in the SDNY. That could have and should have been
avoided, given that no one would have sought pretrial detention.

The arrest caused an international incident. It was an election
year in India, and the ruling Congress Party was in danger of an
electoral bloodbath loss to the Indian nationalist BJP. The BJP,
the party of the future prime minister Narendra Modi, shrewdly
seized upon this supposed Western insult to Indian sovereignty
and caused a crisis for the Congress Party. Khobragade's father,
who had his own political ambitions in India, announced a hunger strike, though there is no evidence that he ever sacrificed a
single calorie after making his dramatic announcement. But the
drama was joined. The then secretary of state, John Kerry, was
pressured to make the case go away. The Indians threatened
retaliation against our embassy in New Delhi and suggested
taking privileges away from American diplomats. At one point,
as the Indian government raged, our largest democratic ally in
the world—in its most hostile action—removed security barriers
from the outside of the U.S. embassy.

I am proud of the case and how we upheld the rule of law.
I defended our work, loudly. Because I was the U.S. Attorney
and I happened to be Indian-born, an avalanche of vitriol and
bile came my way. Never mind that the case was initiated and
investigated by career law enforcement officials, and I personally

became aware of it only the day before the arrest. The Indian government and press decided that the case was brought by me—an Indian American—for all manner of nefarious reasons.

Talk show hosts in India took to calling me a self-loathing Indian who made it a point to go after people from the country of his birth. My colleagues and I found all of it a bit odd, because the alleged *victim* in the case was also Indian. An Indian official asked on television, "Who the hell is Preet Bharara?" I was identified on another program as the most hated man in that country.

The criticism grew more and more intense, which might not have bothered me so much had my parents not been reading every word of it. It upset them greatly. Then came the evening when my daughter overheard a conversation in the living room. She asked me, "Daddy, what is an Uncle Tom?" Because that's what I was being called by journalists in South Asia. That was not pleasant.

As the accusations grew more and more absurd, they became downright comical. Indian critics were angry because even though I hailed from India, I appeared to be going out of my way to act "American" and serve the interests of America. The thing is, I *am* American and the words "United States" were actually in my title.

Finally, I saw a peculiar line of attack in the foreign press, which was this: in a brazen betrayal of my roots, I had undertaken this case for only one reason—to serve my "white masters."

My white masters. These were, presumably, Eric Holder and Barack Obama.

Why am I rehashing all this? Because attacks on prosecutors and investigators by their targets come with the territory. It's not quite Newtonian; for each accusation, there is not an equal and opposite accusation. But the attacks can be sharp and unfair.

You have to deal with them. And you are comforted knowing that it will all be resolved, before too long, in a court of law. In some places and in some circumstances, the targets may be powerful enough to do more than merely muddy the waters or hurl invective. This is when the appropriate bleeds into outright interference and worse.

What happens when criminal justice knocks on the door of people close to the president of a country? What powers does the nation's commander in chief bring to bear on the pesky and intrusive disrupters who have the temerity to think themselves independent, to believe no one is above the law? What ability does the one person with a megaphone louder than any prosecutor's have to undermine the investigation not just rhetorically but actually?

Consider one of the more bizarre international incidents caused by a straightforward criminal case we brought:

In March 2016, a man named Reza Zarrab traveled with his family from Turkey to Disney World for a vacation. Zarrab was an Iranian gold trader who was a dual citizen of Iran and Turkey. He was well connected and close to President Erdogan and other high-ranking politicians and businessmen in Turkey, including Zafer Caglayan, the Turkish economy minister, and Suleyman Aslan, the former general manager of Halkbank, one of the largest Turkish state-owned banks.

Unbeknownst to Zarrab, he had been indicted under seal by an SDNY grand jury for conspiring to evade U.S. sanctions against Iran. The case had been primarily investigated by a tall, quiet, intense prosecutor named Michael Lockard. Michael brought charges against Zarrab and seven other defendants for money laundering and conspiring to violate U.S. sanctions against Iran through a massive, billion-dollar scheme in which they lied to American officials, created fake companies, fabricated documents, and bribed various Turkish government officials in order to trade gold for oil. Zarrab's leading role had earned him significant social and fiscal capital in his country, reportedly orchestrating deals worth almost $10 billion in 2012 alone; his hubris once prompted him to promise his wife, a Turkish pop star, that he would buy her the planet Mars.

I barely knew about the case; we charge people from time to time under seal in cases so that targets are not alerted and may be so reckless as to travel to the United States at their peril. I quickly learned a lot more about Michael's case and about Reza Zarrab. The reaction in Turkey to his arrest was mind-boggling. It was the perfect mirror image of what happened in India after the arrest of the diplomat Devyani Khobragade. Whereas in India I was vilified for a by-the-book prosecution that I knew little about, in Turkey I was immediately lionized for a similarly by-the-book prosecution that I knew equally little about. I was an overnight sensation once again.

This is not an exaggeration.

Within hours, my official Twitter account exploded: followers rose from 8,000 to almost 250,000. Almost every single one of them a jubilant Turk. My name, because it appeared on the indictment, was splashed all over Turkish television. My picture too. People from Turkey offered me praise, thanks, and kabobs. One very generous Twitter user offered me "Turkish raki, Shish Kebab, Lokuum, Turkish Carpet." To which I replied, "Well, I do love shish kebab but I don't think I can accept gifts just for doing my job." For weeks and months, U.S.-based Turkish reporters followed me to events. Songs were written about me. Poems penned also. There were proclamations of love, even the hashtag #welovepreetbharara started to trend online.

Why all the celebration? Why all the acclamation? This is why: Some years earlier, in 2013, Turkey prosecutors had built a case against Reza Zarrab. The allegations were that Zarrab had led a corrupt scheme that included fraud, gold smuggling, and bribery, at the highest levels of the Turkish government, to purchase Iranian gas with gold and to evade American sanctions in order to boost the country's trade exports. You see the overlap with our charges.

What happened to the charges in Turkey? Zarrab escaped them. He was not convicted. But he wasn't acquitted either, because there was never any trial. Reza Zarrab had a get-out-of-jail-free card named Recep Tayyip Erdogan, the president of the country. The case against Zarrab implicated Erdogan's own government, several of his cabinet members and their sons, and even Erdogan's own son Bilal. Zarrab, the son of the environment minister, the son of the economy minister, and the son of the interior minister were part of the scores of people who were arrested and detained in December of that year.

At first Erdogan was merely irate. He attacked the case publicly. He attacked the prosecutors. He attacked the police. He called the investigation a "judicial coup" and accused Fethullah Gulen, a Turkish Muslim cleric living in exile in Pennsylvania and the face of an influential Islamic network in Turkey, of orchestrating the investigation to unseat him. Erdogan used the press to distract the Turkish people from the charges by accusing others of wrongdoing. He continued to frame himself as the target of a conspiracy. But ultimately, Erdogan did more. He didn't just criticize the prosecutors; he didn't just use his bully pulpit. He used his actual power.

First, he removed the prosecutors. He demoted and reassigned thousands of police officers. He reassigned judges. And he released Zarrab and the cabinet ministers' sons from jail after seventy days behind bars. He blocked journalists from investigating government actions. He was incensed.

Then he fired police officers, including the Istanbul police chief. He disbarred and arrested prosecutors. He ordered investigations into the prosecutors who were leading the corruption investigation. He investigated and arrested police officers, judges, journalists. He shut down media outlets. He appointed new prosecutors who closed the meddlesome cases for good.

He went still further. He introduced legislation that would consolidate more power over the judiciary with the justice minister, including the power to start (or stop) investigations of council members. And he expanded his own presidential power to propose members for the High Council of Judges and Prosecutors, which appoints and removes judges across the entire country.

In Turkey, the case against Reza Zarrab went away. Many of the people who tried to bring that case were made to go away also. And essentially half of the country was enraged. Enraged at the cronyism, enraged at the obstruction, enraged at the injustice. It stuck in the craw of tens of millions of Turks. There would never be any accountability for Reza Zarrab. Until, that is, Michael Lockard's secret sanctions case was unsealed. To the people of Turkey who experienced the miscarriage of justice in 2013, this was karmic comeuppance. Zarrab would see his day in court.

Now, just because Zarrab was suddenly facing justice in an American courtroom doesn't mean that Erdogan sat silently by. Not by a long shot. The president of that NATO ally tried to influence our prosecution. He publicly lied about me and said I was a disciple of Fethullah Gulen. I had never even heard of Gulen until he was mentioned in the press after the indictment was unsealed. Erdogan also accused me of helping to aid the unsuccessful coup against his government in 2016. I have never set foot in Turkey, though I wish I had visited that beautiful country.

He did more than that too. As reported in the press, in the final weeks of the Obama administration Erdogan personally met with Vice President Biden. The president of a foreign nation thought he could come to Washington, attack a sitting U.S. Attorney, insert himself into an American criminal proceeding, and have his way. He had two principal agenda items. He demanded that I be fired and that Zarrab be released. He reportedly spent half of his ninety-minute conversation with Vice President Biden discussing Zarrab's prosecution. Erdogan's wife even brought up the case with Jill Biden. The Turkish justice minister at the time visited the then attorney general, Loretta Lynch, and demanded Zarrab's release. Erdogan discussed the case in phone calls with President Obama too. Imagine that. I was not fired (then), and Zarrab was not set free.

Ultimately, after months in jail, Zarrab flipped, pled guilty, testified against his co-defendant, and implicated Erdogan in corruption during a trial that took place after I was fired.

What is to be learned from the Zarrab case and the attendant nuttiness? Probably many things, but here are two lessons.

One is this: Justice is delicate. Attacks on prosecutors by the prosecuted are par for the course. If you can't take the heat, get out of the courtroom. But there are limits, dangerous if breached. When leaders of nations—whether the president of Turkey, Russia, or the United States—join the attacks, hurl the invective, demonize the justice seekers, it jeopardizes justice and threatens to destroy any remaining faith in it. And it may not be a big jump from mere rhetoric to radical abuse of power. Ever since Erdogan undid the case against his erstwhile ally in 2013, Turkey has descended into greater and greater autocracy. The press is muzzled. Freedoms are fewer. Erdogan's paranoia and self-protection were amplified by the coup attempt, no doubt. But make no mistake that a milestone along his unfortunate path to autocracy was his decision to interfere personally in a duly launched criminal case. And nothing says that can't also happen in America.

A second and related lesson is this: People hunger for justice. And the appearance of justice. I mention it because this unbelievable outpouring toward me in Turkey was due to this hunger. The hope is that no man is above the law; that power and privilege do not immunize you from accountability and punishment; that corruption can be fought. And that there are people brave enough to fight it. It shows the universal craving for honest government and the rule of law. Because as it turns out, the dream of honest government, where no one is above the law and the oath of office matters, is the dream of civilized people everywhere. Bringing the powerful and corrupt to justice gives people faith in *all* cases, big and small.

And here's the other thing: People can make too much of prosecutors. They are law enforcers, not saviors. Now that I am at some remove from these events, I think from time to time, with a smile, this: Prosecutors are sometimes empty vessels in whom the public will pour their hopes or hatreds. I was a villain in India, a hero in Turkey, and wholly undeserving of either label.

PART III

Judgment

Introduction

You've finished your investigation. You've swallowed hard and made your accusation. You've charged someone with robbery or assault or fraud or murder. Justice now enters its more public (and accountable) phase. The issues are joined. Suddenly it's no longer just insular law enforcers on the field, aggressively investigating and unilaterally bringing charges, operating on their own terms, subject to only their own judgments, agendas, and priorities. Now many other characters stride onto the stage—judges, defense lawyers, jurors. There is judicial and public scrutiny.

This phase—judgment—is the adjudication of the allegations or accusations. It is the settling of the ultimate question. The possibilities are not infinite. There are only four basic outcomes: charges admitted (guilty plea), charges withdrawn (dismissal), charges proved (guilty verdict), or charges defeated (not-guilty verdict). There is also the chance, I suppose, of a mixed verdict or the accused becoming a fugitive and escaping reckoning altogether, but essentially those are the four potential outcomes. There is, notably, no such thing as a verdict of innocence in our system.

As I said, in this judgment phase, there are many stakeholders. The prosecutor, the defendant, the court, the public. One constituency sometimes gets short shrift—the victim. Not all crimes and bad deeds have identifiable victims. But when they do, an important question to ask is, what treatment do they deserve? What degree of solicitousness, care, protection, empathy, is owed by the prosecutor and by the court? How do we make sure a credible victim who is nonetheless disbelieved and powerless gets her day in court? You'll see the issue through the prism of a case involving a troubled woman named SueAnn, who struggled to get her day in court. She serves, in a way, as a proxy for so many nameless, faceless, forgotten victims who receive only second-class treatment by the system.

Any rendering of definitive judgment requires a presiding officer. That is the umpire or referee in sports; the arbitrator in a business dispute; or the parent in a sibling squabble. One reason there is no satisfying judgment in any congressional inquiry is that there is no neutral arbiter. No one is in charge. Conclusions are based on political power, rather than on detached rulings by disinterested outsiders.

In criminal trials, the presiding officer is the judge, who has a profoundly important role. The judge has a central bearing on the proceedings, can alter the course of events, can advance or thwart truth and justice. The judge's presence, personality, and preferences permeate the unfolding drama in court. A careless or callous judge can easily place a thumb on the scales of justice. For this reason, the very first question anyone asks about a case is this: "Who's the judge?" The myth that the identity of the judge doesn't matter is nonsense. You won't find a reasonable practicing attorney—for the prosecution or the defense—anywhere in America who would tell you otherwise. Anyone who doesn't take into account the individual characteristics and proclivities of the judge is committing a form of legal malpractice.

Like the prosecutor, the judge must follow the law. The judge has no client but the general public and no mandate but to do justice. But, robes notwithstanding, judges can fall short just like everyone else. Most are fair-minded and principled, hardworking and wise. But they are not perfect or infallible; they have good days and bad days; they have insights and also blind spots.

Some are perceived as pro-defense, others as pro-prosecution, and most lawyers can predict based on the judge assignment whether the trial will be a pleasant experience or a difficult ordeal.

I deliver here not a treatise on judging but some select observations about the nature of the judges' job, their role in doing justice, and how to interact with them, especially the difficult ones.

If there is no out-of-court resolution, if there is no admission to the accusations, there is the constitutionally required showstopper, rapidly vanishing from the landscape—the criminal trial.

The prosecutor has said someone is guilty. That is not enough. Now either the accused admits guilt or the prosecutor has to prove it—beyond a reasonable doubt—to twelve ordinary people who are not only strangers to you but also strangers to each other.

The inquiry and accusation phases are about proving the case to yourself. Trial is about proving what you already believe to *other* people. At its essence, a trial is a tour de force of communication, of understanding how other people think, of presenting evidence interwoven with logically compelling stories.

Incidentally, the elements that make a criminal trial an effective and fair process for determinations of truth are a model for debate and truth seeking away from the courtroom as well. They supply something sorely lacking in our debates in the public square. The rationality and rigidity of the trial process, combined with an on-the-field umpire, yield more just (and more satisfactory and acceptable) outcomes than what passes for political debate nowadays.

Day in Court

One year, I nominated my chief of violent crimes, Laurie Korenbaum, for an award called the Stimson Medal. The honor, bestowed by the New York City Bar Association, is named for the legendary SDNY U.S. Attorney Henry Stimson, who served over a century ago, before duty as secretary of state and secretary of war. The Stimson Medal is the highest honor an assistant U.S. Attorney can receive. Laurie was never interested in securities fraud, cyber crime, or public corruption. Her life's work was pursuing violent crime, gang offenses, and especially homicides. In her Stimson acceptance speech, she focused on the victims of violent crime. This is what she said:

> In my job, as interesting and rewarding as it is to solve and try homicide cases, it really is all about the victims and the families of the victims, delivering some sense of justice to them, helping them heal, if only just a little bit. And, while it is true that the victims of many of the murders I prosecute are themselves criminals, sometimes they are not. Sometimes they are a fourteen-year-old girl in the back of a hallway on Bathgate Avenue in the Bronx when an assassin begins to fire through the doorway at his drug rival. Sometimes they are the very young wife of a drug dealer, the mother of two small children, sleeping in bed with her husband when his killers begin shooting into the bedroom. And sometimes they are a

three-year-old boy in his bed who sees his mother murdered in front of his eyes. He is just a little boy in his superhero underwear, but he's old enough to be able to identify his mother's killer, and so he is shot and killed as well.

And, even when the victim is a criminal, he often leaves behind those who love him despite that, those who see a side of him that we don't. These people are victims, too, and we do this work to vindicate them as well.

We are prosecutors, not judges. We take our victims as we find them and try to get them justice. That is my real reward for doing the work that I love to do and, hopefully, doing it well enough to make a small difference in someone's life.

That was and is the mission.

SueAnn was in her early thirties, living in an apartment with a roommate in the Wakefield section of the Bronx. She was self-employed and made good money. Perhaps unwisely, she kept her cash earnings at home. One weekday morning, she was awakened by a loud banging at the door. Two men burst in, both in face masks, one of them armed. They bound SueAnn with duct tape and beat her severely. They pistol-whipped her, which caused her to have an epileptic seizure and pass out. They ransacked the apartment until they found $11,000 in cash and took it. Before leaving, one of the men might also have sexually assaulted her.

The attack sent SueAnn to the ICU for ten days and landed her another six days on bed rest. Her injuries included a broken nose, broken rib, busted lip, damaged neck, and facial bruising.

Although the men had concealed their faces, SueAnn was certain she recognized the voice of one of them as her roommate's ex-boyfriend, Lamont Rolle, nicknamed Bam. This might have been a simple case where a victim was robbed and brutally assaulted and could positively identify at least one perpetrator. But the case was not so straightforward. Among other things, there was no fingerprint evidence, no surveillance video, and no DNA linking Bam to the crime scene.

Moreover, the sole witness to the crime was the victim herself. And this victim-witness came, to put it mildly, with issues. SueAnn was a working prostitute, and the $11,000 in cash stolen from her was revenue from her sex work. SueAnn, moreover, suffered from asthma, anxiety, and bipolar disorder. She was also a drug addict, with a rap sheet full of narcotics and prostitution arrests. On top of that, she was on parole.

People like SueAnn are easy marks. They are frequent victims of crime and brutality; less frequently are they star witnesses against their abusers. They seldom get their day in court. If there's anything I can do without consequences, cowards like Bam must think, it is to beat and rob a drug-addicted hooker with no allies and no protectors. He must have presumed that SueAnn would make an unsympathetic, unreliable, and unbelievable accuser, if she had the guts to come forward at all. He was almost right. SueAnn mistakenly identified a man as Bam's accomplice, a man who matched the description, found a few blocks away by police right after the robbery but who turned out to have an airtight alibi, forcing the Bronx DA to drop the charges his office brought against the supposed accomplice. This misidentification, combined with their assessment that SueAnn was a very difficult and unstable witness, caused the DA to decline to prosecute Bam.

Despite the brick wall in the Bronx, an NYPD detective from the Bronx robbery squad, Sean Butler, did not give up. He thought it was a hard case but a worthy cause. So Detective Butler brought it to my office, where it landed on the desks of Kan Nawaday, a veteran gang prosecutor, and Tatiana Martins, then a junior narcotics AUSA who later became chief of public corruption. This was not a typical federal prosecution; we barely had federal jurisdiction, and one DA had already rejected it. But my folks are an intrepid lot, and impressed by the earnest insistence of Detective Butler, they opened the investigation.

The SueAnn that Tatiana later met was an aggressive, angry, and damaged woman. Life had not been easy on her. She was a mess of a witness—hard to talk to, tough to keep calm, and impossible to keep focused. And she was, understandably, very, very angry. If SDNY were ever going to charge Bam, Tatiana would be the one putting SueAnn on the stand, and she would have her hands full.

First Kan and Tatiana needed more corroboration. They needed to place Bam definitively at the crime scene. They triangulated Bam's general location through GPS information obtained from Bam's mobile service provider. They were able to show that Bam's phone moved in a way consistent with his coming from his home to SueAnn's apartment before the attack and departing from her apartment back to his home. The problem is that GPS tracking is only accurate within a few blocks. It was decent corroboration, but not a slam dunk. So, it was a hard case with a tough victim-witness, but based on that evidence, they obtained an arrest warrant.

Bam was taken into custody on January 9, 2014. We seized his mobile phone and immediately got a search warrant for its contents. The phone dump yielded, curiously, pictures of the suspect holding wads of cash and photographs of dozens of bills in various denominations—$20s, $50s, $100s—fanned across his bed. Metadata showed the snaps had been taken after the robbery. And it gave Tatiana an offbeat idea: What if SueAnn had taken pictures of *her* money? If she had and you could match bills in a picture taken pre-robbery with the bills found on Bam's phone taken post-robbery, that would be smoking-gun proof.

So, on a long-shot lark, Tatiana asked SueAnn if she had ever taken photographs of her money before it was stolen.

Proving that Hail Mary questions have a sacred place in law enforcement, SueAnn said, well, as a matter of fact she had. Why? The explanation will tell you a good amount about this woman's spirit: SueAnn worked solo and marketed herself on the internet. Recently, a man had come out of the woodwork and offered his services, arguing that if they joined forces, he could make her a lot of money. SueAnn was, among her many other qualities, rather prideful. She said to herself, *I'm my best pimp.* She wanted to prove to this aspiring sex manager that, as she put it, "I don't need a pimp to make money. I can make my own money." And so, as luck would have it, shortly before the robbery, SueAnn had arrayed a recent haul of cash on her own bedspread, taken pictures, and texted them to this fellow to demonstrate her financial independence.

She still had the photos, and the prosecutors couldn't believe their luck. They spent hours obsessively zooming in on Bam's money shots, comparing them with SueAnn's, desperately looking for a match. Tatiana studied the serial numbers and markings on every unobscured bill. One of the $100 bills from SueAnn's stash had the word "MAY" handwritten in the top left corner, but she couldn't find a counterpart in Bam's stash. She looked until her eyes went bleary. But hard as she searched, no match presented itself.

Fast-forward to the eve of trial, to the Friday before jury selection, as the team was pulling everything together. Suddenly someone recalled something: At the time of Bam's arrest, they hadn't taken just his phone. They had also taken his wallet. What was in his wallet? Eleven hundred dollars in cash, that's what.

The wallet was, at that very moment, resting comfortably in a locked vault at ATF (Bureau of Alcohol, Tobacco, Firearms, and Explosives) headquarters nearby in the Financial District, seized as evidence in the case. They looked at each other. The arrest took place well after the robbery so the odds were long that any bills stolen from SueAnn would still be sitting in the defendant's wallet. Still, Agent Keltar Mui raced to retrieve it. When he returned, they spread the $1,177 in cash across Kan's desk in his fourth-floor office.

Tatiana had stared at the markings and serial numbers in SueAnn's photographs for so long they were practically tattooed on her brain. Even before the file of SueAnn's collection of images was pulled up on Kan's computer, Tatiana felt her heart leap into her mouth. She saw that one of the bills from Bam's wallet had the telltale word "MAY" in the top left corner. She recognized the serial number too: L12440340A. "Open up the pictures!" she yelled.

Confirmation was swift. There it was, clear as the nose on Ben Franklin's face. The note from Bam's wallet bore the same serial number and "MAY" marking as the bottom-most bill in SueAnn's pre-robbery photograph. Three more bills matched too. By holy luck, two long months after the robbery, Bam had still been walking the streets with *four* $100 bills from the robbery. Jackpot.

Meanwhile, the trial was Monday. The first question was this: Should they tell the defense about this devastating proof? The defense attorneys already had all the pictures, and they were given immediate notice of our intention to use the money from Bam's wallet as evidence and invited to come inspect that evidence. We also provided pictures of the currency in the wallet. All of the relevant evidence was in the defense's possession; there was no ethical requirement or other reason for us to do their homework for them.

One consideration loomed. Spoon-feeding the defense on the matter of the currency matches might prompt a guilty plea, avoiding the need for a trial, avoiding the need for SueAnn to testify. But something counseled against that. SueAnn, unlike many victims in her position, was champing at the bit to testify. She was not afraid. She was angry, enraged even. Although she knew the defense had obnoxiously signaled they would attack her character, credibility, and lifestyle, she wanted to testify. She wanted to tell her story. She wanted the truth to come out. *She wanted her day in court.* She wanted the man who abused her, assaulted her, and robbed her to have to face her. She couldn't believe he had almost gotten away with it when the Bronx DA declined to prosecute.

Tatiana and Kan also believed the case should go to trial. Why? Because SueAnn deserved it. As Tatiana put it, "SueAnn was a drug-addicted, epileptic prostitute who had been abused throughout her life. She'd been disbelieved and cast aside. She wanted her day in court. And we wanted her to have it. We wanted her to have her conviction, and we wanted to show her that in America a person like her could get justice."

So they went to trial.

In her opening statement, Tatiana made out the case, to devastating effect. In the defense opening, Jennifer Brown of the federal defenders had no response to the currency matches. Instead, as promised, as the prosecutors put it, the defense put SueAnn on trial, "slut-shamed" her, and tried to make her the victim for the second time.

The defense lawyers focused on SueAnn's lifestyle, including the company she kept and the environment she lived in. Every question that focused on SueAnn's prior criminal history, her line of work, and her drug usage only reinforced that the defense was attempting to win this case by revictimizing SueAnn. In one line of questioning, Ms. Brown crossed SueAnn extensively about her work and her clients: "So you are very good at what you do, is that right? You have a lot of customers, yes? And in order to be good at what you do, you have to make the customers feel satisfied, right? . . . You tell them what they want to hear, right? Some men like to hear how good they are, right?"

It's not too much of a stretch to say that the defense approached SueAnn with the same mentality Bam did: Why would anyone believe that she could be a victim? Kan explained to the jury, "She was easy prey for the defendant. She was a prostitute on parole. Who was going to believe her? She was an easy target. It was easy money."

Despite the character attacks, the belittling gibes, and the arrogant slanders, whom did the jury believe? They believed SueAnn.

Given her background and baggage, a biased system had rendered her not credible. When the verdict came—guilty—SueAnn fell to her knees, on the ground, crying. In her thanks to the prosecution team, she said, "No one has ever taken me seriously."

Kan and Tatiana tried a lot of significant cases in SDNY. For her part, Tatiana convicted the New York State Senate majority leader Dean Skelos at his first trial and later convicted New York State Assembly Speaker Sheldon Silver at his retrial. But among her many successes in court, Tatiana has told me the case against Lamont Rolle, a.k.a. Bam, was, in a way, one of the most satisfying convictions of them all because it made such a significant difference to a particular person's life.

And as I took in the details of the case—almost all of which I was not aware of, because this is not the kind of case that people bring to the U.S. Attorney's attention—it occurred to me that it is as meaningful as any case we brought. Meaningful not just to the victim, meaningful not just to the trial team, but meaningful also for what it says about the possibility of justice for everyone. It also occurred to me that justice for all is not possible without an office full of people like Tatiana and Kan and Detective Butler who are there to fight for it.

In lines of work where pain and drama are common, there lurks a danger that ordinary people who suffer harm will recede in importance, become part of the occupational furniture, rather than flesh-and-blood human beings. There is a risk that the professionals charged with helping them will become inured and desensitized to their particular pain. I presume it takes a special kind of oncologist to be as empathetic toward, and solicitous of, the thousandth patient she diagnoses with cancer as she was with the very first. Over time for some, I imagine, the compassion and care needed for hand-holding and sympathetic bedside manner become an afterthought or a nuisance. Even the excellent doctor may focus on the disease as an abstraction rather than the real human being who is its victim.

In the preface to his book *The Man Who Mistook His Wife for a Hat,* the famed neurologist Dr. Oliver Sacks announced that he was "equally interested in diseases and people." He describes the limitations of the tool Hippocrates gave to medicine: the case history. Case histories describe, clinically, the course of a disease. Sacks says that is all well and good but deficient, because "they tell us nothing about the individual and *his* history; they convey nothing of the person, and the experience of the person, as he faces, and struggles to survive, his disease."

The illness, Sacks implores, must not be disembodied from the actual and unique person in whom the illness has taken up residence:

> There is no "subject" in a narrow case history; modern case histories allude to the subject in a cursory phrase ("a trisomic albino female of 21"), which could as well apply to a rat as a human being. To restore the human subject at the centre— the suffering, afflicted, fighting, human subject—we must deepen a case history to a narrative or tale; only then do we have a "who" as well as a "what," a real person, a patient, in relation to disease—in relation to the physical.

An identical phenomenon can befall the prosecutor, who must be similarly and equally interested in crime *and* people.

Of course many crimes don't have an identifiable victim. But when they do, the dynamic is and should be different. Even an excellent prosecutor can become so consumed with proving the elements of the crime, with great legal and investigative skill, that she loses sight of the softer work of tending to the crime's victims. As the prosecutor or the law enforcement agent is combing through phone records or reviewing surveillance tapes or drafting, late into the night, tedious applications for search warrants and wiretaps, the flesh-and-blood victims of crimes can float out of mind. This kind of inattention is insidious.

In fairness, of course, some detachment is necessary. If an oncologist or homicide detective, after years on the job, still fell to pieces upon every dire diagnosis or callous murder, we would say she is not up to the task, not fit for the job. Both doctors and cops need to be able to handle blood and death without crying or passing out.

At the same time, undue remove in the name of professionalism can corrode the enterprise and distort just decision making. If you don't make efforts to keep the victim in mind—the "suffering, afflicted, fighting, human subject"—then one danger is that your calculation as to whether she gets her day in court will be compromised. You must *want* to fight for the victim because it's just too easy to see the weaknesses in your case, to find excuses not to proceed.

Because let's face facts. Without a strong orientation toward the victim—especially a vulnerable, powerless, troubled, or unsympathetic victim—a tendency to risk aversion can overpower the impulse to give people their shot at justice. Victims of crimes, like human beings generally, come with baggage. They can be unlikable, difficult, stupid, untruthful, obstinate, hyperbolic, emotional, bombastic, volatile, vengeful, and perplexing. They can be too reluctant or too eager. Both are a problem. They can make mistakes, as SueAnn did in misidentifying Bam's accomplice. That can affect the decision making in a case and inform whether the case can be successfully prosecuted, as it did for the Bronx DA.

Is it more difficult for some people to get justice? Of course it is. Terrible as it is to say—and one wishes for it to be otherwise—there is something of a caste system among victims of crimes. Questions are asked, calculations made. When an unknown accuses a powerful person, will she be believed? When a poor person accuses a privileged person, will he be believed? And even if the prosecutor believes the witness, what about the jury? That is no idle consideration. Sometimes victims come with so many issues that prosecutors shrink from the challenge or believe that such a victim—whether of sexual assault or rape or robbery—must be hyper-corroborated before bringing a case.

There is, for so many reasons, a built-in risk aversion on the part of many prosecutors, but there is a special and additional layer of skittishness that comes from having a vulnerable and imperfect victim-witness. And this is when it's especially necessary to care about the victim, the one who seems less likely to get justice, the invisible and weak prey of some more powerful person. Perhaps that victim wants, needs, *deserves* justice just a little bit more than the well-heeled, perfectly presentable, issue-free one. It may be that special care and compassion for that kind of victim give you the passion, the fight, the indignation to work a little harder, to dig a little deeper to right the wrong. It may be that this engagement alters the analysis, propels you forward even when obstacles abound.

There is a swirling controversy in the country about the degree to which women's claims of sexual abuse and assault by powerful men fall on deaf ears. Any particular case is hard to evaluate, but there is truth in the perception that certain kinds of people, namely men with power and prestige, can get away with anything because they can silence and scare their victims with impunity. Countless women have been harassed, abused, assaulted, and worse, with little justice even in the subset of cases where they have come forward with credible claims. Prosecutors may consider the difficulty of resolving whom to believe (he said, she said) and the daunting task of doing battle against a titan with a bottomless legal budget. There is also the lasting reputational damage to both the high-profile accused and the prosecutor's office itself if a jury fails to convict.

So in close but valid cases, risk-averse law enforcers may not take the chance, especially if they have been burned before. Justice—even a good-faith *attempt* at justice—is not preordained by the law or the facts alone when imperfect and tremulous human beings are making the call.

The mind-set matters.

The questions are these: How badly do you want to make the case? What effort are you willing to exert? What risk are you willing to absorb? What criticism are you willing to endure to vindicate the victim you believe?

The #metoo movement that took off in 2017 in America has resulted in the toppling of many once-mighty titans and a widespread, though very incomplete, reckoning. But the movement has had another palpable effect too. It has perceptibly altered the calculus of prosecutors—that delicate balance between risk and the importance of vindicating real victims. The first time around, famously, the Manhattan District Attorney's Office did not charge the Hollywood mogul Harvey Weinstein with sexual assault despite credible evidence from a 2015 police sting operation that yielded a recording with an apparent admission by Weinstein to nonconsensual touching of his alleged victim. But then came the #metoo movement and the testimonials of multiple women about monstrous conduct, followed by Weinstein's precipitous professional fall. He was sacked. Similar stories of violence and harassment ensued—more than eighty in total—and other powerful men also suffered career consequences. Amid scorching criticism, the DA's Office in Manhattan reopened the Weinstein case and in 2018 charged him with the serious crimes of rape and sexual assault based on incidents with three different women. What had changed? Had more evidence developed? Certainly. But what really changed, in all likelihood, was the will to pursue it. A shift in priority, in risk assessment, and in focus was wrought by a burning national outrage, righteous and long overdue. The will to justice matters.

Sometimes we forget the victims. Sometimes we doubt them. Sometimes we judge them. But ultimately, the system is supposed to serve them and give them their day in court, consistent with the requirements of justice. This is true whether the victim is a purely innocent three-year-old child in his bed, a sick and troubled soul like SueAnn, or a young woman sexually abused by a powerful man.

The Judge

I once found myself at a function speaking to a noted film director. He had no idea who I was but after someone's introduction understood I was a prosecutor of some kind. Attentive and curious, the director asked me, "So what's new in your world?"

Somehow—I can't remember why—we got into a conversation about judges. What he wanted to know was this: "How does a judge get picked for a criminal case?"

So I told him about the wheel. I said there's a wheel with names inside. A magistrate judge turns the handle on the creaky wooden wheel to mix up the cards and then draws one out. And that's the assigned trial judge. This was unremarkable to me, but the director expressed delighted surprise. "There's an actual wheel?" I could see him trying to picture it.

I said, "There sure is."

He smiled, in thought. Perhaps he was taken by the quaintness of it, the anachronism of it. Maybe he was struck by the drama of it. He said he could imagine a television show or movie called *The Wheel*, stories spinning out from that fateful moment of selection.

I've kept an eye out, but no drama series of that sort, to my knowledge, ever materialized. I had never really thought about it from an outsider's perspective—until this filmmaker fixated on the dramatic potential of the wheeling out of a judge assignment. He was onto something important. Judges are not interchangeable. They're not fungible, as an economist might say. The identity of the presiding judge makes a difference. Sometimes a world of difference—especially in punishment. There are almost infinite ways that the conduct, demeanor, and decisions of the judge can shape just or unjust outcomes and the faith of participants in the fairness of the process.

But first, back to the wheel. In SDNY, there are actually three wheels, not one, and they all have locks on them. They sit just behind the bench in the low-ceilinged main magistrate's courtroom on the fifth floor of the modern courthouse at 500 Pearl Street. There are three wheels—labeled A, B, and C—to account for the varying lengths of trial. Not every judge participates in every wheel. The wheels themselves are geometric in shape—octagonal—and fashioned from dark wood. They've been there forever. The envelopes holding the individual judges' names are often sealed so tight a letter opener is needed to extricate the card inside. When the duty magistrate slowly turns the wheel upon the filing of an indictment, it's a singular moment because a lot rides on it. We were not above superstition, and sometimes we sent a "lucky" prosecutor for the wheel out.

Here's the interesting thing: The physical wheels are wholly unnecessary. It's simple enough to generate random judge assignments electronically. In fact, in the very same district—SDNY—when a *civil* case is filed by my office, a judge is assigned just that way, by a randomizing computer program. That's been true in civil cases for many years. Yet these literal wheels of justice persist in criminal cases. To be sure, the rules require that the event triggering the need for a judge assignment—the return of a grand jury indictment—must happen in open court. Why the wheels, though? It's as if this quaint ritual—this vestige of a bygone era—furthers the need to approximate a solemn lottery, to uphold a public appearance of blind justice, made more urgent in a criminal case because liberty is at stake.

The judge is the robed oracle, the voice of God; if your fate is in a judge's hands, she might as well be holding a wand as a gavel. But the principal thing to know about any judge is that he or she is a human being who maybe has just had a better career than most people. Judges have good days and bad days. They have points of view. They have tempers. They have weak spots. They're just people.

The other human part of it is this: knowing who the judge is will tell you how pleasant the experience will be. You'll know which trials will keep you up until 2:00 a.m., which judges will make you feel small and rip you up in front of other people and which won't. You can predict to a fairly decent degree how long the trials will take. If the identity of the judge is something that determines the outcome, then what does that mean as a practical matter?

You may not be a practicing litigator, but you have dealt with judges or judge-like figures your whole life. You might have come across actual judges if you've faced a traffic infraction, gone through a divorce, or had a "small claim." If you've been arrested or sued or if you've sued someone else, you've dealt with the looming presence of a judge.

But judges are everywhere. The teacher who decides a punishment in school; the boss who adjudicates a personnel matter; the executive who chooses someone to promote; the parent who settles a dispute between siblings. Also the referee in soccer and the umpire in baseball. These are all judges. If you've ever engaged in competition or work or sport, you've dealt with some kind of judge. We have all been judged, and we have all sat in judgment.

Consider your perception of these everyday judges' neutrality, judgment, and wisdom. Your view of their calls likely depends on your sense of their fairness or unfairness (people tend to think people who rule against them are inherently unfair; it's a natural bias).

Just as important, what was your strategy for dealing with

these consequential judge-like figures? Back talk? Belligerence? Deference? Stoicism? Surrender?

How well lawyers navigate judges in the courtroom often has its roots more in common sense and human nature than in legal expertise, just like in the rest of life. A judge's role is to allow the truth to be discovered, without bias, favoritism, or a thumb on the scale, while treating both sides with dignity and respect. Mostly that happens. But sometimes other people in the process—prosecutors, defense lawyers—may have to steer the court back to these values. That's how ultimate justice is done.

It was my great honor to practice in a district with some of the most thoughtful, most intelligent, most ethical judges in the country. When I worked in the U.S. Senate, part of my job was to identify, vet, and shepherd the most accomplished lawyers in New York for federal judgeships. I cared deeply about the quality of the court and helped to assure it. SDNY has long been dubbed the Mother Court. This is a sign as much of its excellence as of its own self-regard. But for this storied court, that reputation was richly deserved. This does not mean everyone was perfect.

Judges may sometimes act in ways that seem more self-preserving than justice seeking. It's a surprising thing, because you don't normally think of a judge as someone with skin in the game. The judge's name, after all, does not appear on either side of the v. Judges want to succeed in their jobs, whatever that means for them. For those who believe that being reversed by an appeals court is the judicial version of a job setback, they may do things to avoid it.

We once had a high-profile national security case. In the lead-up to trial, the presiding judge suppressed certain evidence after a motion by the defense; she would not let in some incriminating statements the defendant made to federal agents after his arrest in another country. It was good evidence, but it wasn't critical, given the abundance of other proof in the case. More troublingly, in rendering her opinion, the judge made what is called an adverse credibility finding against the two principal federal agents who were handling the case; she found their denials about making threatening statements to the defendant not believable. Like my team, I thought the finding against the agents was baseless and detrimental. Their careers would be harmed by it. Her ruling could trigger ethics investigations and also make it more difficult for them to testify at future trials. The judge had just handed future defense lawyers bombshell cross-examination material against these agents for all time.

The suppressed evidence we could live without; it was not critical.

But the credibility finding was upsetting and hard to stomach. The judge could have made her ruling without slapping down the agents, both of whom I happened to know well and had worked with personally when I was a line prosecutor and both of whom I believed over the self-interested accusations of the defendant. We were mad. I was mad.

The suppression ruling was what we call appeal-proof, and was deliberately so. Credibility findings made by a trial judge are granted great deference, and appeals judges are loath to second-guess them. What we strongly suspected the judge had done was set forth a reasonable basis for suppressing the evidence but then, to immunize it further, she larded on the adverse credibility finding for good measure. And that she didn't firmly believe it.

In my irritation, I did something unusual, something I never did before or after. I made a public statement that we would consider appealing the decision. This caught the judge's attention.

The judge called for an immediate conference with the parties, for the very next day. That afternoon we strategized in my office in the usual spot around the coffee table. The trial prosecutors on the case were two of the best and smartest I ever worked with, Anjan Sahni and Brendan McGuire, each of whom I twice promoted to supervisory positions. Along with Rich Zabel and Boyd Johnson, we discussed how they should approach the conference. We decided Anjan and Brendan should say that what was most bothersome was the unfair adverse credibility finding, and, if pressed, make clear we would not seek an appeal if that portion were withdrawn. There was some chance she would be put off by the request to remove the offensive basis. Such an approach would have been unthinkable with most judges, because it smacked of barter.

Was she put off? No, she was not. Once we made clear that we wouldn't appeal, the judge was quickly amenable to reissuing her ruling and opinion without the adverse credibility findings. She did it in a day. A different judge later found that one of these agents could be cross-examined about his potential bias for the government because of our advocacy on his behalf to have the adverse credibility finding withdrawn, so the damage was not impermanent.

What did we think of this? On the one hand, we had done right by the case and by the facts and by the agents. We were pleased that the judge had retracted her findings. On the other hand, the speed with which she was willing to undo a career blot on these two agents indicated how transactional and ends-driven her decision to impose the permanent stain was in the first place. To make such a finding, knowingly and personally harmful to longtime agents, you would think that the judge would have believed it strongly and felt it necessary to make it a part of the decision, not lightly withdrawn. You would be mistaken.

There are judges across the country who test the waters: If I rule in this way, will the parties take an appeal? There is a pregame choreography. This is not necessarily bad—this effort at accommodating everyone's interests in a negotiated way—but there's no denying that some of what is at play is the self-preservation instinct of highly successful professionals. That is also not necessarily a bad thing.

In this case, bartering an adverse credibility finding in exchange for certainty on appeal doesn't seem very principled, does it? It wasn't. But there it was, and we had to deal with it. We take our credibility seriously, and we think that if someone is going to cast aspersions, it is done with great thought; to withdraw them so easily suggested she was not so wedded to that view originally.

I'm not suggesting this cynical scenario is common. Hopefully it is not. But it happens and I'm sure it also happens in halls less hallowed than those found in the SDNY courthouse.

The point is this: The judge is not always a fully disinterested figure, merely applying law to facts, merely calling balls and strikes. The judge is not always above it all. There are tactics and strategies pursued by all people, even judges. They are not always above bartering. A prosecutor who knows that a particular judge cares about reversal has a lever to push. The lesson is awareness—as with the everyday judges you come across at home, at school, at work—awareness of what makes them tick, and what can be done to mitigate potential self-interest, conceit, or bias.

Doing the best you can to advance justice, and its appearance, requires, I think, constant vigilance, but also constant growth and evolution. For a peculiar structural reason, trial judges have a handicap in this regard.

Judges, in my experience, are generally smart and curious. They are also rigorous and detail oriented. They are well-trained lawyers who believe in excellence and understand that cases can turn on the interpretation of a clause or a comma. But there's a peculiarity in the nature of judging that I think holds these robed ones back from improving over time like other professionals. Sure, a judge will improve from experience. She will become more knowledgeable about the law over time just by reading more briefs and conducting more trials.

But there's another kind of learning and training that trial judges—almost uniquely—don't get. It is the vital education gained by watching *other* people do the same job. Trial lawyers watch other trial lawyers in court. They see what works, what doesn't. They may copy tone or timing or tactics. When I was U.S. Attorney, I urged young prosecutors to watch their colleagues perform, as often as they could. Also to watch the best defense lawyers. Of course you learn by doing. But you also learn (and improve) by watching. This principle is not limited to lawyering. Athletes study other athletes, both during competitions and in highlight reels. Boxers watch other boxers; quarterbacks and pitchers and golfers do the same. And they up their own game by observing the best. The same for business leaders and journalists and actors.

Trial judges are a little bit different.

To be sure, many will have had substantial careers appearing before many different judges with varying styles and levels of competence. Many will have clerked for a judge after law school, so they will have some idea of how to inhabit the role. But once they actually don the robe, this kind of learning ends. They are kings of their own courtrooms. But they are also prisoners of them. They no longer appear before other judges, get to see how another might handle a complex objection or a difficult witness or a disrespectful lawyer or a confused juror. Their observational experience is largely stopped in time at the moment of being sworn in. This is not unexpected of course. Kings and queens seldom spend time in other monarchs' castles. But something is lost as a result, I think. Some aspect of continuing education— the humbling revelation that the rest of us have, from time to time, in seeing someone do something better than *we* would do it. And so through no fault of their own, relegated to their own insular chambers, judges who go to the bench with bad habits or unhelpful demeanors tend to persist in them. This can be damaging to the way justice is perceived (and done).

I'm speaking here of the trial judges, who preside alone and who need not concern themselves with what happens outside their individual palace walls. They can set peculiar and eccentric individual rules for their own courtrooms. Some judges demand you never stray from the lectern. Or that you don't drink water from a bottle. Or that you always ask permission before approaching a witness. Or that you never thank the court (seriously). It's sometimes difficult to remember which thing will tick off which judge. (Judges who sit on courts of appeals—like justices on the Supreme Court—do their courtroom work in panels, so they can see and observe and learn from colleagues over time.)

I don't mean to overstate the problem. Part of a judge's work is to write legal opinions, and every judge reads countless opinions written by others in addition to authoring their own. So that is a continuing learning process. But behavior in the courtroom is important too.

As I've said, judges are masters and commanders of the courtroom. They set the tone, from the time of the defendant's first appearance. Everyone looks up to the judge. This is literally true because the judge sits at an elevated level on the bench, swathed in a black robe and armed with a wooden gavel. Everyone stands when the judge enters and again when the judge leaves. The stage is always set for respect and deference. What each judge does with this authoritative prestige varies.

Some judges do not appreciate their unique power to legitimize a proceeding or to delegitimize it.

Let me offer an example.

Many judges begin court proceedings by heartily acknowledging only the lawyers—"Good morning, Ms. Prosecutor. And good morning, Mr. Defense Lawyer." Very convivial and very respectful. And then, looking at no one in particular, the judge says, "I note the presence of the defendant." That is a formal nod to the defendant's constitutional right to assist in his defense and participate in every meaningful proceeding, done so that the court stenographer will place it on the record. As if noting the presence of a cactus. It may seem like a small thing, but it goes a long way toward undermining the dignity of the person who is the reason everyone is there—the defendant. The defendant is the only one whose liberty is at risk, the only one who will be judged, the only one whose entire life and existence are in peril.

The former chief judge in my district, Loretta A. Preska, and some others did it differently. They did it better. Judge Preska was always immaculate, coiffed, and magisterial bordering on regal. I appeared in her courtroom many, many times. Her proceedings were always formal but friendly. She also invariably began with a smiling "Good morning, Ms. Prosecutor" and "Good morning, Mr. Defense Lawyer." Then she would turn to the defendant—the reason for our presence—and say with a smile, "Good morning, Mr. Defendant." She treated that person like a human being, someone worthy of respect and dignity. We forget that. Prosecutors can forget it. Judges forget it too. But for there to be overall trust in the system, for there to be faith that everyone is getting a fair shake, not only must the rules be good, but people have to behave in ways that respect other people's humanity and dignity.

It is just a pleasantry. There are more important things, I suppose. But I have often wondered what that human defendant is supposed to think about his place in the system and the fairness of the process when he cannot get even the simple courtesy of a "good morning" from the presiding judge. Does he feel invisible? Can he trust the proceedings? It is alienating and unnecessarily so, and small diminishments like that undermine confidence in justice.

There is a lot of shape-shifting in the courtroom. We exalt the judge and dehumanize the defendant. But neither cuffs nor robes change the truth that both are human beings.

A judge can get a bit too involved in the proceedings, provide a bit too much running color commentary, act more like an announcer than an umpire.

At the end of the summer of 2018, the country was closely following the federal criminal trial of President Trump's 2016 campaign manager Paul Manafort. It was interesting for many reasons—for the defendant's close association with a sitting president, for one thing. But it was notable also for the amount of attention the judge received. He was a much-talked-about figure and conspicuous character in the play. That is the judge's right, just as a film auteur has the right to cast himself in his own film. Typically, that kind of ego is a mistake (although there are exceptions; Orson Welles did star in his greatest film, *Citizen Kane*).

The presiding judge in the Manafort case was T. S. Ellis III, a seventy-eight-year-old Reagan appointee, with degrees from Princeton, Harvard, and Oxford, as well as an advanced degree in Curmudgeonry. As *The New York Times* observed during the trial, Judge Ellis "has routinely broken in on questioning, limited admission of evidence and exhorted lawyers to 'expedite'—all the while entertaining spectators with humorous asides about his age, his wife, his Navy past, his lack of an email address, the jury's lunch menu, split infinitives and the noise produced by a machine intended to keep bench conferences from being overheard."

In the view of some, judges—notwithstanding their title and place of work—should not be "holding court." But people possessed of wit, judges included, like to wield it, especially to captive audiences.

How to manage a judge who wants to be the center of attention and insert himself unduly into the proceedings?

Judge Ellis, to his credit, did possess some self-awareness. He said at one point, "I am a Caesar in my own Rome," duly and humbly noting, "It's a pretty small Rome." Like some other judges, he bestrode his small world like a colossus. There is a certain proprietary affect that permeates the judiciary. Judges say this is *my* courtroom. There is a whole pecking order, determined by seniority, in how courtrooms are assigned. Junior judges wait eagerly in the queue for better courtrooms. The competition for superior courtroom assignments in SDNY by life-tenured judges is not unlike the angling for spacious corner offices in any law firm or company. Comfort and status matter to everyone, it turns out.

Even before the Manafort trial commenced, Judge Ellis put on an angry display. In a tirade excitedly seized upon by Manafort's supporters as a sign that Judge Ellis would soon throw the whole case out, Ellis questioned the scope of the special counsel's authority. From the bench, he intoned, "What we don't want in this country is we don't want anyone with unfettered power. So it's unlikely you're going to persuade me that the special prosecutor has unlimited powers to do anything he or she wants." The special counsel had not argued any such thing. The judge vented but denied the defense motion to dismiss the indictment, and the case sped to trial.

Ellis sparred with the advocates. He belittled. He lost his temper. He mused aloud. These are not the hallmarks of a good referee. Judges do better in the background. When a judge becomes famous for a trial he is presiding over, that's usually a bad sign. See, for example, Judge Lance Ito in the O. J. Simpson trial. The best judges are not scene-stealers, because scene-stealing can look like advocacy and, unlike the prosecutor and defense lawyer, the judge is never to be an advocate for a side.

Judge Ellis picked on the prosecution team especially. That included reminding prosecutors to answer with "yes" instead of "yeah" or "yup." Fair enough.

But it got so contentious that there was a back-and-forth about . . . facial expressions. He told them during the first week of trial to "rein in their facial expressions."

JUDGE ELLIS: Look at me when you're talking to me.

PROSECUTOR ANDRES: I'm sorry, Judge, I was.

ELLIS: No, you weren't. You were looking down.

ANDRES: Because I don't want to get in trouble for some facial expression. I don't want to get yelled at again by the court for having some facial expression when I'm not doing anything wrong, but trying my case.

Bizarrely, at one point, Judge Ellis accused Greg Andres, a stoic and seasoned prosecutor, of crying in court.

ELLIS: Well, I understand how frustrated you are. In fact, there's tears in your eyes right now.

ANDRES: There are not tears in my eyes, Judge.

ELLIS: Well, they're watery. Look, I want you to focus sharply on what you need to prove—to prove the crime. And I don't understand what a lot of these questions have to do with it.

Andres had put the Bonanno family crime boss Vincent Basciano behind bars and had a security detail for a time because of credible death threats. This was not his first—or tenth—rodeo. He was not apt to have tears in his eyes.

At the same time, Ellis did show some additional disarming self-awareness. He said to the parties, "Judges should be patient. They made a mistake when they confirmed me."

This antic behavior is sometimes viewed warmly by jurors and journalists alike—this effort to break up the monotony, to puncture the sterile air, to move things along, to relieve the drag of the day. Spectators delight in judicial badgering of advocates and witnesses. The lawyers, of course, detest it. It adds obstacles and increases stress and unpredictability. Lawyers are like financial markets: they love stability and hate uncertainty. How is the judge going to rule on this piece of evidence? Will it depend on his mood? His whim? Will he forget what he said yesterday, reverse his own favorable ruling?

Finally came an issue of importance. Prosecutors called to the stand an expert witness who had been in the courtroom for the trial proceedings after getting express permission from the judge on day one. Typically, a judge will exclude testifying witnesses from the courtroom so they can't tailor their testimony. For this reason, prosecutors asked explicitly for an exemption for their expert. When Ellis realized the expert had not been excluded, he exploded.

Prosecutors reminded him that he had approved it on the first day and would "check the transcript."

The government nonetheless earned a sharp reprimand, in front of the jury.

After this episode, prosecutors filed a motion with the court requesting that the judge explain to the jury that the prosecution hadn't done anything wrong, noting that the judge's action left a "negative impression" of the Mueller team. This was a thumb on the scale: "The Court's sharp reprimand of government counsel in front of the jury on August 8 was . . . erroneous. And, while mistakes are a natural part of the trial process, the mistake here prejudiced the government."

Ellis, upon reflection and a review of the record, agreed. And he was contrite. He told the jury, "Put aside any criticism."

Chastened, Judge Ellis also said this in open court, perhaps his truest words: "This robe doesn't make me anything other than human." Headstrong judges can be humbled too.

Throughout the ordeal and Judge Ellis's outbursts, the prosecutors stuck to their guns, stood up to him, called him out when he was wrong, and just tried their case. With respect to the expert witness issue, they secured a correction of the record, a rare apology, and an even more rare admission of fallibility.

Paul Manafort was convicted on eight counts. Shortly thereafter, he pled guilty to another set of charges before a second scheduled trial in Washington, D.C. The prosecutors did their job. Even when a judge has misbehaved or misremembered or misrepresented, if the lawyers keep their heads down, do their job, follow the rules, the just and right result can still prevail. That is the power of our justice system.

Sometimes, if the moment is right, even in the most tense standoff with a judge, standing up for yourself with a quick human (and humorous) reaction can disarm the court and advance your cause.

Here are two quick examples from before my time in the SDNY.

Judge Kevin Duffy was appointed to the bench at the astonishingly young age of thirty-nine and had grown over decades, perhaps out of boredom, into one of the most curmudgeonly judges on the bench. He could treat lawyers in his courtroom like a cat might toy with a terrified mouse. One day an AUSA was examining a witness and veered into a line of questioning that the judge believed violated one of his rulings. He erupted. In open court, his voice cut the air: "If you do that again, I'm going to have your balls!" The courtroom went silent. This was a peculiar threat, insofar as the prosecutor was female. The AUSA looked back at the judge and replied, "You know, Judge, if you can find 'em you can have 'em." The tension broke. The judge laughed. At that moment, she became one of Judge Duffy's favorites.

Here's another story: Andrew McCarthy, a headstrong prosecutor (later a strident opinion writer for *National Review*), was in a spirited exchange with Judge Whitman Knapp one day during trial. The jury was not present. At one point, Judge Knapp snapped, "Basically, Mr. McCarthy, your position is fuck you."

"No," Andy quickly corrected him. "My position is fuck you, *Your Honor.*"

Judge Knapp laughed.

The key point in these stories is that the people laughed. And thank goodness. Laughter and jokes in some environments, say, in a high-stakes trial or in an operating room or on a military mission, may seem horrendously off-key, inappropriate, and disrespectful. I hope that is not always so. The reason? Every pressure cooker needs a release valve.

There is a theatrical quality to the courtroom. People analogize trials to plays or movies, prosecutors believing they are the directors and principal actors in the production. But there's another artificiality, maybe a necessary one. Notwithstanding the moments of levity described above, for the most part judges display an aura of utter seriousness in open court. Good judges feel some natural pressure not to be themselves. Not to be too casual, too relaxed, because every proceeding has weight. Every proceeding is solemn to some degree. They sit elevated and robed, gavel at the ready. You can forget that they are just people. Sometimes I think *they* forget.

When I was a young prosecutor doing a tour in the White Plains office of SDNY, there was an especially officious magistrate judge, Mark D. Fox. He barked at the prosecutors. He hewed militantly to the clock at the back of his courtroom, which was often kept a few minutes fast. This meant that if you were right on time, you were late.

Just into my second year in the office, I had a narcotics trial scheduled for a March Monday in White Plains. The Friday before, I finished drafting my opening statement late in the evening and needed a break. I decided to take Dalya to dinner at a nice restaurant in Union Square close to where we lived. Afterward, around 11:30 p.m., on the way home we stopped at the Chase bank ATM machine on the corner of Fourteenth Street and Fifth Avenue. We were two blocks from home. Dalya was seven and a half months pregnant. Suddenly two men grabbed us from behind on Fifteenth Street—just yards from our doorway—and pushed us down several concrete steps leading into another building. They had seen me take out money and now demanded it at knifepoint. I suffered a concussion and a hairline fracture of the skull, and Dalya went into contractions that evening. Everything turned out fine. Dalya was okay. I recovered. Beautiful Maya was born healthy six weeks later. I missed a week of work.

One day that week, Dalya brought up the mail. In the pile was the most affecting note I received during the entire ordeal. It was handwritten on personal stationery. It was warm and kind. It was from Judge Fox. No other judge—and I knew many—sent such a personal and heartfelt note. I carried it in my briefcase for a long time. As a reminder of something. As a reminder of a small kindness of course. But also, I think, as one of many reminders over a lifetime that everyone is a human being, judges included.

Once I became intensely frustrated with a judge before whom we were trying a tough white-collar case. I felt we were being treated unfairly, that many rulings were wrong, that there was a thumb on the scale. We considered moving to recuse the judge if there was a hung jury and a retrial. The defendant was acquitted. Against my good judgment, at a closed and off-the-record office dinner not long after, I made a harsh joke about the competence of the judge. It was not intended to be made public beyond the room, and it was part of an attaboy comment to the trial team who had worked very hard and felt stymied. My remark ended up in the press. Mortified, I wrote a note of apology to the judge. I also sought advice and counsel from some other judges about how I might make amends.

I went to see one of the most respected judges in SDNY. We talked in her chambers one afternoon, and she was reflective and frank. She was not unduly critical of me, but she made clear I had made a huge and hurtful error. And she said something that has stayed with me. She said that while judges have considerable authority in the courtroom, they are fairly powerless in another respect. They are powerless to counter public criticism, no matter how unfair. This judge I was visiting had been raked over the coals by a newspaper editorial page time and time again, recently and in rough language. But tradition and ethics render a federal judge virtually silent outside the courtroom.

"How do you handle it?" I asked. The judge smiled.

She said, "Well, Preet. What I do is I call over some dear friends and we sit on my couch and we drink a big bottle of white wine. And then I go to work the next day. Like any other day."

I have been awed by judges, and also disappointed by them. The former experience has been far and away more common. We ask a lot of them. We ask them to do justice, even when the most just outcome—in sentencing, for example—may be unknowable. We ask them to pass judgment on other people. We ask them to decide human fates, withhold liberty, and disrupt livelihoods. We ask them to leave their emotions at the door, to wear permanent poker faces, to model perfect behavior, to endure public criticism in silence, to get it right always.

They are just human beings, though we ask them to be a little superhuman.

The Trial

A crisis persists in public discourse and political debate. It is coarse and vicious and tone-deaf. Truth is a victim of self-interest and extreme tribalism, as are decorum and respect. The very notion of civility—and even the need for it—are hotly debated. Meanwhile, political tribes insulate themselves more than ever. More than ever, people seek out only like-minded voices, only comfortable viewpoints, avoiding challenge, debate, and inconvenient facts. They stick to their side no matter what the evidence; openness to changing your mind is not only rare but seen as weak and disloyal somehow. Fewer people than ever adhere to Cromwell's admonition— *think ye may be wrong.* Meanwhile, when debates are joined—on cable television or on the internet—name-calling, innuendo, and character assassination are more favored tactics than logic and reason.

It may be hard to believe, but criminal trials have something to teach us. Why? Because they are object lessons in persuasion, truth, and even civility.

Criminal trials are remarkable, and they should inspire awe. But they are funny things. We say public trials are about finding the truth, and while this is correct, there are certain paradoxes. Criminal trials are, for example, suffused with elaborate concealments. We hide a lot from the jury. We hide the defendant's criminal history; we hide the potential punishment; we suppress certain evidence. If the defendant is dangerous and incarcerated, we hide that from the jury as well; the defendant is led into the courtroom and unshackled before the jury can see his bondage.

We conceal the lawyers' personal views about guilt and innocence, about the credibility of the witnesses, though this is often obvious. We don't let the jury hear the legal arguments made at sidebar, don't tell them how much lawyers are being paid.

We don't advise the jury—because it is not relevant—whether the judge was appointed by a Democrat or a Republican, whether the prosecutor has donated to Republicans or Democrats, even in a public corruption trial, again, because it's not relevant. We don't say whether the judge is reversed on appeal often or never. We tell jurors not to educate themselves in any way, to do no outside research on the case or on the parties. This is to ensure, among other things, their minds are not poisoned by unfiltered opinion, false information, or prejudicial facts about the defendant or the witnesses.

There are subtler concealments also as the participants in the courtroom resort to a kind of acting, maintaining poker faces in the wake of damaging testimony or harmful rulings. A scene from the movie *Liar Liar* illustrates the point comically. In the film, Jim Carrey plays a prevaricating trial lawyer whose son makes a wish that for twenty-four hours his father not tell a lie. Lo and behold, the wish comes true, and for a very long day Carrey is straitjacketed by brutal honesty. At one point, his character objects to some testimony in court, and the judge asks the basis for the objection. Carrey, unable to lie, answers, "Because it's devastating to my case!"

"Overruled," says the judge.

This prompts more honesty from Carrey: "Good call!"

In the end, justice (and truth) are served by good-faith concealments. Consider the blind grading of exams: the identity of the students is hidden from professors to strip away potential bias; the evaluation is based solely on merit. Or take medical drug trials, done blindly; they are an effort to prevent bias and corrupt considerations from infecting the search for truth. This type of secondary hiding is in the service of a primary goal—fairness. Insisting that the evidence be relevant and that certain arguments are off-limits is vital to producing a just result. We blind you to irrelevancy to train your eyes on the truth.

The courtroom is governed, for the most part, by hard rules. Not norms, but *rules*. Rules of evidence, of procedure, of professional ethics. Just as in a competitive sport like boxing or football, there are concrete rules—no punching below the belt or holding the receiver, for example. In the courtroom, the rules are enforceable by the judge and punishable by contempt, bar sanction, or adverse ruling. The consequences for an intentional lie by an attorney at trial are dire and, if serious enough, existential because you can be disbarred. There is, of course, considerable discretion in flagging an infraction, especially in close cases, just as with sports umpires and referees. But the rules matter, and brazen violations are seldom tolerated; gross breaches of rules and protocols will be not only challenged by the participants but condemned by outside observers. Radically different from how debates unfold in real life.

Here's the other thing. The rules of court are designed to bring closure. There is an end: a judgment or a verdict (or a settlement) always looms. There is a *decision;* there is finality. Other kinds of proceedings—even if they are governed by a gavel or a set of procedural rules—are left wanting in this way. Take Congress, for example. Congressional hearings held on matters other than legislation (on which some finality comes with a vote) are deeply unsatisfying; they generate little light. Members can ramble, embrace irrelevancies, attack character, make speeches; witnesses also can filibuster, evade, run out the clock.

All successful prosecutors tell compelling stories; it's what convincing persuaders do. You can have facts and figures and statistics, but they are powerless and unpersuasive if not woven into a compelling narrative, an understandable story. Good prosecutors know not to present their cases as checklists. Trials are not box-checking exercises.

It surprises people to learn that a criminal's *motive*—which is what books and movies and police procedurals sometimes obsess over—is generally *not* an element of the crime. Intent, as I've said before, is relevant to guilt and often hard to prove, but intent and motive are distinct concepts. Intent is that you meant to do the thing—pull the trigger, kill your victim—that it wasn't an accident or a mistake; motive is *why* you did it.

Why someone robbed a bank or killed a person or cooked the books is most often legally irrelevant to guilt. But it is deeply relevant to the jury who must decide guilt. Without addressing motive, the story is incomplete, and incomplete stories are less compelling. That's why prosecutors talk about greed and power and jealousy and revenge, not because the statute demands it, but because jurors need to *understand* the case, not just in their brains, but in their guts, so they can carry out the terrifying duty of rendering a verdict. That's also why good prosecutors use anecdotes and analogies and, occasionally, metaphors. And, throughout, simple language.

Sometimes young prosecutors have to be reminded of this.

The same principle is true for the defense. The defense story can be as simple as this: the government, in its zeal, got the wrong guy.

Or this: the cooperators lied and framed my guy to save their own skins.

Or this (as we will see): it was just a father helping his son.

This is not to say you throw logic in the trash bin; stories have (and need) internal logic too. Stories propel and teach. If the defense has a good, easily understandable story, then the prosecutor needs a better one.

At trial, the trick for the prosecution is figuring out how—consistent with the constraints—to best get your point across. At the inquiry and accusation phases, you are mostly proving the case to yourself, hopefully after a rigorous, open-minded, unbiased internal review. Presumably you have convinced yourself beyond doubt of the defendant's guilt. You are persuaded you have the right person, the right charges, the right evidence.

But now all that remains is the small matter of proving guilt to *other people*. They are your jurors. You also, of course, need to persuade the judge you have a case.

This requires putting yourself in someone else's shoes. And it requires anticipating other people's arguments. The strength of the evidence, the excellence of the investigation, the persuasiveness of the pretrial motions, all shape the outcome as well, but how the case is presented in the courtroom matters a great deal, especially in cases that are close or complicated by emotional issues.

It requires more than cursory understanding of the opposing view; you have to put yourself in your adversary's shoes. You must look at the world from her perspective, her belief system, her biases and interests and goals. Understand her point of view, her assumptions, as well as or better than you know your own. Supreme Court justice Felix Frankfurter, who served as an AUSA in SDNY once upon a time, reminiscing about the U.S. Attorney he served, Henry Stimson, recalled that Stimson "very early instilled in me that you must prepare the other fellow's case at least as well as he prepares it, usually better, so that there are no surprises, no nothing."

Prepare the other fellow's case at least as well as your own. Such preparation can be complicated. It can be hard to know how to respond to the emotional story lines of your adversary.

In 2015, the two most significant New York public corruption trials in a generation were looming in SDNY. One was against the Speaker of the New York State Assembly, Sheldon Silver, for various violations of federal law. The other was against the New York State Senate majority leader, Dean Skelos, for similar breaches of his duty of honest services to his constituents. Both cases were set to go to trial at almost the same time at the end of 2015. In the summer of that year, as we thought about how to present the cases effectively, I grew concerned, not about the sufficiency of the evidence or the relevant law. The legal cases were strong (at least until the Supreme Court changed the law after the first set of trial convictions). The complication was that we had charged Dean Skelos in a conspiracy with his own son.

In a nutshell, we alleged that Senator Skelos—one of the three most powerful people in the state, one of the three men in a room—extorted various businesses to either hire his son, Adam, in a no-show job or otherwise pay him money he didn't earn. We had not only documentary evidence and compelling testimony but wiretaps too. There was one especially helpful recorded call. At a time when our scrutiny of corruption was well-known, Adam Skelos, increasingly nervous about all the heat, called his father to complain: "It's like fucking Preet Bharara is listening to every fucking phone call. It's just fucking frustrating." Well, not every phone call, but we were definitely listening to that one. This is what we call powerful evidence of consciousness of guilt.

On the one hand, the evidence was strong. On the other hand, the defense would argue that the case was much ado about nothing, that Dean Skelos was just a good father trying to help his son. So, the argument—the defense story line—was this: Dean Skelos, the most powerful man in the state senate, was just being a good dad. I for one thought this was nonsense, but maybe this had to do with my own upbringing; my strict Indian-immigrant dad would have sooner disowned me than put the arm on other people to help me inappropriately.

But would such a defense resonate, as some worried it might, or backfire, as I expected? Though the facts and the law were on our side, trials are about more than that. They're about commonsense justice. They're about presenting a narrative that ordinary people will find compelling enough to vote to convict someone. Prosecutors in particular rely on jurors' common sense, their everyday pragmatism and humanity. But given the unusual nature of this case and the father-son wrinkle, it was conceivable that jurors' personal experiences would cut against us. The universal impulse for all parents is to help their children—even if they are ne'er-do-wells. And so, unlike our usual legalistic discussions about the scope of the bribery statute, the definition of "official action," or the admissibility of certain proof, these conversations around the coffee table in my office devolved into a debate about competing philosophies of parenting. Hand-holding and pampering your child versus tough love and self-reliance. Some parents give their kids everything they want, and some parents make their kids earn it. In the real world, to each his own, but at this trial we had a worry that instead of focusing on the facts and the law and the abuse of power, the trial would become a referendum on the parenting choices of an undeniably loving father.

To the extent a trial is about convincing other people of your point of view, it is really about putting yourself in the shoes of other people, anticipating the intellectual and emotional reactions of other people to the facts and arguments you present. Maybe I wasn't doing that. Maybe I looked at the situation too much from my own perspective and background. Based on how I grew up, the idea that Dean Skelos was being a good parent was preposterous.

For the first time I could remember, I wasn't sure we had a handle on the message, a beat on the right story. Then, a radical thought. I asked Ed Tyrrell, our office manager, to swing by. Ed was much more than our long-serving office manager. He was the glue in that office. He handled the staff, the budget, and hundreds of sundry needs to support the mission of the place. Ed was friend, confidant, coach, and maybe the most beloved person in SDNY. He sported a gray-and-white beard, an eternally cheerful demeanor, and the low resting pulse of a compulsive runner. If you ever asked Ed how he was, he didn't say "okay" or "fine." He roared, "Great!" Ed could be tough too, but mostly he was a walking morale boost.

I explained now to Ed that we were talking about the Skelos case and asked what did he think about our hiring jury consultants to help game out the father-son defense. It felt unseemly somehow, plus I wasn't sure we could afford it. Ed reminded me that the last time the office did so was for the trial of Martha Stewart, years earlier. Ed said the budget was ample, and so we did it.

That summer, a load of us showed up at a nondescript building in midtown Manhattan early on a Friday morning and took the elevator up to a windowless suite of offices where several rooms were retrofitted either as mock courtrooms or as jury deliberation rooms, miked for sound and with one-way internal windows. One AUSA presented the prosecution's case in abbreviated form, and another presented for the Skeloses—complete with opening statement, presentation of evidence, and closing. It consumed half a day. It occurred to me then, by the way, that though it was a lot of extra work, it might be useful in every case to make prosecutors prepare the jury addresses of the adversary. Literally, *prepare the other fellow's case at least as well as your own.*

The prosecution summarized all the corrupt acts Skelos performed in favor of Adam: how he put the arm on three businesses; how Dean got Adam a job for $78,000 per year (plus health benefits) at one insurance company, even though Adam sold no insurance and didn't even have a license; how Adam threatened to "bash in the skull" of a supervisor for daring to question why Adam claimed to work thirty-five hours and only worked *one;* how Dean shook down a real estate company to send Adam $20,000; and on and on.

The mock defense attacked the various allegations but also argued that the case was about a committed father's helping his child.

After the simulated trial, a group of us eavesdropped from leather chairs, through the one-way glass, on the focus group's "deliberations." There were indeed flashes of sympathy for the proposition that Dean was just a good father, but there was also great hostility. Some "jurors" reminded others that Adam was not an adolescent or dependent child but rather a fully grown thirty-three-year-old man with a job and a decent income, seeing the conduct less as loving parenting and more as the abuse of power that it was. This was encouraging. One older and well-spoken juror, who worked as a supervisor at a transportation authority, stood up and quietly but stridently said, "Even though I had the power to do so, I would never have called anyone to get my son a job because that's just not what you do." I had the feeling that for him this was not merely a matter of personal ethics but a heartfelt principle of parenting.

There was no great revelation or epiphany from the exercise, just confirmation that there would be the subtext of parental love nibbling away at the otherwise inexorable logic of guilt. And so, it was not an accident that the prosecutors went out of their way, at the real trial, to describe Adam as a grown man and an "able-bodied adult son." They worked hard to remind the jury that Dean was no ordinary parent, that he had enormous power, and that if he had wanted to help his son in his personal capacity, terrific. They also took care to acknowledge and respect Dean's obvious love for his son, not to dismiss it, denigrate it, or doubt it. As Jason Masimore said in the rebuttal, "No one questions the love a father has for a son and no one questions the love this father has for this son. But loving your son is not an excuse for committing crimes." And then he went on, perhaps channeling some of the focus group's reactions: "The argument itself is offensive."

Dean and Adam Skelos were convicted twice on all counts (a retrial was necessary after the U.S. Supreme Court changed the law of what constitutes corrupt official action after the first trial). In the end, the continued emphasis on a father's love did not work at either trial and backfired at sentencing. They were sentenced to fifty-one and forty-eight months, respectively.

As I've said, trial lawyers, perhaps more than any other professionals, must understand what is going on in the heads and hearts of other people. You can't put your head in the sand, can't use sophistry, faulty logic, insults, taunts, non sequiturs. You are forced to worry about your credibility with people who are not already on your team—like the judge and the jury.

That sounds basic and obvious, doesn't it? But consider how radically different this is from much of modern social interaction, especially with respect to debates of the day. In regular life, you can shut out opposing views. You can swim in your own controversy-free lane at all times. You can avoid people with different views, different backgrounds, different experiences. You don't have to hear them, read them, see them, engage them. You can always just change the channel. I think too many people take advantage of their right to cloister, to live in their little echo chambers, to settle into small societies of like-minded souls, never taking the time to test and strengthen the rightness of their beliefs through searching inquiry, vigorous debate, and open dialogue.

There is no such luxury at a criminal trial. There you cannot hide in your self-absorbed bunker, especially if you are the
prosecutor. People are *paid* and obliged by *oath* and blessed by
the *Constitution*. To do what? To attack every single allegation
and argument you have made. And to do it with great zeal. So
in that world you have to engage with your critics. And you
must engage using facts, truth, and logic. You cannot just say, "I
believe this" or "These are my alternative facts." Honest engagement is the essence of the job.

And it is the most exhilarating thing in the world.

We malign lawyers as litigious and combative, often deservedly so, but I vastly prefer the spirit of respectful engagement
and combat to what we have now in so many parts of society—
siloed self-congratulation, self-affirmation, without risk of challenge or dissent or real and respectful debate.

Now, in order to meet arguments, you have to consider flaws
in your own arguments, which means you sometimes have to
concede things. Oh, the thrill of a concession. When was the
last time you saw a politician or a TV debater concede a point,
refine an argument on the fly in the face of a well-articulated
objection?

What is the key to the courtroom? Preparation, command,
eloquence, sure. Those all matter. But the key to the courtroom
is credibility. Credibility is what makes your story believable.
Concessions are a sign of strength, not weakness, because they
enhance your credibility. It's always better to volunteer a weakness than to have your adversary point it out. I would always
advise this: If you have an incriminating conversation but no
tape, say so. If there are discrepancies in the testimony of your
witnesses, say so. If your cooperator is likely to come off like
a jerk, say so.

Defense lawyers know this. Renowned criminal defense lawyer Ben Brafman recently represented one of the most disliked
defendants in recent times, Martin Shkreli. Shkreli had been

charged with defrauding his investors but earned special status as "America's most hated man" because he hiked up the price of Daraprim, a previously affordable drug used to treat patients with HIV/AIDS, by as much as 5,000 percent—an astronomical rise that left many unable to afford the lifesaving medication. It didn't help that the "Pharma Bro" responded to any criticism with dismissive snark, like, for example, harassing female journalists and bragging on social media that he'd raise the price on more drugs, if he could. He was thoroughly detestable.

Brafman made it a point to concede that his client's personality was wanting. He said, at sentencing, that he sometimes wanted to punch his own client in the face. That rude concession built credibility, created some separation from his client, forged a connection with the court, and gave Brafman more space to argue on his client's behalf. Many defense lawyers fight every point, every allegation, even those that are irrefutable, irrelevant, ambiguous, or could backfire. This is not strength; it is weakness.

How does failure to consider the other person manifest itself at trial? Principally, I think, through unclear communication.

I have often said this to young lawyers: Much of the time, your most important job as a lawyer is not to talk; it is to listen. You want to be a good lawyer? Work on how you speak. You want to be a *great* lawyer? Work on how you listen. You could substitute "leader" for "lawyer" in both of those sentences and express an even more universal truth. You know what is the most important advice we gave for conducting an effective direct examination? Listen to your witness. For cross-examination? Listen to your witness.

When I took a class on trial practice as a young third-year law student at Columbia Law School, my professors were SDNY judge Michael Mukasey and AUSA Dan Nardello. A quarter century later, I still remember a pointed (and off-color) true story they told us about the critical importance of listening to your witness, no matter how much you have prepared. Here's how I remember it:

There's a sentencing hearing for a defendant who ran a halfway house where he sexually abused young boys. The AUSA dutifully prepares a victim to testify and stresses the importance of telling the court exactly what the defendant said and did, even if vulgar. He tells the victim not to sanitize anything. They go over the testimony many times because the witness is understandably anxious about testifying in open court.

So now the hearing is on, everyone is wearing a suit, and the judge is there in a robe. The young victim-witness nervously takes the stand. The prosecutor asks what happened, and the witness describes the events surrounding his abuse, how he was alone with the defendant, how the defendant unzipped his pants. And the prosecutor asks, "What happened next?"

In that moment, the witness—sanitizing—says, "The defendant asked me to perform oral sex on him." But that's not how they had prepared it.

And the prosecutor, who has stopped listening to the witness, robotically asks his pre-written follow-up question: "And what happened after the defendant told you to suck his cock?"

Failure to listen is fatal and can do more than just embarrass you in federal court.

I am an unabashed admirer of trials and what they represent. Public trials in America are, I think, rightly exalted not just as exhilarating exercises for practitioners but as important expressions and guarantors of democracy for the general public. Trials, after all, are showcase moments for our legal system and for the rule of law; they fulfill the requirement that justice must not only be done but also be *seen* to be done. In many ways, trials are touchstones of our democracy, in its most direct and tactile form. When trials vanish, citizenship also suffers. It is at trial where ordinary people are, for a time, pressed into extraordinary service.

Law professor Paul Butler has put it this way: "Nobody does trials like Americans. We made it an art form. It's almost as fundamental a part of our culture as jazz or rock 'n' roll." I suppose that is right. I'm a big movie fan, so I shudder to think what our cinematic legacy would be if Hollywood screenwriters and directors could not place at the heart of so many films the quintessentially American courtroom clash. Not many people would go see a movie called 12 Angry Mediators. And Arbitration at Nuremberg doesn't sound like a blockbuster.

But there is something else grand about trials and the way they are meant to be conducted. No one much looks to lawyers and lawyering as a model for anything these days, but I think the example of the American criminal trial has something to teach us more broadly—about debate and disagreement and truth and justice.

At a time of headstrong faith that your side is always right and the other side is always wrong, the court of law offers a worthwhile ideal for finding truth and justice generally.

In the courtroom, almost uniquely, the quest for truth depends on evidence and on facts; it relies on examination and cross-examination; it abhors assumption and insinuation.

It relies on the right of both sides to present arguments and to challenge arguments.

And it lets both sides do so, without fear of being shouted down or shut down—so long as the presentations are fairly made, with respect and decorum, and so long as they do not make undue appeals to prejudice or fear or emotion. Neither side is permitted to lie or mispresent, to suggest truth isn't truth, or they will be shut down. You can't call your adversary a "low IQ person" or name-call; you can't argue the prosecution is political; and you can't make sweeping biased statements, like suggesting that Mexicans are rapists or that some witnesses came from "shithole countries." The courtroom rules force truth and prohibit garbage.

And at every phase of the trial, members of the jury are admonished repeatedly—to do what? To keep an open mind. Every day the judge reminds the jury to keep an open mind, to remember the presumption of innocence—until all sides have been heard, until all facts have been offered, until all fair arguments have been made.

In our system, jurors can have distasteful views. They can hate the way the prosecutor looks or dresses. They can take notes, not take notes. Of course, jurors can get kicked off for various infractions—from showing up consistently late to researching facts about the case on the internet. But one basis for removal is notable: a refusal to deliberate.

This is to say the system recognizes—as perhaps society should—that you're entitled to your view but only if you have taken the time to engage with others about it; listened to an opposing opinion; grappled with the issue in some meaningful sense; made at least a show of open-mindedness; given others the respect of being heard. And if you don't, you get the boot.

If you announce your decision before any deliberation, if you close your eyes and ears to all debate, if you physically remove yourself from the discussion, then you are not worthy of being a decision maker in the case. Your view won't be counted, and you will be sent home.

This is the way our law has determined to best discover truth and achieve justice.

There is something special in that; you wonder whether it provides some guidance for the way to search for truth and justice in our society as well.

If society operated that way—with respectful and open-minded debate and full engagement—we can wonder whether we would have better laws and better policies instead of just bad blood.

———

As I've said, trial is about effective storytelling, about convincing other people of what you've already convinced yourself. It is about having enough empathy for the human decision makers—the jury—to know how to express your arguments in the most compelling, understandable, and persuasive way possible. Sometimes you worry about a nagging weakness that the defense can exploit because there's a superficial appeal to their story.

Here's one example: In our first groundbreaking insider-trading trial, I remember we struggled with how to undercut one expected superficial defense. In the case of Raj Rajaratnam's hedge fund, the Galleon Group, we had substantial evidence that scores of stock trades were based on material nonpublic information, on illegal tips. It was simultaneously true, however, that thousands and thousands of other Galleon trades were in fact perfectly legitimate and lawful, based on real market research. The defense, we expected, would wave those reams of research in front of the jury to declare how robust their analysis had been. "Look at all this research!" the defense would shout. Piles of it. Reams of it. They would have research coming out of their pores.

It's a flimsy argument if you scrutinize it, of course—that you often drive under the speed limit does not prove that you don't sometimes speed—but it's not a terrible *story*. Good stories can overwhelm good arguments; the ideal is to have both a good argument *and* a good story. In the spring of 2011, we sat around a table in a windowless conference room on the fifth floor with the trial team, trying to figure out a pithy retort to this story line. Meanwhile, trial approached. We were coming up empty.

Then, one day, the team was prepping an important cooperating witness. The lead AUSA was Jonathan Streeter, a sharp and curly-haired lawyer who also happened to be an accomplished water-skier. Jon put the witness through a mock cross-examination to prepare him for the onslaught he would face on the stand. (A bit of ironic trivia: the witness in this case about a perversion of the financial markets was named Adam Smith.) Jon channeled, with fervor, the defense story line about the research: *But you did research, didn't you? There was all this research, wasn't there?* Finally, exasperated but clear-eyed, Smith explained, "Look, at Galleon, we did our homework, but we cheated too."

That was it. Jon knew immediately that this was a gem for the opening statement, a simple and clear explanation for the jury: "They did their homework. But they cheated too." Only eight words, but eight words that packed a punch. Those eight words simultaneously conceded something (many trades were lawful and research based) and also posited something (other times they broke the law, like with Nvidia, Intel, and Intersil). It was both hammer and shield; it crystallized the issue. We hoped that every time the defense thundered about all that research, those eight words would ring in every juror's ears. Like the prosecutors said, sure, they did their homework, *but they cheated too.*

When you think about it, experience tells you that many high-profile cheaters do a lot of legitimate work. They cheat for the extra edge. The baseball star Barry Bonds was—even without any enhancement—one of the greatest players of his time. Lance Armstrong, same. They were colossally talented. They practiced and trained and worked hard. *They did their homework, but they cheated too.* Just like Raj Rajaratnam and the Galleon Group.

It worked.

Consider once more the case against Dean and Adam Skelos. In addition to the father-son defense, there was a superficially persuasive defense story that we fought to undercut.

As a reminder, the bulk of the case charged Dean Skelos with extortion; he extorted benefits and payments to his son from people who relied on his legislative good graces. But when laypeople think of extortion, they think of threats like those the mob makes—waving baseball bats and all of that. In the public corruption context, however, the crime is literally to commit "extortion under color of official right." That's simply a fancy way of saying bending someone to your will by virtue of the official governmental authority that you have. Rarely in the history of public corruption prosecutions are there direct threats. They aren't necessary. Why? Because the nature of raw political power is ever present in every discussion where favors are demanded. It is the ever-present elephant in the room.

The weekend before summations in the Skelos case, Joon Kim, Joan Loughnane, Dan Stein, and I gathered in the eighth-floor library with the trial team. I was anxious and interested to see how the summations were coming along after the case had been so well tried. Jason Masimore was slated to rebut. I peered at him from the head of the table and saw a sheepish grin come over his face. I wondered why. He said he was thinking about citing a poem during his rebuttal.

I gave him a skeptical look. Government summations are not platforms for poetry. Then Jason said the poem he intended to invoke was from a *children's* book. And not just any children's book, but a famous one called *Where the Sidewalk Ends* by Shel Silverstein. I had read it to my own children. I raised an eyebrow. I'm sure Jason worried that I would nix it. He passed me his draft rebuttal, which I read with his eyes on me. I looked back at him and smiled.

Finally I said, "I love it." Not because it was different or creative, but because it gave the jury a quick and concrete understanding of why Dean Skelos never needed to be explicit in his threats. And so we all gave him an enthusiastic thumbs-up. To me it showed a masterful understanding of what *other* people needed to understand, in an instant, the bogusness of the defense argument. It was a better story than their story. And it was more true.

Here's what Jason said at trial: "At the end of the book is a particular poem. And on one side of the page there is an illustration. And it's this little kid, happy little kid. And he's riding on top of this gigantic gorilla."

Jason described the imposing animal: "This thing is huge. It's giant. It's scary. Its knuckles are literally dragging on the ground. And the kid is on top of the gorilla in this book and he's smiling. He's happy." The child is having a ball riding on the gorilla's back, and he's on his way to school. And then Jason said, "But the gist of it is, and it's told from the kid's perspective, the gist of it is: Hey, ever since I started bringing my gorilla to school everyone has been really nice to me. Since I started bringing the gorilla to school, kids, they're bringing me presents. My teachers are letting me chew gum in class. They're saying great job. I'm allowed to cheat on my tests. And I'm getting all As ever since I brought my gorilla to school."

Jason asked the rhetorical question: "Why is this happening?" He gave the response: "They're all afraid that the gorilla is going to rip their arms off, and that's why he's getting As on his tests and all of that. And they should be scared of this gorilla because it has no business being in a school." Then Jason brought the point home: "It's like what you heard in this case. The gorilla in this case that you heard about, it's the power of the office of the senate majority leader." It was his power to make or break a business, to exercise his clout however he wanted.

The jury ate it up. Something about this smart, snappy metaphor—charmingly delivered—did the trick better than paragraphs of argument could have.

I had gone to many days of the trial and always sat unobtrusively in the back of the courtroom. Just after Jason's riff, a reporter sitting way in the front lifted his head, turned around, made direct eye contact with me, and nodded, as if to say, "That was something else." And it was.

It was the kind of advocacy that anyone's nine-year-old nephew could readily understand.

Three Men in a Room

There are many reasons why public speaking can be important for a U.S. Attorney. Federal prosecutors are supposed to not only hold people accountable for crimes committed but also prevent crime. Almost no one has the voice, mandate, and pulpit that federal prosecutors do, all of which can be used to reassure, explain, educate. There is a general lack of trust in government institutions (now more than ever), so it was important to me to adhere to the old maxim: justice must not only be done; it must be seen to be done. The public cares that there's a cop on the beat, that people will be held accountable for egregious crimes, and that the entire process is done openly and transparently. Sometimes that means speaking up on issues related to crime and public safety, issues that have real impact on people's lives.

I was tough at news conferences announcing criminal charges. I took seriously the possibility of deterring other people from committing the same crimes, especially white-collar crimes committed by smart and privileged people who should know better and whose cost-benefit analysis I thought we could influence by publicizing the prosecutions of their peers. Though I resorted to the occasional flourish, I was careful not to ad-lib, careful to hew to the publicly available facts. Every word I uttered in my prepared remarks, moreover, was vetted by my deputy, by the public affairs office, and by the career line prosecutors who had brought the charges; in fact, the lawyers on the case usually wrote the first draft.

I spoke often outside the context of standard arrest announce-ments too. I spoke about the opioid crisis because it was a cri-sis. I spoke about the gang crisis because it was a crisis. And I spoke about public corruption. Why? Because it was a crisis too. Nobody complains when a prosecutor rails against murder or robbery or drug trafficking or corporate fraud. I did not believe that the epidemic of corruption in Albany was worthy of soft-pedaling or less attention than other crimes. It was pervasive and grotesque. So I spoke about it. I spoke about it at conferences and at academic institutions.

Speaking about it—not just prosecuting it—I believe is what prompted Governor Andrew Cuomo to establish a corruption-fighting panel called the Moreland Commission, which was supposed to be dedicated to investigating corruption and pre-venting it. And when the governor prematurely and question-ably disbanded the Moreland Commission under suspicious circumstances, I spoke about that. And then we seized the More-land Commission files, continued its work, and opened up an investigation of its closure. I was already scheduled to be on a popular public radio program the day after we took the files, *The Brian Lehrer Show* on WNYC. And I didn't pull any punches. I said, "The plain facts are that it was disbanded before its time. Nine months may be the proper and natural gestation period for a child, but in our experience not the amount of time necessary for a public corruption prosecution to mature."

I make no apology for having been generally outspoken, for drawing attention to the problems of opioids or gangs or insider trading or public corruption. I stayed always within the four cor-ners of the public charging documents, didn't gild the lily. Was I sometimes sharp-edged and glib and sarcastic? Probably yes. It is perhaps preferable to be quieter. I can see the argument for that. It depends a bit on how one sees the job and its potential impact. Is it purely to prosecute or also to prevent? Also to edu-cate? Also to warn? Also to deter? The important thing was not to affect any particular defendant's right to a fair trial. Which I made sure I never did.

There is a speech I once gave, the morning after we charged the New York State Assembly Speaker Sheldon Silver, which drew significant attention and a sharp judicial rebuke.

The New York Law School CityLaw Breakfast speech in 2015 was long planned for January 23, 2015, well before I knew the precise date when we would charge Silver. I had a whole other speech ready on some topic I no longer remember. But it seemed odd to show up there and ignore our arrest just the day before of one of the most powerful men in New York State.

The night before the speech, Joon Kim and I went to the Odeon, a restaurant near the office, for a drink and a bite and to digest the day. It had been a significant one. We talked about not just the particular facts of the case we had unsealed against the assembly Speaker but also the political and power dynamic that enabled such deep corruption—the so-called three men in a room, who famously made all important decisions for the people of New York, mostly behind closed doors: Governor Andrew Cuomo, the state senate majority leader, Dean Skelos (whom we would arrest on corruption charges just weeks later), and the assembly Speaker, Sheldon Silver. We talked about the absurdity of it, the perversity of it, and also the comedy of it. I jotted down some notes from my conversation with Joon, making fun of this preposterous way of doing the people's business in New York.

Like lots of people, I was angry about this state of affairs. The senate ethics committee had never held a hearing. The legislature did no self-policing. In fact, a senate chief counsel once notoriously advised legislators to hand deliver their financial disclosure forms to avoid violating the federal mail fraud statute. As I have already mentioned, a New York state senator was more likely to be indicted than defeated at the polls. That was the landscape. Rather than attack the problem, politicians mostly attacked prosecutors, who were fellow public servants. Lots of people were angry about the three men in a room. But, of course, I was not just anyone. I was the U.S. Attorney who twenty-four hours earlier had charged this powerful New York icon. And I chose to speak about it.

The next morning, at 8:00, I strolled into a large wood-paneled hall on the second floor of New York Law School in lower Manhattan. The room was packed to capacity, standing room only. The school had to set up an overflow room with a video feed. I had never seen so much energy at a breakfast speech. These were typically sleepy affairs.

I went to the stage and delivered a scathing critique of New York state politics. Among other things, I said this: "Politicians are supposed to be on the people's payroll; not on secret retainer to wealthy special interests they do favors for . . . Money often seems to be the core of the problem." I made an observation, which would be quoted a bit: "Power in New York state, as far as we can tell, is unduly concentrated in the hands of just a few men. Some say . . . just 3 men. There are by my count 213 men and women in the state legislature and yet it is common knowledge that only 3 men wield all the power." And this: "When did twenty million New Yorkers agree to be ruled like a triumvirate in Roman times?"

Then I made some jokes: "I have a little bit of a hard time getting my head around this concept of 'three men in a room.' Maybe it's just me. I'm an immigrant from India, which is overpopulated, so for me it's like a billion men in a room . . . Why does it have to be three men? Can there be women? Do they always have to be white? How small is the room that they can fit three men? Is it three men in a closet? Are there cigars? Can they have Cuban cigars now? After a while, doesn't it get a little gamey?"

As the crowd ate it up, I pushed it further: "It seems to be that if you're one of the three men in the room and you have all the power and you always have, and everyone knows that, you don't tolerate dissent, because you don't have to. You don't allow debate, because you don't have to. You don't favor change or foster reform, because you don't have to and because the status quo always benefits you. And on the other side of the coin, if you're one of the three men in the room, you keep people in the dark . . . because you can. You punish independent thinking . . . because you can. You demand lockstep loyalty . . . because you can. You get swept up in the power and the trappings because you were never challenged and because you can easily forget who put you there in the first place."

Now, I knew full well that nothing I said would affect Silver's right to a fair trial; that event was far off, and voir dire assures that any potential juror who might have been affected would be struck. Still, I might have thought better of the timing of my rant. I might have stuck to my preplanned speech rather than inflame passions the day after the bombshell charges. I might have shown a little less exuberance. Reading these lines now, more than three years later, I can see how it sounds like something bordering on a political speech, a call to arms. That was not my intention. I was speaking out of earnest frustration about the political cesspool, and I was channeling the frustration of every New Yorker. But are prosecutors allowed to be frustrated, allowed to vent their frustration? Something about the speech felt satisfying, felt good. That should have been the warning sign: if it feels good, it's probably a bad idea.

One reason for caution might have been to make sure I wouldn't affect the case in any way. The trial was eventually assigned to Judge Valerie Caproni, former general counsel to the FBI director Robert Mueller and probably the most press-averse judge on the bench. When Silver's lawyers lobbed a non-meritorious Hail Mary pass to dismiss the indictment on the grounds of pretrial publicity, my public remarks were the centerpiece. There was no chance the judge was going to dismiss the case, but my folks had to defend my remarks in legal briefs. At the end of the day, Judge Caproni ruled against the defense but not before slapping me hard and repeatedly castigating me for my "media blitz."

I got word of the court's opinion while on a plane. Her ruling was favorable, but her language was tough. I felt as if I'd been punched in the stomach. But it had the effect I assume was desired. I was more careful after that, as one news article described me later, "more subdued."

Ironically, when Judge Caproni finally sentenced Silver in 2018, though she was punishing only one individual, her rhetoric swept far beyond his singular transgressions. She said, "Corruption cases have touched, directly or indirectly, all three of the infamous men in the room. And yet it was those three men who cut a deal to shut down the Moreland Commission . . . This has to stop. New York State has to get its act together and do something institutionally to head off corruption." I couldn't have said it better myself.

Public corruption makes people angry, angry in a way I didn't perceive in any other area we prosecuted, which is understandable. One needs to be careful about tapping into that, about fomenting a mob mentality. But it should also be noted that these were not members of a poor, downtrodden, underdog community mercilessly made out to be victims of malicious prosecution. These were the most powerful elected leaders in the state, who too often violated their oaths, betrayed their voters, and monetized their offices. They did not merit coddling.

The Verdict

It's May 2011. We are in the midst of trial against the hedge fund billionaire Raj Rajaratnam. We've charged him with insider trading and alleged his fund's whole business model is basically corrupt. It is the most high-profile insider-trading case in a generation. It is the first to use wiretaps. We have been aggressive and prolific, and our drumbeat of insider-trading cases has sent shock waves through the hedge fund industry.

But this is our first big test.

The courtroom is packed every day, and the trial receives saturation coverage in the business pages and on the financial news networks. It is bitterly fought, with Rajaratnam's pit-bull lawyer John Dowd—yes, Donald Trump's former lawyer John Dowd—not just assailing the government's case in court but also attacking me personally throughout the litigation.

But the team does a superb job, and the case goes in beautifully. We hope for a quick verdict.

No such luck. For days we hold our breath. Every day members of the jury arrive at Judge Richard Holwell's courtroom, look inscrutable, occasionally ask for exhibits or the reading back of the testimony, and return the next morning, as indecisive as the day before. Occasionally, I visit the trial room to make sure the team is hanging in there. They pretend to be, but everyone is stressed, myself included. The weekend comes and still no decision. What is taking so long?

On day ten (ten!) of deliberations, I have to fly to Washington, D.C., to give a speech to a Columbia Law School alumni group. I don't want to leave and risk missing the verdict, but it's too late to cancel. I wake up Wednesday morning in the JW Marriott on Pennsylvania Avenue to fly back. I'm about to walk out the door when Boyd calls. There's a verdict.

I'm surprised at how tense I get. I remind myself of what a supervisor once told me when I was awaiting a jury verdict in one of my own cases years earlier: "Remember, whatever happens, you get to go home. Think of how the defendant feels."

I turn on the television in my hotel room and tune in to CNBC. The anchors are breathlessly reporting the breaking news of the verdict. They speculate aloud about how devastating a loss would be for our "crusade" against insider trading and also for me personally. I brace for an acquittal and for the disappointment and recriminations that will follow.

Finally, Boyd texts me from inside the courtroom: "Guilty all counts." One minute later, the CNBC anchors confirm it.

The next day, along with news stories about the conviction, *The New York Times* runs an article titled "U.S. Attorney Sends a Message to Wall Street." A nice flattering piece. It's possible I pick up an extra copy or four after work that night.

When I arrive home, my daughter is sitting in the family room. I think it is just before dinnertime. Maya is ten but precocious, which is an evidence-based observation, not just a parental boast. A copy of the *Times* is in my hand. The piece is written in straightforward prose, nothing too technical, and it occurs to me maybe I should have her read it.

And so, for the first time ever, I ask my daughter to read something about her father. I figure maybe it will make her a little bit proud of me. There is even a pretty nice picture. I ask if she would read it.

"Sure, Daddy," she says.

I open the paper to the business section and put it in her hands. She turns her young, bespectacled face to the page and dutifully begins to read. I watch her. She is expressionless. As she reaches the end of the article, she lingers for a moment on the last line, which quotes me bemoaning rampant insider trading at some news conference: "I wish I could say we were just about finished, but sadly we are not."

My beautiful little ten-year-old finally puts the paper down. I await her response like a mini-jury verdict. She looks straight at me, tilts her head, and in a flat voice she says, "Daddy, why are you such a drama queen?"

The wait for a jury verdict in a criminal case is excruciating. Not just for the defendant, but for the prosecutor too, though obviously with much less life consequence. It is not only the defense lawyers who pace. It might seem odd, this prosecutorial angst, given that prosecutors traditionally enjoy an extremely high success rate. The rate of conviction at trial in my former office, for example, has always been just a few points shy of 100 percent.

The government lawyers are nonetheless nervous because they know a cardinal truth: once the case goes to twelve ordinary Americans, anything can happen. Those twelve inscrutable decision makers, about whom you have only the barest information, can base their judgment, the court's legal instructions notwithstanding, on anything they wish. There is no guarantee of a particular result, and everyone has stories of surprise. I know I do.

Sometimes juries find fatal flaws in your case. Or they don't believe—or simply despise—your cooperating witnesses. Or they hate the case, or they feel sympathy for the defendant, or they are charmed by the defense attorney. And they acquit. Or maybe the jurors favoring conviction are fainter of heart than those opposed, and as the days drag on, the former group just wants to get the hell out of there and they cave. Acquittal.

Or all the jurors stick to their guns, and at an impasse the jury hangs. Mistrial. And you have to go through the whole tortured process all over again, only the next time the defense lawyers know all your witnesses' strengths and weaknesses, know all your best and worst arguments. Retrials are not usually better for the government. Many prosecutors secretly pray—justice or no justice—that above all things please, Lord, let the jury not hang, don't make me have to do this again.

I have long marveled that anyone gets convicted of anything—given the stakes, the standard of proof, and the requirement of unanimity. Try getting twelve people to agree on what kind of pizza to order. Requiring unanimity in that context would cause riots.

So as the verdict approaches, the prosecutors are nervous and uncertain too. Some cases, to be sure, are very strong. But there is no sure thing.

Here's how you know the moment of truth is at hand. The judge, through the courtroom deputy or a clerk, sends word: there's a verdict. It is a sobering announcement because judgment is near. If you are in the courtroom already, you stiffen and wait. If you are back at the office on a call, you hang up and make haste. If you are at lunch, you finish chewing what's in your mouth and rush out.

People collect. Attorneys for the government, lawyers for the defense, courtroom personnel like the deputy and the assigned clerk, though typically all the clerks like to be ringside for the final decision. If it's a press-worthy case, reporters with small flip notebooks come into the gallery also, likely with conviction stories pre-written, given the odds. Oftentimes the defense has supporters in force—spouse, kids, parents, siblings, friends, clergy, co-workers, neighbors. Other times, the accused and his lawyer sit alone at the defense table, without cheerleaders, feigning stoicism until the foreperson speaks. Typically, deputy U.S. marshals will take up silent sentry against the wall. They are armed because violence, though rare, is always possible.

Finally, there comes the boom of a deputy marshal's fist

pounding three times on the door from inside the deliberation room. "Jury entering!"

Everyone stands as the jury files into the wood-paneled courtroom now thick with anticipation, dread, and prayer. All eyes are fixed on the ordinary men and women who walk toward the jury box, a casual caravan of sweaters, jeans, slacks, flats, and sneakers. Mostly their gazes are directed indifferently forward, as if riding an elevator. The stakeholders staring from the well see only tea leaves, not faces, straining to catch a hint of the looming judgment from a telltale glance or expression. Sometimes jurors are crying; rarely are they jovial at this moment.

The prosecutors, for their part, wear intentional poker faces. The first time I sat in the well waiting for the foreperson to announce the verdict, my trial partner leaned in and whispered forcefully into my ear, "Remember, no emotion. No reaction. No matter what." Acquittal or conviction, the poker face is a must. This is a matter of etiquette and also, I think, a conspicuous show of respect and humility.

You think you tried a good case, you believe the defendant is guilty, you don't know whether the jury bought it, whether the jury liked you. You run the reel of your best and worst moments, and you brace. I remember being astonished when the jury at my first trial convicted and astonished again when the jury at my fifth trial acquitted. And astonished is an understatement for how I felt sitting in the courtroom for the verdict in our case against al-Qaeda's Ahmed Ghailani, the last man brought to America from Guantánamo Bay to face civilian trial. Charged with 285 counts for the murder of 224 people in the horrific bombing of U.S. embassies in Kenya and Tanzania, he was acquitted by the jury of 284 counts, convicted only of count 5: conspiracy to destroy property and buildings of the United States. Inexplicable to the point of absurdity. To this day we have no logical explanation, except that some lopsided compromise must have been struck in the black box of a jury room.

So everyone waits nervously for judgment—by unanimous reckoning—to be pronounced not by the robed judge but by an ordinary American plucked from some local neighborhood for this extraordinary service. Finally, the foreperson stands in the jury box, before a motionless courtroom, and speaks the verdict.

And then it is done.

It may be surprising to hear that the right-minded prosecutor does not feel joy at that moment of "Guilty." Hours later there will be drinks, gratification, pats on the back, job well done. Professional reputation intact. The moment of conviction is the most somber and sobering moment in civilian civic life. There is nothing else like it. I was present on the floor of the U.S. Senate for the confirmation of two Supreme Court justices as the roll was called, aye and nay ringing out as C-SPAN recorded history. That doesn't come close to the mood I experienced at every jury verdict in a criminal case. It is grave and sad, even if just.

In many courtrooms in SDNY, the defense table is situated behind the prosecution's so it's impossible to witness the response of the person with the most at stake. At best you hear it, above the sound of your own beating heart, a sigh or a gasp or, most commonly, no sound at all.

That is not always true in the gallery. The spouse may cry; the child may wail. A defendant now knows his fate. The presumption of innocence is no more. Sometimes the prosecutors move for remand on the spot, and the defendant leaves the courtroom through the side door, in cuffs, straight into lockup.

Particular verdicts are expected when cases are very strong or very weak. Facts matter, and there is a feeling of probability on the part of the lawyers at least. But probability is not certainty, and the uncertainty is always palpable. That uncertainty is proof that the thing is not fixed, not rigged. It gives the trial result credibility, just as uncertainty about elections lends credibility to democracy.

On the eve of the 2016 U.S. presidential sweepstakes, famed

chess champion, human rights activist, and self-exiled Russian Garry Kasparov posted this on social media: "That nervous feeling you have about tomorrow, Americans? That's democracy working. Unpredictable elections, what a luxury!" After Trump won the presidency the next day, against all odds, Kasparov later offered this optimistic observation: "Trump's election is greatest proof of democracy. You don't know the results in advance!"

The same should be said about verdicts in criminal cases. That nervous feeling you have when the jury comes out, prosecutors? That is justice working. Unpredictable verdicts, what a luxury.

PART IV

Punishment

Introduction

Perhaps the most bewildering and consequential questions about justice relate to punishment. What sentence is sufficient but not more than necessary to satisfy what a just society seeks—retribution as well as rehabilitation, incapacitation as well as deterrence? How to balance the need for uniformity in punishment against the goal of doing individual justice in every case? Do we focus only on the criminal act? Or do we take account of the circumstances peculiar to the transgressor—family circumstances, upbringing, motivations? In the end, what is the precise number of weeks, months, or years to deprive someone of liberty in the interests of justice? No one can truly know.

And so the final phase of justice—punishment—can take on a deep moral, emotional, and even religious dimension, despite modern efforts to reduce the issue to a mathematical computation. The best-known theory of punishment—though long rejected in our jurisprudence—is the biblical one: an eye for an eye. Laypeople may not understand the technicalities of wiretapping, the law of conspiracy, the job of a grand jury, or the arcane procedures of trial. The fairness of these tools and rules is hazy to the average person. But people do believe they understand punishment. Reactions to particular punishments are visceral—whether deemed too light or too harsh. Because we've all imposed punishments and been punished—whether grounding a child, disciplining a subordinate, or giving someone the silent treatment. Punishments are felt in the gut, by individuals and also communities.

For a long time here, and in some places still, punishment was a public event, intended to be consumed as spectacle by the citizenry. The stockade, the gallows, the guillotine, the cross. The stoning of infidels or the lashing of thieves. These were symbols of the state's wrath and occasions for communal catharsis and purge. Also potent warnings to future wrongdoers.

Punishment is more tucked away now. It's a bit out of sight. We have done away with punishment in the public square. Our prisons, too, are out of sight and out of mind. Once upon a time, we constructed our correctional facilities right in the heart of the city. The first modern U.S. penitentiary, Eastern State, was built in Philadelphia proper, in 1829. Now convicted felons are shipped far and wide to serve their terms, away from civilian populations and out of easy visiting distance for relatives.

But even though punishment is not endured publicly, its announcement still takes place at a public proceeding, in a court of law, where judges pronounce—sometimes after a visible struggle—prison sentences with reference to the federal sentencing guidelines. The current sentencing system tries to make all of this into a math exercise, with numerical scores assigned to different crimes, loss amounts, criminal histories, aggravating factors, mitigating circumstances. It is a crude and cold method of calculation, literally embodied in a formal chart that more resembles a bingo card than a thoughtful recipe for justice for real human beings.

That is of course the crux of the matter and the source of most deliberative anguish—the presence of human beings. How to apply both formula and conscience to serve justice when flesh-and-blood people are involved? The victims of crimes are human beings, but the perpetrators are also, and sorting out what is fair and just, what is principled and proportional, is a labor that no judge relishes. Because they are human beings too. And so in case after case, once guilt has been established, there comes the final torture of setting a proper punishment. Probation or prison? Months or years? Life or death?

Sometimes the prosecutor can put an anvil on the scale by employing a statute carrying a mandatory minimum sentence, effectively becoming the sentencing judge. As you will read, we came up against this quandary in the sad case of a long-unsolved baby kidnapping. Amid roiling emotion and tragic loss, combined with the prospect of visiting a second hell upon a young victim by gambling on a trial, the question of the right punishment was far from formulaic. You can decide for yourself whether we made the right decisions.

Sentencing has a feeling of finality about it, of closure. I used to think this is where the prosecutor's concern rightly ended, at the prison's perimeter. An inquiry fairly conducted, an accusation rightly made, a judgment properly rendered, and then a punishment judiciously imposed. On to the next case! But that is not the end, at least not if we care about overall justice, because the other consequence of our jails and prisons being out of sight is that we don't see the physical and moral rot pervasive in them. This is a feature of justice too. How we treat the human beings we deem dangerous or depraved enough to imprison is a moral imperative for everyone, prosecutors included.

On a policy level, we must rethink sentence length, mandatory minimums, discretion in charging, cash bail, and so many other things. Significant criminal justice reform has recently passed.

But we also need to humanize the conditions of confinement. The entrenched violence at the New York City jail known as Rikers Island—which violence my office deeply investigated, punished, and tried to abate—provides object lessons in the brutality of confinement, the depravity of bad-faith prison guards, and the need for humanity and hope in even the darkest places. Learning these lessons is necessary not just for the redemption of the people housed there but for all of us.

Baby Carlina

The moral quandary of what constitutes fair and effective punishment is not unique to life-tenured jurists presiding over criminal cases. It will be familiar and irksome to many people: to the regulator who must penalize a rogue company; to the supervisor who must handle a misbehaving employee; and even to the parent who has to discipline an unruly child. What is proportional? What is effective? What will, in the future, deter that person specifically and everyone else generally? What action is sufficient but not greater than necessary?

As I've said, these questions have no precise or certain answers, and yet every day orderly society demands that they be answered. And every day mere mortals try to meet that challenge as best they can.

Carlina Renae White entered the world at Harlem Hospital in New York on a mild midsummer day in 1987. At eight pounds even, she was healthy and beautiful, with light brown skin, curly hair, and a birthmark on her right arm. Though her young unmarried parents hadn't planned the pregnancy, they were in love and resolved to raise their daughter together. Carlina's mother, Joy White, was just sixteen and still in high school; the baby's father, Carl Tyson, was twenty-two and holding down two jobs, driving a truck by day and working nights in a parking garage. There were no riches, but baby Carlina was welcomed into the home of her mother, Joy, and her grandmother Elizabeth, where she would receive care and love and the normal doting.

When Carlina was nineteen days old, she fell sick with fever. The couple took no chances and brought her back to Harlem Hospital late on the night of August 4. Doctors were concerned enough that they admitted Carlina overnight and ran an IV tube into her foot. Having entrusted Carlina to the hospital's care, Joy ran home at about 12:30 a.m. to fetch some things so she could come back and spend the night.

Joy would never learn the medical diagnosis for her daughter's illness, because sometime in the predawn hours of August 5, Carlina was taken from the seventeenth-floor pediatric ward of Harlem Hospital. The kidnapper had unhooked the IV tube, scooped up the baby, and walked out into the night, undetected—"simple as a bodega shoplifting," as a news report later put it.

The toll on Carlina's young parents was severe. They tried to keep up hope that their baby would return. Carl would later say, "I always felt that my daughter was going to come back." But days turned to weeks and weeks to months, while police leads didn't actually lead anywhere.

Joy's grief was deep. She had been blessed with a child but permitted only nineteen days with her, nineteen days to "bathe her, wash her hair, and then get her a bottle of milk and rock her to sleep." Joy became depressed, took Valium, entered therapy. She dropped out of school, and eventually, under the weight of the loss, she and Carl broke up.

What had happened to little Carlina White? And who was the cruel thief who snatched her?

It took twenty-three long years for the mystery to be solved. On the night that Carlina disappeared, a woman with a minor arrest record named Ann Pettway lurked in the hallways of

Harlem Hospital. There were reports she wore a nurse's dress, but she was not a nurse. For some time, Pettway had struggled to have a child of her own. Several miscarriages had left her desperate.

Pettway was on the pediatric floor when Joy came in with her sick baby. Feigning concern, she even made a pretense at comforting the new mother, telling her everything would be all right. A short while later, observing Carlina unattended, Pettway took the child. No one stopped her. There would eventually be a lawsuit for negligence against the city, but every legal and law enforcement effort to find Carlina and her kidnapper came up empty.

Pettway took Carlina just outside New York City to her home in Connecticut, renamed her Nejdra, and proclaimed the new baby hers. Carlina, now known as Netty, was raised by Pettway first in Connecticut and then in Georgia.

The case of Carlina's kidnapping stumped police investigators for decades. But more than twenty-three years after a high fever helped deliver Carlina into the hands of Ann Pettway, the sleuth who ended up solving the case was none other than Carlina herself. As Carlina grew up, people would comment that she didn't look like her mother. There was no resemblance in their African American features, and while Carlina was light-skinned, Pettway was dark. Carlina didn't think much of it until she herself became pregnant at sixteen and needed proof of birth to sign up for prenatal care. When Pettway couldn't produce a birth certificate, Carlina became deeply suspicious. The older woman broke down in tears and made a partial confession: she admitted Carlina wasn't her daughter but insisted, cryptically and without credible detail, that a stranger had given her Carlina as an infant and then never came back. That was all she would say.

Over the next several years, Carlina's suspicions mounted, and she wondered who she really was. She began doing internet searches on missing kids from the 1980s. Finally, close to Christmas 2010, she contacted the National Center for Missing and Exploited Children (NCMEC). Based on her age, telltale birthmark, and other details, NCMEC quickly narrowed the search to two abduction cases. One of those was the case of Carlina White. Photographs of the newborn Carlina compared with infant pictures of "Netty" confirmed what was becoming clear: the woman who had always known herself as Netty was in fact the kidnapped Carlina White.

Meanwhile, more than two decades on, Joy had never stopped thinking about her missing baby. Though she eventually married and had other children, Joy had never stopped grieving for the daughter taken by a stranger in the middle of the night. She still kept a framed baby picture on her dresser and even used Carlina's name in her email address. She could never have expected the call she got from NCMEC telling her that her baby was alive and well.

Even before the DNA tests came back definitively, Carlina began speaking to Joy from Atlanta. They were soon together again in New York. Their reunion was emotional and overwhelming. Carlina met her real mother, her real father, her grandmother, a sister and brother she didn't know she had, and untold aunts and cousins.

It was at this time, in January 2011, that the tragic, twisting tale of a long-lost stolen baby made its way to my desk as the U.S. Attorney in Manhattan. The prosecutor put in charge was Andrea Surratt, a young rising star in the office. Andrea was fair and tough, and her skills outside the courtroom included being a certified pilot and a skilled marksman.

The mystery of baby Carlina now solved, it was time for Ann Pettway to face justice. The Manhattan District Attorney's Office made a brief play, but with the statute of limitations long expired on the relevant state charge, federal prosecution was the only option. The case was ours.

After seeing herself on television, Pettway finally surrendered to an FBI field office. There she confessed to FBI special agent Maria Johnson, saying she had suffered multiple miscarriages in the 1980s, wanted a child, and took Carlina from Harlem Hospital. In a written statement, she said she was "truly sorry."

The criminal case against Pettway was fairly straightforward. In our minds, she was undeniably guilty of violating the federal kidnapping statute. There was some posturing about a defense case from her lawyer, Robert Baum. Pettway's story could change; she could try to suppress her confession; and, to be sure, there was no reliable eyewitness who could definitively put Carlina in Pettway's hands leaving the hospital that night. But all things considered, the risk of losing was slight, and so on the issue of guilt, justice was likely to be swift and sure.

Guilt was the easy part in this case. Determining the just punishment for Pettway's heinous act, on the other hand, was a wholly separate legal (and moral) question and would occupy our thoughts and discussions for some time.

Most prosecutors I know are more skilled at getting convictions than at making sentencing recommendations. For a prosecutor, guilt is often relatively easy to argue for. There is, typically, moral clarity. Each count in an indictment presents a binary choice—guilty or not guilty. There are no shades. A defendant cannot be a little guilty any more than a woman can be a little bit pregnant. Indeed, the system rejects gray. For the jury to convict, guilt must be all but certain, to be pronounced only if the question is answered beyond any and all reasonable doubt. On the issue of deciding guilt, then, justice seems fairly assured and achievable. Even when an apparently guilty man is acquitted, if the jury did its job, if the judge kept her foot off the scale, if the lawyers were constitutionally competent, we say the jury has spoken, justice was done, and we move on.

Sentencing is different. As the question moves from guilt to punishment, the sky gets cloudy and the terrain foggy. The choices are no longer binary but overwhelmingly varied and numerous. If no mandatory minimum is at stake and the crime is serious enough, a vast continuum of punishment is available. Time served, life imprisonment, and anything in between. Then matters of restitution, financial penalty, conditions of confinement, and post-sentence restrictions further multiply the punishment options.

I think many prosecutors are less focused and sure of themselves in advocating particular punishment not because they don't care but because it is hard. Also because they know the ultimate burden, thankfully, belongs to the judge. They have done their job securing the conviction through guilty plea or trial, and they are happy to leave the godlike task of deciding the precise deprivation of liberty to someone else. This is one reason I have never aspired to be a judge. I never wanted to play God in that way. How to know, with certainty, if the right punishment is seventy months or eighty? How to know the rehabilitative effect of an extra day or week in prison, or the opposite?

The judge's grave duty is to impose just punishment where punishment is called for. A federal judge is guided by all manner of scores and set numbers based on criminal history, nature of the offense, aggravating factors, and mitigating facts, but ultimately the law requires only that a judge impose a sentence that is "sufficient but not greater than necessary." If you think this must be excruciatingly difficult to calibrate, you are right. Most every judge will candidly confess that the toughest burden of the robe is to calculate the sentence that is "sufficient but not greater than necessary." Many judges naturally chafe when their options are choked off by mandatory minimums, but unfettered discretion over the life and liberty of another human being isn't any kind of picnic either.

The very notion that a just sentence can be "calculated" is one of the long-standing fetishes of crime and punishment. That mathematical fetish may be important to justice insofar as fairness begs for standards and uniformity across racial, regional, and other differences, but we should never be under any illusion that fallible humans can achieve perfect justice in punishment. "Sufficient but not greater than necessary" is a Goldilocks standard and an inherently impossible one.

So what to do about Ann Pettway?

As it happens, an early charging decision set the stage for many days of discussion and debate over Pettway's fate. There was a mandatory minimum sentence called for under one subsection of the relevant statute: twenty years if the kidnapping victim was a minor and the kidnapper was not a relative. This fit the facts, and so this is what we charged. That meant if Pettway were convicted, the judge would have no discretion to go under twenty years, and Pettway would serve at least that much time in prison, without parole.

That did not seem in any way outlandish, unfair, or disproportionate. There is much debate about the fairness and propriety of mandatory minimums, but it would be hard to feel heartburn in a case like this. The sheer anguish Pettway had visited upon Joy and Carl, who remained pained and angry, seemed to justify it. Add to that traditional considerations like deterrence, and this seemed a fair outcome. So that is how we proceeded at first.

The hiccup came a bit later. Pettway's lawyer ultimately said his client was prepared to plead guilty but the twenty-year mandatory minimum was a deal breaker. She might, however, plead guilty to another section of the statute, and everyone could make arguments to the judge, who would be free to sentence her to twenty years, or a lot less or a lot more.

This was a tougher decision than many I can remember. On the one hand was the suffering of the biological parents, Joy and

Carl. They made it clear that they wanted harsh punishment—twenty-three years for Pettway for the twenty-three years Carlina had been taken from them. Eye for an eye. But in this case there was another victim, not in the same position, but profoundly victimized—Carlina herself. She was something of an understandable mess, and at any trial Carlina would have to be a witness. Victims need to be vindicated, but they are arguably the most biased and conflicted people in the whole drama. And different sets of victims have different interests. Balancing those interests is tricky. What Carlina wanted was different from what her parents wanted.

Carlina's life with Pettway had its ups and downs. Carlina was popular and outgoing in school, and she dreamed of becoming a famous performer one day. At the same time, she would later say, Pettway was often doing drugs and could be a "monster." Carlina would see weapons. Sometimes Pettway struck her, though Carlina insisted she was not abused: "I'm not going to say she was the best mom ever, but she did what she had to do to make me who I am."

Life with Pettway had been far from perfect, but having discovered the truth of her identity and still loving the woman who raised her, Carlina had zero interest in cooperating to put Pettway in prison perhaps until her death. There was also her half brother, Pettway's other child, still a minor at only fourteen years old, who would be collateral damage in the machinery of justice.

We had a lot of meetings that spring in 2011 in my office on the eighth floor of One St. Andrew's Plaza. The issue was clear, though the answer was not: Do we pursue the letter of the law, the clearly applicable and fitting mandatory minimum statute and arguably undermine justice by jeopardizing the conviction at trial and visit more suffering upon the kidnap victim? Or do we permit a plea to a different subsection and arguably undermine justice by allowing the possibility of a too-light sentence?

At each discussion around the coffee table in my office, we

gave free range and voice to all these considerations. And I was struck by something that has stayed with me since. Right or wrong, my thoughts kept turning to my own young children, then aged ten, eight, and six, and back to their births at Columbia Presbyterian, without question the three happiest days of my life. I thought about the life I had with them, the life I knew I would have with them. And then I compared my joy as a father with the emptiness and loss that Ann Pettway had forced on Carlina's parents. If you allow yourself to go down that road for even five minutes, you will find a lot of vicarious pain and anger well up. If you are any kind of human being, that will affect your views of what justice requires.

And the question could be asked: Is this natural and appropriate empathy for a crime victim, or is it a source of bias and dangerous emotion? Do we want our prosecutors to think and feel in this way? What does it mean to be passionate about justice but dispassionate and fair-minded about a particular case? On one occasion, I asked for a vote and went around the room. There were about eight of us—line prosecutor, supervisors, and all my top deputies. We were spending a lot of time trying to figure out what the right thing to do was, and it was weighing on all of us.

There is another submerged feature to this debate: Did it matter how Pettway had raised Carlina? Was her parenting style relevant? Is it okay to think differently about a kidnapper's sentencing based on what she provided her stolen charge? Any difference if Pettway had been a model mother, had turned Carlina into a Rhodes scholar?

The vote was lopsided. Most in favor of going with the mandatory twenty years, some in favor of getting the certain guilty plea and leaving open the possibility of an unacceptably light sentence. It took me a minute to realize what might have accounted for the split. It was not along lines of seniority or gender or general reputation for toughness or softness. This is what

I realized: every prosecutor who had a child voted for twenty years, and every prosecutor in the room who did not voted the other way. So what to do? What you do is you hug your kids a little tighter that night and you sleep on it.

It took me some time, but I ultimately authorized the milder course. In the end, the victim's well-being carried the day. We didn't want to re-traumatize Carlina by forcing a trial where she would have to testify. There was, frankly, a tactical issue too: Carlina would no longer have been a friendly witness. At some point, she stopped being cooperative with the FBI and my prosecutors. If there were to be a trial, she would require a subpoena and would have been volatile and utterly unpredictable, not what you want at a trial. The trauma would arguably be revictimizing her. We maintained our right to argue for the twenty-year sentence, which we thought was just. We were merely giving up our ability to mandate such a sentence by requiring a plea to the mandatory minimum charge; now it would be up to the judge. Some might say that's always how it should be. So, we got certainty and closure and we spared Carlina.

Pettway pled guilty. Joy and Carl were upset at our decision. At sentencing, they spoke softly and with dignity, their words soaked in pain. Carl went first: "What I have to say is it's been twenty-three years, Ann, you have me suffering. Put a scar in my heart. You took something away from me very precious. And I never got a chance to have my daughter her first birthday party. I never had a chance to watch my daughter go to school. I never had a chance to even put her on a school bus. You hurt me so bad. I didn't even give my daughter her first birthday, her sixteen-year birthday party. You did damage to me . . . What they should give you is twenty-three years, which you took away from me." It was hard to argue with this logic.

Such baby kidnappings are rare, but they happen. Even as I was writing this book, there was news of a baby girl who was stolen from a Jacksonville hospital in 1998 and not reunited with her biological parents for eighteen years. The parents in that case asked for the death penalty.

This was an irreplaceable loss, and Carlina's parents were not the only ones crushed by it. As Joy said, "This tragedy has impacted my life, my daughter's life, my family, her grand-mother, her aunts, and all of her little sisters and brothers. Our lives will never be the same from the day forward that Carlina was missing . . . My daughter has found me, but I still have not found my daughter." Something would always be missing; a hole would never be filled.

Judge Kevin Castel noted at sentencing the broad discretion he had, the wide range of possibilities for punishment: "The Court has the authority to give this defendant a sentence of time served, basically, the time that she has served in prison to date, all of the way up to a term of life imprisonment without parole."

So, what did he decide? He gave Pettway twelve years. Joy and Carl were devastated. My prosecutors were disappointed. Carlina was not present. The judge recounted the troubling details of the kidnapping. But he also recounted Pettway's dif-ficult childhood, which included a history of sexual abuse, drug abuse, mental illness, and a series of miscarriages. And he spoke to the total and absolute grief that Carlina's birth parents expe-rienced as a result of the kidnapping, a "continuing crime" that stole twenty-three years of relationships, of family, of Carlina's own identity.

But perhaps most telling were these lines: "I have considered the need for just punishment. This was not a crime of greed, it was not a crime of vengeance. But it was an act of selfishness, a crime of selfishness." There is something to be said about our system of justice, which intentionally rejects the antiquated, biblical notion of eye-for-an-eye justice. Whether or not the judge calibrated it perfectly in this particular case, just punishment requires empathy not only for the victim but for the per-petrator too, not in the same way or to the same degree, but the reasons for the crime—both mitigating and aggravating—and the whole of the defendant must be taken into account, consid-ered, and balanced. It is an impossible balance to strike, I think, but the judge's job is to strike it.

Was this the right result? Was justice done? I was not sure, and I will never be, though I think about the gut-wrenching case of the stolen baby still.

Lord of the Flies

One of my favorite people is Steve Martin. Not the comedian and actor, though I am a big fan of his work also. The Steve Martin I got to know well during my last couple of years at SDNY has been working in and out of prisons for forty-six years, first in the sprawling Texas system as a guard, later as general counsel of the Texas Department of Corrections, and more recently as a smart and thoughtful reformer helping correctional facilities solve their epidemics of violence and excessive force.

With his lanky frame, lined face, gray mustache, and southern drawl, Martin resembles a kinder version of Sam Elliott, the actor known for playing tough cowboys and ranchers in the movies. Martin was the court-appointed monitor selected to help reform the New York City jail system known as Rikers Island.

I am not an expert on prisons or prison reform. Most prosecutors are not. They work hard to prove guilt, advocate for some sentence with varying degrees of stridency, and then move on to the next case. They think little about life for the defendants they prosecute after they are shipped to their far-flung lockups.

I had only one prior experience sticking up for the rights of an inmate, more than two decades earlier. When I was a very young lawyer in private practice, I and others at my firm represented, pro bono, a man named Paul Jolly. Jolly was serving a life sentence in Attica for murdering a man in front of his five children. Shot him to death. We didn't represent Jolly in his criminal case. We aided him in his effort to practice his Rastafarian religion, which was his legal and constitutional right, even behind bars. Because he refused, for religious reasons, to submit to a non-conclusive test for latent tuberculosis, he was confined to "medical keeplock," solitary confinement at all times except for one ten-minute shower a week.

My secretary at the firm asked me when we took the case what our client had done to land himself in Attica. I told her about the murder conviction. She refused to work on the case, and so I did all the mundane tasks—copying, printing, and correspondence—myself. I respected her bright line, though I was taken by the intensity of it. I was able to separate what Jolly had done—his atrocious, unspeakable crime—from his entitlement to decent treatment in prison, his continuing right to the protections of the Constitution. They were different things in my mind. It was a lot of work and a formative experience for me—depositions (my first), motion practice, preliminary injunctions, and eventually trials in related cases. We won the case and Jolly's release from solitary.

Twenty years later, two AUSAs in the Civil Division, Emily Daughtry and Jeff Powell, spearheaded a groundbreaking investigation into the treatment of adolescents at Rikers Island. Their shocking findings opened my eyes to the malignant problems at New York's most notorious facility and in prisons generally. The findings were particular to Rikers Island, of course, but there are lessons and warnings for all prisons, all places where we separate human beings from their freedom. Well into my tenure, our work on Rikers drove me to think about conditions of confinement, made me believe there is a moral reason to care about the state of correctional institutions. We should always care what a just and fair society should look like. In a just and fair society, the healthy should care about the sick; the rich should care about the poor; the mighty should care about the weak;

and the prosecutor should care about the prisoner. Rikers was an object lesson.

When I was a college freshman, I took a course on the phenomenon of genocide. The class shook me. There's an argument to be made that the subject should be required study for everyone—the extremes of cruelty that people can visit upon fellow human beings. The syllabus included what are, to this day, three of the most important works I've ever read: Stanley Milgram's *Obedience to Authority,* Joseph Conrad's *Heart of Darkness,* and a write-up of Professor Philip Zimbardo's infamous Stanford prison experiment. We also read Hannah Arendt and studied, like so many thousands of students, her theory about the banality of evil. Those works—like the murder of Jessica's parents' friends at the hands of their sons—shattered something for me, *Obedience to Authority* the most of all. I have read it many times since college, more than once as U.S. Attorney. For the unfamiliar, Milgram conducted a series of 1960s-era experiments testing the boundaries of human obedience to commands to hurt other people. Milgram himself was astonished that ordinary people would, under the mundane conditions of an academic experiment, blithely subject other human beings to tremendous pain by personally administering what they believed were high-voltage shocks. Why? Because a man in a lab coat told them to.

Professor Milgram wrote this five decades ago: "This is, perhaps, the most fundamental lesson of our study: ordinary people, simply doing their jobs, and without any particular hostility on their part, can become agents in a terrible destructive process."

Decades later, in my own workplace, I heard Arendt's famous phrase again—the "banality of evil"—out of the mouth of Steve Martin. He used it to explain how it can be that even good human beings, when operating in the confined and charged environs of a prison under dehumanizing rules, could act so cruelly to their fellow humans.

In the Stanford prison experiment—one of the most famous psychology experiments of the twentieth century—Philip Zimbardo and his assistants selected twenty-four ostensibly stable Stanford students, all male, and randomly assigned them to roles as guards or prisoners via coin flip. The experiment was meant to last two weeks. It was canceled after six days. Why? Because guards became increasingly sadistic—employing "psychological pressure," waking inmates up at 2:00 a.m., placing them in "solitary confinement," and forcing them to engage in physically humiliating acts. Zimbardo later testified to Congress that he ended the experiment because he realized that he "could easily have traded places" with the "most brutal guard" or the "weakest prisoner." Over the years, there have been articles discrediting the study because of evidence the "guards" were pushed or coached, but the jarring lesson of well-heeled Stanford students quickly taking to abusing and dehumanizing fellow students stands.

Whether exaggerated or flawed, the Stanford prison experiment has for five decades endured in the public consciousness because its purported results were both shocking and *believable*. As Mikhail Khodorkovsky, a railroaded billionaire incarcerated in a Russian penal colony for more than ten years, wrote in *My Fellow Prisoners,* "Prison has a terrible effect on the majority of both prisoners and guards. It's not yet clear, in fact, which group is affected more. Society has to do something about this human tragedy. And for a start people need to know about it."

Steve Martin wants to do something about this human tragedy. He believes that people can be incarcerated humanely, that prisons need not be lethal cesspools of violence and corruption. And he has spent his whole career fighting for that vision.

What circumstances combine to give rise to barbarism and cruelty? The answer has to do with both culture and individuals.

Every prison environment is impossible pretty much by definition: the inmates are charged with (or convicted of) crimes,
many are mentally ill, and by order of a court they are denied
liberty. This is already one step to subhuman status. This is not
to say prison is, in concept, inhumane or unnecessary. So long
as there are people who must be justly incapacitated because of
fair punishment or because they are dangers to the community
or risks of flight, incarceration is necessary.

The point is that you begin with a powder keg. Prisons
and jails are crucibles of dehumanization. The very dynamic
of a prison—as crystallized in the Zimbardo experiment—
rationalizes and rewards subjugation. Policies and practices
adopted for efficiency and safety easily dehumanize. There
are, Steve says, so many ways to dehumanize people in prison,
countless ways to treat them like cattle. There is the complete
stripping away of privacy; the drab identical uniforms; identification by number; the en masse herding to meals. There is
the baseline powerlessness and the perception of the jailers'
omnipotence.

Also it is a matter of ease. The road to hell is paved with
laziness. Punitiveness doesn't require brainpower. Force is easy;
restraint is hard. Someone resists, he gets a fist to the head.
Someone violates, he gets solitary. It is easy to deal with most
problems with brute force. In many cultures, the use of force is
rewarded. Steve began as a correction officer at age twenty-two
in Texas. In his telling, he felt himself sliding down the slippery
slope, becoming more inclined to violence as the months passed.
By age twenty-four, he felt he had changed, become more violent, not unlike the guards in the Stanford experiment, except
this was real life. He decided to leave that employment track but
remained committed to the mission of bringing humane conditions to prisons. He said to me once, "I could have risen high if
I had been more willing to kick ass, indiscriminately."

Not everyone who causes harm sets out to do it; not every

institution embraces cruel practices with the purpose of hurting those in their charge. It's not all malice and intentional evil. Take the example of the Eastern State Penitentiary—America's very first penitentiary, opened in 1829, established by Quakers. There, inmates endured brutal solitary confinement, all of them. But this was not meant solely to punish; it was meant to rehabilitate. One of its supporters, Dr. Benjamin Rush, proposed a "house of repentance" where prisoners could experience true remorse through solitary reflection. It was intended to heal; it was considered humane. The theory was that inmates would be solitary, alone with their thoughts—to reflect and to repent. The root of "penitentiary," after all, is "penitent." That was the social experiment. Eventually, the ills of locking people up alone became known. By 1913, Eastern State Penitentiary ended its practice of automatic solitary confinement, realizing that it was a cruel and inhumane form of punishment. The experiment was abandoned, but it had begun in good faith.

Incompetence and shallow thinking play their part, as they do in many awful stories. During one of our regular meetings in the eighth-floor library, Steve told me another story that stayed with me. In the early 2000s, Steve was brought in by the Ohio Department of Youth Services to investigate excessive use of force at a youth facility for girls in Scioto, Ohio, a small town whose other claim to fame is that it's where golf great Jack Nicklaus learned to play the game.

Steve found an astonishingly high incidence of arm injuries there—fractured and broken wrists, elbows, and shoulders. He'd been around a lot of years and never seen anything like it. But as he said, "There's always an explanation if you dig for patterns." So Steve went and observed on-site. He quickly saw the cause: it was how the guards were escorting prisoners from one location to another. He saw guards, inexplicably, using a tight and restrictive C-grip: extending each inmate's arm straight out from her body, locking the elbow, and maintaining the lock

by putting a hard C-shaped grip on the elbow, which placed tremendous strain on virtually every joint in the arm. I had Steve
demonstrate on me. He gripped me tight, locked my elbow.
I couldn't imagine walking a few steps that way, much less a
long distance, especially if I were in a state of agitation. One
false move and something was definitely going to break. When
questioned about the practice, the captain said, "That's just how
we escort people."

Steve was dumbfounded. How do you take girls long dis-
tances with their arms locked like that? It's basically a method
of "pain compliance." Even horses aren't moved along that way.
What was especially troubling was that the restrictive grip was
the *routine* method of escort, not to stop a fight or defuse dis-
obedience. Steve went to the warden, even before submitting his
report, and advised that the grip had to be corrected: don't lock
the elbow, escort with a firm hand on the waist rather than the
arm. That's it. The fractures stopped overnight.

Sometimes, of course, the trouble is not benign incompetence. Sometimes there are evil people to blame, overwhelmed
by an impossible environment, enabled by weak systems, and
protected by a corrupt culture.

Rikers Island is a broken hellhole. The primary jail complex
for New York City and one of the largest in the country, Rikers
is a four-hundred-acre institution floating between the Bronx
and Queens with ten facilities that house men, women, and
adolescents. The population is mostly pretrial detainees who
have been convicted of nothing. They are disproportionately
men of color, and close to 40 percent of the population suffers
from mental illness (we found the number rose to 51 percent
among adolescent inmates). Since opening in the 1930s, Rikers
has been known for its deeply entrenched culture of violence.
It is notoriously one of the worst correctional facilities anywhere. There was a persistent pattern and practice of conduct

at Rikers that violates the constitutional rights of inmates. We found Rikers to be a fundamentally broken place where brute force is the first impulse rather than the last resort; where verbal insults are repaid with physical injuries; where beatings are routine but accountability rare; and where a culture of violence endures even while a code of silence prevails. As we prepared to announce our findings in 2014, Rich Zabel suggested a fitting literary reference to put the situation in context: it was like *Lord of the Flies*.

A Rikers-related tragedy rightly received considerable attention in 2015. At age sixteen, a boy named Kalief Browder was locked up and charged with—but never convicted of—the theft of a backpack. Two of his three years at Rikers Island were spent in debilitating solitary confinement. He was assaulted and harassed by both officers and other inmates. Charges were eventually dropped, and Browder tried to start his life again, telling his story to raise awareness about abuses behind bars. Two years after his release, he killed himself. Life inside Rikers no doubt played a part. It is a heartbreaking story, and there are other terrible deaths—stories of assault and murder within the walls of Rikers too.

In 2014, my office released a lengthy and damning report detailing the culture of violence at Rikers, replete with alarming findings, facts, and statistics. Ultimately, we negotiated a judicial consent decree, informed by the problems we found. It required new policies to reduce excessive violence and protect the safety and rights of inmates; the enforcement of use-of-force investigations; the installation of seventy-eight hundred cameras by 2018; a new pilot program for body cameras; the development of new programs, recruitment tactics, and training for staff and new guidelines for inmates under nineteen, including the end of solitary confinement and efforts to find alternative housing off Rikers Island. These reforms would be tracked by an outside monitor and regular progress reports.

Stories, however, jar more than stats. These two are worth

unspooling in some detail. A summary report that an inmate was beaten to death does not do justice to the life snuffed out. Consider the final miserable minutes of two men who never left that island.

This was the first sentence of AUSA Lara Eshkenazi's opening statement at the criminal trial of a Rikers officer named Terrence Pendergrass: "Jason Echevarria died alone in a tiny jail cell on Rikers Island after hours of being in pain, gasping for breath, vomiting, and pleading for help."

It was a bleak end for a troubled soul. Echevarria was a twenty-five-year-old Bronx man who had been charged with robbery and burglary. He was arrested in September 2011 and housed at Rikers Island while awaiting trial.

Echevarria struggled with bipolar disorder. Mental illness is common among inmates at Rikers. As *The New York Times* reported in 2014, Rikers Island housed more mentally ill inmates than "all of New York State's 24 psychiatric hospitals combined." At the time of his death, Echevarria was in solitary confinement in the Mental Health Assessment Unit for Infracted Inmates (MHAUII). He had been moved to the MHAUII—unit 11A—after repeatedly causing disruptions in another unit. He had attempted suicide multiple times.

On August 18, 2012—in a stark example of the wretched physical conditions at Rikers—the toilets in unit 11A backed up, spewing raw sewage into the cells. An inexperienced correction officer distributed "soap balls" to the inmates to clean up their own cells. This was not an over-the-counter product but a highly concentrated toxic detergent that must be diluted in water before distribution. This the officer failed to do.

Echevarria—not in his right mind, long chafing at being in solitary, and angling for reassignment to the infirmary—ate and swallowed the soap ball. It was a meal of pure bleach. He had purposefully ingested poison. This was at 4:30 p.m. on August 18.

Over the next eighteen hours, Echevarria was the victim of shocking neglect. Upon swallowing the chemical, he became immediately and visibly ill. He vomited violently as the chemical burned through his mouth, throat, and stomach.

He shouted for Raymond Castro, a young correction officer assigned to patrol unit 11A that day. Echevarria was frantic, panting, yelling at the top of his lungs that he had swallowed a soap ball with bleach, that he couldn't breathe, that he needed a doctor. Castro had joined Rikers Island only months earlier, in January 2012. He had no experience with such emergencies, so he reported the alarming news to his captain.

The captain on duty was a surly, longtime officer named Terrence Pendergrass, employed at Rikers for sixteen years. He had the power, responsibility, and duty to help Echevarria. He did not. Pendergrass responded, "Don't call me if you have live breathing bodies. Only call me if you need a cell extraction or if you have a dead body."

Officer Castro went back to Echevarria's cell and saw him vomiting. He alerted Officer Pendergrass for a *second* time. And a second time Pendergrass refused to help, saying that Echevarria should "hold it."

At 5:35 p.m., a pharmacy technician and Angel Lazarte, another correction officer, arrived at the unit and looked inside Echevarria's cell. They too saw him vomiting. His face was red, he was hunched over, his voice was breathy and short. "Help" was all he could get out. "He could die," the tech said to Lazarte.

Lazarte and Castro went to Officer Pendergrass's office and alerted him to Echevarria's condition. This was the *third* alert. Pendergrass again dismissed their concerns and told Lazarte to fill out a report. Finally, Officer Pendergrass walked—slowly— over to Echevarria's cell to look at him for the first time. He peeked in and walked away. He stopped Lazarte from finishing a report and told him to hang up the phone when he tried to call for medical assistance.

At 8:35 a.m. the next day, Echevarria was found dead. His cell was filled with sewage. There was white froth and blood around his mouth, black-and-blue discoloration around his neck, and vomit in the toilet in his cell. There was blood in his sheets, on his undershirt, and at his ankles. His body was cold. He had chemical burns on his tongue and mouth, the back of his throat, his intestinal and respiratory tracts. Fluid had entered his lungs. While Echevarria's body attempted to expel the chemical, uninterrupted exposure resulted in a slow, excruciating, and preventable death. The medical examiner later declared Echevarria's death a homicide, caused by medical "neglect."

We arrested Pendergrass in March 2014, the first Rikers Island officer to be charged with civil rights abuses in more than ten years. Lara and her trial partner Dan Richenthal persuaded the jury to convict him of deliberate indifference to Echevarria's medical needs.

I met Jason Echevarria's father, Ramon, after the trial. We both sat down with the weekly TV newsmagazine *60 Minutes* to talk about the case and the rot at Rikers. Ramon was a slight and talkative man who spoke softly but quickly. Jason was the child he had always worried about, he said. As he sat in a large wing chair across the coffee table in my office, he shook his head a lot. And he said to me a version of what he said on camera: "Why couldn't you just call an ambulance for him? Okay, he's a prisoner; he's an inmate. He's a human being. He's a human being."

Here's the second story:

You may recall how the investigator Steve Braccini flipped the Rikers correction officer Anthony Torres at a Port Chester diner. This is the rest of that story.

Brian Coll was a middle-aged correction officer working the night shift in the North Infirmary Command, housing for detainees who have chronic or serious medical conditions. On December 18, 2012, a week before Christmas, Coll's posting started at 11:00 p.m. and ended at 7:00 a.m.

Ronald Spear was one of Coll's detainees. Like Echevarria, Spear was a medical mess. Awaiting trial on burglary charges, he was a fifty-two-year-old with diabetes, heart disease, and end-stage renal disorder, which required regular dialysis. He needed glasses and walked with a cane. He wore a bracelet emblazoned with the warning "Risk of Fall."

Spear had been held at Rikers for almost three months and was known among the staff and other inmates for his complaints about the lack of adequate medical care. He was in pain—so much so that he filed his own lawsuit claiming that he'd been denied his medications for hypertension at Rikers. His efforts to reclaim his rights, in a place where he was brutally stripped of them, made him a target. In blighted places like Rikers, trouble-makers are targets.

On December 18, 2012, Coll was on duty when Spear approached, trying to see the doctor. It had been at least six days since he'd received dialysis. Coll told Spear to come back later. The exchange was heated, and Spear was belligerent. But Spear was turned around. "This guy is a real dick," Coll remarked about the infirm Ronald Spear to a nearby officer.

When Spear returned just before 5:00 a.m. on December 19, Coll again stopped him. Desperate for his medication, Spear tried to push past Coll into the doctor's office. Disrespected, Coll exploded. He punched Spear, multiple times, in the face and stomach. Officer Torres heard the altercation and went into the hallway, where he threw an arm around Spear. He restrained Spear and brought him to the ground, where he was laid facedown. As another officer, Byron Taylor, approached to help restrain Spear, Officer Nancy Duplessy went to quiet the inmates who were watching the entire episode. Inmates were yelling, "They're killing him, they're killing him!" Spear was lying prone on the hard floor, spent. Torres was positioned on top of him.

Then Brian Coll killed Ronald Spear.

This is how AUSA Jeannette Vargas described what happened after Spear stopped resisting and was fully restrained, in her opening statement in federal court almost two years after the fact:

> On that December morning, two correction officers held Ronald Spear's face down on the ground. The defendant stood over Mr. Spear. He wore heavy work boots. He brought his foot back and he kicked Mr. Spear. He kicked him in the head and then he kicked him again and again. He kicked him so hard that Mr. Spear started bleeding on the inside of his skull. Then the defendant knelt down, he grabbed Ronald Spear's head, and he lifted it off the ground and the defendant said: "That's what you get for fucking with me. Remember that I'm the one that did this to you." And then the defendant dropped Mr. Spear's head onto the hard tile floor. Ronald Spear died on that prison floor.

Spear did not try to stop the kicks. His shaking body absorbed every one, and he emitted a noise each time Coll's boot slammed into the side of his head. Those kicks killed him. And then Spear's inert body was handcuffed.

The cover-up began immediately, before the body was even cold. The officers on the scene quickly created a false narrative. In this alternate reality, Coll was merely acting in self-defense against a violent Spear, who raised a cane on him. The group went so far as to retrieve a spare cane from a supply closet five hours after Spear died to bolster their lies.

The officers lied to supervisors at Rikers, lied to the Bronx DA's Office, lied to a grand jury. The DA's Office declined to bring charges against the officers because they believed, given the exculpatory party line, that they couldn't prove guilt beyond a reasonable doubt.

Coll thought he was in the clear, and he might have remained so, might have remained in a position to beat and abuse more vulnerable people in his charge, might have killed other inmates. As I described earlier, the break came when SDNY investigator Steve Braccini confronted Officer Torres at a diner in Port Chester. Torres flipped and finally told the story, the real story, about Spear's death on December 19, 2012. When asked about how Coll had kicked the prone Spear's head, Torres testified at trial, "He kicked him like he was kicking a field goal."

Prosecutors Jeannette Vargas, Brooke Cucinella, and Martin Bell tried the case to a jury. After two days of deliberation, the jury convicted Coll of murdering Ronald Spear and obstructing justice by covering up the crime. He was sentenced to thirty years in prison.

How to explain such brutality and sadism on the part of law enforcement officers sworn to uphold the Constitution? Culture plays a part; an institution's culture can incubate depravity. Terrence Pendergrass, in the minds of the prosecutors, was not necessarily an evil person. Pendergrass, who was convicted of the crime of deliberate indifference, was not necessarily irredeemable. In sixteen years, he had never been the subject of an excessive force report. He had no particular beef with Echevarria. He didn't kill him with his bare hands, but nor did he lift a finger to save him. Pendergrass might have developed, after so many years, an awful, callous indifference. It may be that after sixteen years of dealing daily with the tension, the trauma, the mental illness, the hostility of that place, he just didn't care anymore. He discounted the distress signals of inmates because he had stopped seeing them as human beings, as members of the same species.

Only one time, as Echevarria lay dying in his cell, did Pendergrass bother even to check on him. Even after being advised about the vomiting and the blood and the poison, Pendergrass walked to the cell window with zero urgency. In fact, the trial video showed Pendergrass walking so slowly to the cell window that the defense claimed prosecutors had purposely slowed down the tape. They had not. It is sad to watch, Pendergrass's sluggish, ambling indifference, a quietly evocative piece of evidence that helped to convict him.

Brian Coll was a whole different story. A physically small man, Coll was short and paunchy and pug-faced. He sat through his trial with a vacant look on his face. He barely interacted with his attorneys. His own family was afraid of him and skipped the trial, and not one of them was prepared to post bail for him.

Officer Coll, it is possible, was a sociopath, utterly irredeemable. The best evidence of his pathology was this: As shown at trial, Coll had clipped a newspaper article from *The Village Voice* about the death of Ronald Spear, the man he killed. The story described how another inmate had broken the news to Spear's sister, to tell her that Ronald was dead, that "they beat him to death." The article featured a photo of a smiling and healthy-looking Ronald Spear. Coll had cut out this article, framed it, and hung it over his bed like a macabre hunter's trophy. What kind of a person does that? Perhaps only a sociopath.

But sociopaths can't get away with their crimes unless they are enabled and protected by compromised colleagues and a rancid culture. It may be that Coll lay at an extreme end on the cruelty spectrum, but the protective latticework that let him almost get away with it was already in place. He knew he had a safety net, the conspiratorial pledge of silence. He knew that everyone would have his back. Everybody knew that that safety net existed. That was the enabling. That was the larger corruption.

Pendergrass committed a crime of omission, while Coll committed a deliberate act of physical brutality. But each transgression produced the same horrific result: a human being, awaiting trial, while presumed innocent, was dead.

There is a tradition in our office. On the occasion of a jury address, a member of the trial team sends an office-wide email so that colleagues can come watch and provide support. When

I was a line AUSA, I thrilled at watching my peers argue to the jury. Martin Bell, who gave the summation in the Coll case, wrote this in an email announcing Jeannette Vargas was about to open in *United States v. Coll:* "And the world is full of complex problems, but sometimes, honestly, what we all really need is to see justice done in places no one thinks justice reaches."

Amen.

Sometimes rays of hope and reform are allowed to penetrate the cold confines of institutions like Rikers Island.

You are more than the worst thing you've ever done. That was the grounding principle of Defy Ventures, an innovative nonprofit group that worked with inmates. Defy's mission was to properly equip incarcerated folks for reentry and educate the rest of the population about the unique struggles they face. The group did many things to ready inmates for the future, including teaching basic job application skills and résumé writing and, most excitingly, developing their entrepreneurial skills, holding out the prospect of funding and capital for good ideas.

In December 2016, I visited Rikers Island to view the facility and any progress made under the terms of our consent decree. There was apparently no way to do this quietly. With a huge entourage and several layers of security, I felt like a visiting Western dignitary to some autocratic foreign country where the sanitized tour took me to only the best places, washed and cleaned especially for the occasion. As we came upon one mess hall in the jail, there was actually carrot cake laid out for me and the other visitors.

While at Rikers, I participated in one of Defy's workshops. It was shocking and eye-opening to be in that place, hugging and clasping hands with inmates, while two rings of armed security looked on.

And then to judge—à la *Shark Tank*—hopeful business plans from future entrepreneurs, still incarcerated, was surreal. I sat at a table with my business-minded brother, whom I'd brought just for this purpose, as people approached us with their carefully crafted pitches. There was the budding locksmith, and there was the inmate who imagined a mobile recording studio for aspiring artists and rappers. You could almost forget you were at Rikers Island.

At the close of the day, there was a startling participatory exercise: Step to the Line. Volunteers and inmates faced each other, forming a corridor, with volunteers on one side and inmates on the other. Someone would read a phrase out loud, and if it applied to your life and circumstances, you stepped forward to the center line. The point was radical honesty to provoke clarity and, of course, empathy. The prompts varied, but here are some of the most poignant ones that I remember:

Step to the line if you went to college.

Step to the line if you have lost a parent.

If you heard gunshots in your neighborhood growing up.

If you have been shot or stabbed.

If you have ever felt ashamed.

For some of the questions almost all of the inmates were at the line. Other times, all the volunteers. Sometimes a mixture of the two.

Then this prompt:

Step to the line if you have done something you could have been arrested for but weren't.

I think every single person stepped to the line, volunteers and inmates both. Upon every prompt, you learned something about other people, about yourself, about how much you were different, about how much you were the same.

An unshakable belief in the brains of some law enforcement people and politicians who deem themselves tough is that policies seeking to be humane are a form of coddling. They scoff at anything that smacks of comfort or kindness, even if the program might smartly minimize violence, improve safety, and enhance successful reentry. Intelligent rehabilitation, on the other hand, takes thought and effort. Too often it has to battle against the macho mentality that prison life must be painful, that suffering toughens up the inmate, is a necessary rite of passage.

There is always also the baseline tension between inmates and guards. Something is seldom mentioned in these discussions: how brutally difficult, bordering on impossible, the job of prison guard is. It is, I think, the most difficult job in all of law enforcement. It is tense, stressful, dangerous, tedious, violent, low paying, and thankless. And so, a certain mentality is not so hard to comprehend. Life is hard for the guard, and so life should be much harder for the inmate. The ethic is simple and understandable: prisoners don't deserve perks. Why do *they* get free classes? guards may think. Where's *my* free college course? they may ask. As if any consideration given to inmates were an insult to the guards. These are real tensions and real conflicts, and without buy-in from the correction officers, well-meaning programs are easily undermined. Prisons are natural hotbeds of resentment.

Enter man's best friend. The concept of a unique new program, dubbed Rikers Rovers, is simple: adolescent inmates train rescue dogs and get them ready for adoption. The dogs came from the New York City Animal Care and Control shelter and live in Rikers housing units where inmates, who must apply to the program, are the dogs' primary caretakers for nine weeks. Duties are divvied up and shared on a rotating schedule, inmates taking turns with different responsibilities. You wake up before 6:00 a.m. You feed your dog and walk her on a special track multiple times a day. You wash your dog. You take your dog to classes and teach her basic commands like sit, stay, and fetch. Inevitably, you bond with your canine. In the initial program, there was a pit bull named Roxy. There was a Rhodesian ridgeback and a Plott hound named Lenny, a black Lab mix named Ace. There was Shadow, Angel, Gigi, Bey, Kody, and Marie. When I visited Rikers, I met a pit bull named Perez. The majority were pit bulls, in fact, who were constitutionally less intimidated by the harsh and cold jail environment. One time they brought in a poodle. That was a mistake. The poodle was having none of it, and she had to be removed from the program.

This was the reaction of the correction officers when the program began: they laughed and sneered and mocked the program. The hostility came from two impulses. First, it didn't square with the tough-guy image of prison; playing with puppies is just not how you envision time behind bars. Second, it stoked ever-present, corrosive resentments. It seemed a reward to give dogs to people accused of crimes. Why should they get such a gift? Officers also thought this was another program that would put an extra burden on them. What if an inmate slashed a dog? Skepticism mixed with resentment. To sum up the general sentiment: *So now we're giving puppies to inmates? What's next, ponies?* But the then commissioner of the Department of Correction, Joseph Ponte, persisted, notwithstanding the eye rolls that went on behind his back among the rank and file.

The positive effect on the inmates was immediate. Everyone felt better; man's best friend made a difference to their psyches. The kids had someone to care for and tend to, individually and in teams. Adolescents with a history of violent behavior began behaving better just to qualify for the program. Not only did adolescents across housing units begin to engage with each other in positive ways, but they also saw how their personal investment in the dogs yielded real results; if a dog was successfully adopted, it was because of the work of each participant. Every team was instructed and encouraged. And it was especially inspiring that these were abandoned dogs brought in to help turn around the lives of abandoned youth, help them develop responsibility, discipline, maturity, and commitment.

If the impact on the inmates of this modest dog program was surprising, the effect on the nay-saying correction officers was even more so. Over time, even the cynical ones saw true value in the program. Officers cheerfully joined in the care and feeding of these abandoned dogs. Against expectations, they stopped rolling their eyes and started rolling up their sleeves to pitch in. In most cases, they became just as invested in the dogs as the incarcerated caretakers were, sometimes sneaking them out for secret extra walks during the day. Here's the other thing: at the end of each dog's nine-week stint at Rikers Island, having been trained, they were available to the public for adoption.

At least forty dogs have been trained at Rikers Island at the time of this writing. Guess who adopted the vast majority of these Rikers Rovers?

Most found homes with the very guards who, as a group, had sneered at the program. As I left the island that December, I pulled aside one of the most senior officials at the jail. He was a big, burly guy, and I asked him about his outlook on the future of Rikers (he was not overly optimistic, and the history of Rikers Island didn't give abundant hope), but I was struck by what he chose to tell me. He said that when they rolled out Rikers Rovers, he was utterly pessimistic: "I thought this was the stupidest thing I'd ever heard of. I thought it was a joke. But you know what? I'm now its biggest supporter. It's a little thing, but it does a lot."

In the now four years after our findings were issued, after the hotly negotiated consent decree with the city on Rikers Island, violence did not much abate. That is disheartening to report. All that work and not so much progress. Hardened cultures, it seems, are tough to fix. There are increasing calls to shut down the Rikers complex and start from scratch, as if violence were baked into the concrete walls like asbestos. And maybe that's right. Maybe the culture at today's Rikers is as irredeemable as Brian Coll. Incremental changes and programs that introduce humanity, soften the experience, prepare residents for the future, these are all good. And they may well bring respite to less troubled places. Puppies are a heartwarming initiative, but if you're being honest, you have to consider that what may be needed for a place like Rikers Island, sadly, is to burn it to the ground and start over.

Beyond Justice

You will not find God or grace in legal concepts, in formal notions of criminal justice. Certain values and ideals are beyond justice. These include mercy, forgiveness, redemption, dignity. Also love.

This crime story is about values larger than mere procedural justice. It is a story that was not so widely covered by the media, but it should have been. I first read about this twisting tale in *The New York Times* in 2011, and it later became the subject of a beautiful book, *The True American,* by Anand Giridharadas. The story begins—like so many terrible (but ultimately uplifting) stories—with the morning of September 11, 2001.

On that day, of course, terror rained down on New York City and on Virginia and also on Pennsylvania. And the world has never been the same.

In the aftermath of that awful day, some misguided individuals thought that they would exact vengeance for those acts. A sad spree of hate crimes followed. Three days after 9/11, a man named Frank Roque declared at a bar that he wanted to kill "ragheads." So he shot and killed Balbir Singh Sodhi, a Sikh American father of three, as he was planting flowers outside the gas station he owned in Mesa, Arizona. Four days after 9/11, three men firebombed a mosque and a Hindu temple in Canada. The FBI's annual report noted that hate crimes increased in the aftermath of 9/11.

Another of those misguided individuals was a man named

Mark Anthony Stroman. A thirty-one-year-old stonecutter living in Dallas, Texas, Stroman was an avowed white supremacist. After 9/11, he decided it was his duty to kill some Arabs.

So, on September 15, 2001, Stroman walked into a Dallas convenience store and came upon forty-six-year-old Waqar Hasan, an immigrant from Pakistan. As Hasan was grilling hamburgers in his small shop, Stroman shot him in the head, killing him.

A few weeks later, on October 4, Stroman walked into a Shell gas station in Mesquite, Texas, where he came upon Vasudev Patel. Patel, a Hindu, was an immigrant from India. Stroman shot him at close range with a .44-caliber pistol, killing him also. Patel is survived by his wife, Alka, and their teenage son.

Stroman was, fortunately, apprehended, and the following year he was tried for the murder of Patel.

According to reports, he showed no remorse at trial. In April 2002, Stroman was found guilty of capital murder. Just two days later, he was sentenced to death.

But there was a third victim of Stroman's violent rampage, one who miraculously survived. And it is that victim I want to tell you about.

You see, in between the two murders back in 2001, Stroman had also walked into a Texaco mini-mart and came upon a man named Rais Bhuiyan. Bhuiyan was a Muslim immigrant from Bangladesh.

Stroman entered the store with a sawed-off, double-barreled shotgun.

Here is how Bhuiyan himself described what happened next: "Business was slow. It was raining cats and dogs . . . I thought it was a robbery. I said, 'Don't shoot me please. Take all the money.' He said, 'Where are you from?' He was four or five feet away from me. I felt cold air in my spine. I said, 'Excuse me?' "

Bhuiyan went on to explain what he then saw and felt: "It was a double-barrel gun. I felt a million bee stings on my face at the same time. Then I heard an explosion. I saw images of my parents, my siblings and my fiancée and then a graveyard and I thought, 'Am I dying today?'

"I looked down and saw blood was pouring from my head. I placed both my hands on my head to get my brains in and I screamed, 'Mom!'"

Stroman left him for dead, but Bhuiyan did not die.

He had thirty-eight pellets lodged in his face, scalp, and eye; he endured a series of surgeries; and he lost most of the sight in one eye.

Bhuiyan is a devout Muslim who prays five times a day. One pellet is embedded in the center of his forehead, and every time his head touches the ground in prayer, he suffers pain.

And so Mark Anthony Stroman did not kill Rais Bhuiyan, but left him to years of physical pain and mental anguish.

It took a long while for Bhuiyan to get his life back on track. Years passed. And then an interesting thing happened.

Bhuiyan thought about the man who had done this to him and who was now sitting on death row in Texas. He thought about the two women who had lost their husbands, and he thought about their children and all the suffering this hateful man had caused.

And then he did something that I think most people, myself included, could never do.

He forgave his would-be killer. And he did more than that. In 2010, Bhuiyan began a campaign to spare Stroman from the death penalty.

As a magazine asked in an article about him, "If someone shot you in the face and left you for dead, would you try to save his life?"

But that is exactly what Bhuiyan did.

He said that he had looked in his heart and had consulted his faith. And there he found love and compassion and grace.

Bhuiyan spent two years trying to spare Stroman's life. He

began an online petition. He filed legal briefs. He fought with the Texas attorney general.

"He's another human being, like me," Bhuiyan would say, often.

He expressed concern and sorrow for Stroman's children, who would be left fatherless if the state's punishment were carried out—concern that Stroman himself had of course never displayed for the children of his victims.

And as Rais Bhuiyan elevated himself from victim to advocate, he was not the only one transformed.

For you see, the man who had tried to kill him and who now sat on death row had learned of Bhuiyan's efforts on his behalf.

Stroman was asked by a reporter for *The New York Times*, in the days before he was scheduled to be executed, "What are you thinking now?"

Stroman wrote this in reply: "I can tell you what im feeling Today, and that's very grateful for Rais Bhuiyan's Efforts to save my life after I tried to end His."

This hateful and murderous man, who had shown no mercy to his victims and no remorse at his trial, was moved to change by the man he had tried to kill, and said, on the eve of his own scheduled execution, "Hopefully something good will come of this."

Among his very last words were these: "Hate is going on in the world and it has to stop. Hate causes a lifetime of pain."

A few minutes later, on July 20, 2011, at 8:53 p.m., almost a decade after his murders, the legal process finally at a close, Mark Anthony Stroman was put to death.

Now, speaking as a prosecutor, I would say that formal justice was done in this case. A jury deliberated, the law was followed, and ultimate punishment was imposed.

But, speaking as an American and as a human being, I believe a much larger lesson looms here.

Perhaps it is this: while we can respect the methodical and

grinding machinery of the law in this case, we can marvel even more at how a victim of hatred grew to be a teacher of tolerance and seemed to transform his own would-be killer in the process.

And so I end this book as I began it.

The law is an amazing tool, but it has limits. Good people, on the other hand, don't have limits.

The law is not in the business of forgiveness or redemption.

The law cannot compel us to love each other or respect each other.

It cannot cancel hate or conquer evil; teach grace or extinguish passions.

The law cannot achieve these things, not by itself.

It takes *people*—brave and strong and extraordinary people.

Acknowledgments

Despite its length, this book hardly scratches the surface of what I hoped to convey about doing justice and about the office I served for thirteen years. I could not tell every story, discuss every lesson, address every setback, highlight every hero. Some little-known cases are treated in detail; many high-profile matters make no appearance at all, or barely so. Nonetheless, it is the sum of all my experiences—in big cases and small, in those I handled personally and in those I oversaw—that animates every smart and stupid thought I set down. The errors are mine, and my debts are many.

I want to thank first my extraordinary editor, Peter Gethers, who I believe was destined to edit this book. Peter reached out to me on a lark, unsolicited and out of the blue some years back, when I was midway through my tenure as U.S. Attorney. No book was in the offing, but a friendship was born. I'm blessed that Peter believed in me as a public servant first and as an author second, which is the right order. He wielded his editorial pencil—yes, pencil, no red pens for Peter—kindly but mercilessly, which has made this thing much better than I could have hoped. Thanks also to Sonny Mehta for his support and faith in this work and all the fine folks at Knopf, including Janna Devinsky, Paul Bogards, Erinn Hartman, Jessica Purcell, Nicholas Latimer, Chris Gillespie, Sara Eagle, and Carol Carson.

My literary agent, Elyse Cheney, was my friend and champion throughout this process. Over lengthy and thoughtful sessions, usually filled with laughter, Elyse and Alice Whitwham helped me sharpen my thinking, flesh out my structure, and find my voice. Thanks also to Claire Gillespie and Alex Jacobs of Elyse Cheney Literary Associates for their work.

I'm supremely grateful to Erik Kahn and Douglas Winters of Bryan Cave for their early support and their legal counsel.

I had loads of help from my colleagues at CAFÉ, where I make my podcasts. In a hundred ways, Vinit—who does double duty as my brother and my boss—helped me write this book, with resources and advice and faith. Several fine people at CAFÉ managed and shepherded so many aspects of this book—Tamara Sepper, Julia Doyle, Vinay Basti, and Jared Milfred, who helped me review, refine, and research. Julia and Vinay in particular burned the candle at both ends, investigating cases, scouring transcripts, proofreading chapters, and turning some of my dictated dreck into passable prose.

I am incredibly grateful to the scholars and students at New York University Law School, where I work under the lofty title Distinguished Scholar in Residence. Thanks first to my superb law student assistants Sara Bodner, Rupinder Garcha, and Ravi Singh for their insight, rigor, research, and keen eyes. I'm also indebted to the terrifically smart students in the Justice seminar I teach at NYU Law, with whom I discussed many of the cases and quandaries elaborated upon in this book. Finally, I am grateful to my friend and NYU Law Dean, Trevor Morrison, for his unfailing encouragement and support.

Here's a confession: I committed at one time or another every sin warned against in these pages—I let a victim's pain float out of my mind; forgot to think I might be mistaken; deviated from exactitude under the press of work; held stubbornly to a view for too long; withheld a question I thought too dumb to verbalize. What saved me, most of the time, was the excellence and integrity of the most hard-working and idealistic people I have ever known—my colleagues in and around the SDNY. This book is, in a way, for and about them. And this book exists only because of them.

My SDNY deputies—Boyd Johnson, Rich Zabel, and Joon Kim—are three of my dearest friends, closest advisers, and greatest influences. They are also superb editors. Each provided inspiration, guidance, and everlasting friendship, which is what one really needs most, in any endeavor.

There are countless more friends and colleagues—too many to mention all by name and I fear I've inadvertently left some out—who sat with me, counseled me, corrected me, steered me, edited me, taught me. Many are mentioned in the telling of these stories, but I also want to thank by name Anirudh Bansal, Rachel Barkow, Marc Berger, Michael Bosworth, Perry Carbone, Chris Conniff, James Cott, Michael Farbiarz, Nicole Friedlander, Jesse Furman, Jessica Goldsmith-Barzilay, Nola Heller, Bill Johnson, Bonnie Jonas, Jonathan Kolodner, Amanda Kramer, Paul Krieger, Joan Loughnane, Brendan McGuire, Anne Milgram, Lou Millione, Lisa Monaco, Marc Racanelli, Mimi Rocah, David Rody, Anjan Sahni, Yusill Scribner, Dan Stein, and Jocelyn Strauber.

I mention a host of SDNY investigators in the book because they are the true unsung heroes of my former office, but I also want to thank their supervisors Eric Blachman and Keith Talbert. There are also too many special agents, cops, inspectors, analysts and others to mention here. I am indebted to all of them—after all, they made the cases that make up this book. FBI heads George Venizelos, Diego Rodriguez, Joe Demarest, Janice Fedarcyk. Also Ray Kelly, Bill Bratton, Jimmy O'Neil, John Miller, and so many others at the NYPD. All the hardworking heroes at DEA, ATF, IRS, HSI, DOI, Postal, and more. I'm forever thankful for their friendship, leadership, and service.

Senator Charles Schumer, for whom I worked during a tumultuous and important time on the Senate Judiciary Committee, gets my eternal thanks and a standalone paragraph because I became the U.S. Attorney only on account of his recommendation to President Obama. He thought I could do that big job before many others did and so, outside of my immediate family, no one has shown more faith in my professional ability than Senator Schumer, the hardest working person I have ever met.

Now, my family: I am deeply thankful to my wife, Dalya, who was the portrait of loving patience. She read every page of every draft and offered inspired edits on every version, over more than eighteen arduous months. She tolerated my absence, my stress, and my petulance. She talked me through each wretched insecurity and writer's block, and her pen saved me considerable embarrassment. She was both encouraging and unsparing, in perfect balance. That is quite a feat and precisely what you wish for in a spousal editor. Thank you.

My three beautiful children—Maya, Jaden, and Rahm—did not line-edit my manuscript, but every day they ground me, enliven me, inspire me, and make me realize how much they deserve to live in a fair and just society. Inasmuch as this book is about the future, it is for them.

I end with thanks and blessings to my Mom and Dad: Jagdish and Desh Bharara. They brought me from India to America as an infant, forty-nine years before I published this book. They are not lawyers, didn't especially want me to become a lawyer. But they were the first to teach me about justice, fairness, and the importance of principle—just by quietly demonstrating those virtues and values every day. As they do still.

Index